Inclusive Place Branding

Place branding is often a response to inter-place competition and discussed as if it operated in a vacuum, ignoring the needs of local communities. It has developed a set of methods – catchy slogans, colourful logos, 'star-chitects', bidding for City of Culture status etc. – that are applied as quick-fix solutions regardless of geographical and socio-political contexts.

Critical views of place branding are emerging which focus on its unexplored consequences on the physical and social fabric of places. These more critical approaches reveal place branding as an essentially political activity, serving hidden agendas and marginalizing social groups. Scholars and practitioners can no longer ignore the need for more responsible and socially sensitive approaches to cater for a wider range of stakeholders, and which fully acknowledge the importance of resident participation in decision-making.

The contributions in this innovative book set out to introduce new critical ways of thinking around place branding and practices that encourage it to be more inclusive and participatory. It will be of interest to researchers and advanced students of branding, critical marketing, and destination marketing as well as critical tourism and environmental design.

Mihalis Kavaratzis is Associate Professor of Marketing at the University of Leicester. A Founding Board Member of the International Place Branding Association, his publications include *Towards Effective Place Brand Management* (with G. J. Ashworth, 2010) and *Rethinking Place Branding* (with G. Warnaby and G. J. Ashworth, 2015).

Massimo Giovanardi is Lecturer in Marketing at the University of Leicester. His research examines from a sociological perspective the marketing, communication and consumption of places. He has published in major academic journals such as *Annals of Tourism Research* and *Marketing Theory*.

Maria Lichrou is a Lecturer in the Department of Management and Marketing, University of Limerick, Ireland. She has published in the *Journal of Marketing Management*, *Journal of Place Management and Development*, *Journal of Strategic Marketing*, *Place Branding and Public Diplomacy*, *Tourism Planning and Development.*

Routledge Studies in Critical Marketing
Edited by Mark Tadajewski and Pauline Maclaran

Marketing has been widely criticised as being probably the least self-critical of all the business disciplines and has never really been able to escape the charge that it is socially, ethically and morally barren in certain respects. Marketers may talk about satisfying the customer, about building close relationships with their clientele, about their ethical and corporate social responsibility initiatives, but increasingly these claims are subjected to critical scrutiny and been found wanting. In a social, economic and political environment in which big business and frequently some of the most marketing adept companies' practices are being questioned, there has emerged a very active community of scholars, practitioners and students interested in Critical Marketing Studies.

Using the types of critical social theory characteristic of Critical Marketing Studies, this series will drive the debate on Critical Marketing into the future. It offers scholars the space to articulate their arguments at the level of sophistication required to underscore the contribution of this domain to other scholars, students, practitioners and public-policy groups interested in the influence of marketing in the structuring of the public sphere and society. It is a forum for rigorously theorised, conceptually and empirically rich studies dealing with some element of marketing theory, thought, pedagogy and practice.

1 **Consumer Vulnerability**
Conditions, contexts and characteristics
Edited by Kathy Hamilton, Susan Dunnett and Maria Piacentini

2 **Islam, Marketing and Consumption**
Critical Perspectives on the intersections
Edited by Aliakbar Jafari and Özlem Sandıkcı

3 **Inclusive Place Branding**
Critical Perspectives on Theory and Practice
Edited by Mihalis Kavaratzis, Massimo Giovanardi and Maria Lichrou

Inclusive Place Branding

Critical Perspectives on Theory and Practice

Edited by Mihalis Kavaratzis, Massimo Giovanardi and Maria Lichrou

LONDON AND NEW YORK

First published 2018 by Routledge

2 Park Square, Milton Park, Abingdon, Oxfordshire OX14 4RN
52 Vanderbilt Avenue, New York, NY 10017

Routledge is an imprint of the Taylor & Francis Group, an informa business

First issued in paperback 2019

British Library Cataloguing in Publication Data
A catalogue record for this book is available from the British Library

Library of Congress Cataloging in Publication Data
Names: Kavaratzis, Mihalis, editor. | Giovanardi, Massimo, 1982– editor. | Lichrou, Maria, 1976– editor.
Title: Inclusive place branding : critical perspectives on theory and practice / [edited by] Mihalis Kavaratzis, Massimo Giovanardi and Maria Lichrou.
Description: Abingdon, Oxon ; New York, NY : Routledge, 2018. | Includes bibliographical references and index.
Identifiers: LCCN 2017035348 (print) | LCCN 2017044514 (ebook) | ISBN 9781315620350 (eBook) | ISBN 9781138659247 (hardback : alk. paper)
Subjects: LCSH: Place marketing–Social aspects.
Classification: LCC G155.A1 (ebook) | LCC G155.A1 .I449 2018 (print) | DDC 910.68/8–dc23
LC record available at https://lccn.loc.gov/2017035348

ISBN: 978-1-138-65924-7 (hbk)
ISBN: 978-0-367-87731-6 (pbk)

Typeset in Times New Roman
by Wearset Ltd, Boldon, Tyne and Wear

Contents

Illustrations

Figures

Tables

Contributors

Skye Akbar, Research Fellow, School of Management, University of South Australia, Adelaide, Australia. Skye has a strong focus on applying her skills and experience to improve outcomes for those who experience disadvantage and vulnerabilities. Growing up on the Eyre Peninsula with family in primary production and being of the Waljen group, of the Wongutha Peoples of the North-Eastern Goldfields of Western Australia, she established her understanding of remote life, communities and economies. Her passion is for research that supports self-determined community economic development and wellbeing for local peoples. Skye aims to continue research in this area in the coming years as it is of considerable importance to people in these communities and to the wider community.

Anne-Marie Broudehoux is Professor at the School of Design, University of Quebec at Montreal, Canada. She has published extensively on urban images and urban marketing and is a leading author on critical perspectives on place branding.

Jan Brown is Senior Lecturer of Marketing at the Liverpool Business School of Liverpool John Moores University, UK, with a track of publications around place branding and services marketing.

Cecilhia Cassinger, PhD, is Assistant Professor and Senior Lecturer at the Department of Strategic Communication, Lund University, Sweden. She has written on research methodology, consumption practices, and the relationship between retail image and narrative.

Aram Eisenschitz is a Senior Lecturer in tourism policy in the Department of Marketing, Branding and Tourism at Middlesex University's Business School. He was previously at the London Chamber of Commerce and Industry and has published in the fields of urban regeneration, social inclusion and place marketing. Current research interests include the political economy of tourism and the sociology of knowledge. He leads the cello section of two North London orchestras.

Daniel L. Fay, PhD, is an Assistant Professor in the Askew School of Public Administration and Policy at The Florida State University. His research interests include organizational theory, diversity issues in public management, veterans' policy, policy diffusion and higher education policy and management. Prior to joining the faculty at The Florida State University, Dr Fay served as an Assistant Professor of Public Administration in the Department of Political Science and Public Administration at Mississippi State University, a Visiting Assistant Professor in the Department of Public Administration and Policy at the University of Georgia and a Postdoctoral Associate at Syracuse University.

Massimo Giovanardi is Lecturer in Marketing at the University of Leicester. His research examines from a sociological perspective the marketing, communication and consumption of places. He has published in major academic journals such as *Annals of Tourism Research* and *Marketing Theory*.

Kevin Fox Gotham is Professor and Associate Dean of Academic Affairs at the School of Liberal Arts, Tulane University, USA. His research interests encompass the areas of social theory, urban sociology and sociology of culture.

Johan Gromark's primary focus is brand orientation, corporate branding and place branding, and he has published articles in the *Journal of Brand Management* and the *Journal of Marketing Management*, while also having served as a reviewer for the *European Journal of Marketing*, the *Journal of Brand Management*, the *Journal of Marketing Management* and the *International Journal of Hospitality Management*. Since 2012, Johan has been working on his PhD dissertation at Lund University in Sweden, where he is a member of The Lund Brand Management Group. Furthermore, Johan also has extensive practical experience, where he has held the position of Managing Director for Label, a brand consultancy within BBDO Worldwide, ever since 2000. During these years, he has undertaken several large-scale place branding projects where he and his colleagues have advised nations, regions and cities in their brand management efforts.

Freya Higgins-Desbiolles, Senior Lecturer, School of Management, University of South Australia, Adelaide, Australia. Freya is a non-Indigenous academic that has researched and taught on the subject of Indigenous engagement with tourism for nearly two decades. Her approach as a critical scholar is to seek the emancipatory capacities of collaborative research to co-create change for better futures.

Cate Irvin is a PhD researcher in Tulane University's City, Culture, and Community department, USA in the Sociology track.

Eva Maria Jernsand is a postdoctoral researcher in marketing at School of Business, Economics and Law at University of Gothenburg, Sweden, and affiliated with the Centre for Tourism at the same university. Her research interests include place branding, participation, innovation, design and sustainable tourism development.

Nadia Kaneva is Associate Professor in the Department of Media, Film, and Journalism Studies at the University of Denver, USA. Her research draws on critical theories of culture and communication, and explores the intersections of media, markets and identities in the post-socialist context.

Mihalis Kavaratzis is Associate Professor of Marketing at the University of Leicester. A Founding Board Member of the International Place Branding Association, his publications include *Towards Effective Place Brand Management* (with G. J. Ashworth, 2010) and *Rethinking Place Branding* (with G. Warnaby and G. J. Ashworth, 2015).

Richard Koeck is Professor and Chair in Architecture and the Visual Arts in the School of Architecture; Director of the Centre for Architecture and the Visual Arts (CAVA), both University of Liverpool, and founding Director of the Film/Digital Media company CineTecture Ltd. He is co-/editor of several books on moving image culture, including *The City and the Moving Image* (2010) and *Cinematic Urban Geographies* (2017), co-/author of numerous articles and book chapters on the visual culture of cities in areas such as film, mobile media and advertising, and author of the monograph *Cine|Scapes: Cinematic Spaces in Architecture and Cities* (2012) and *Inhabiting the Image of the City* (2018 forthcoming).

Helena Kraff is a PhD candidate in Design at the Faculty of Fine, Applied and Performing Arts at University of Gothenburg, Sweden. Her research interests include participatory practices in areas such as design and place branding. She is particularly interested in ethical and methodological challenges with participatory research.

Maria Lichrou is a Lecturer in the Department of Management and Marketing, University of Limerick, Ireland. She has published in the *Journal of Marketing Management*, *Journal of Place Management and Development*, *Journal of Strategic Marketing*, *Place Branding and Public Diplomacy*, and *Tourism Planning & Development*.

Andrea Lucarelli's primary research interest is connected to branding applied to the realm of public places (i.e. cities, regions and nation). More specifically Andrea's research focuses on the spatial and political dimension of place brands. Her secondary research interest is related to the geographical and historical dimension of consumption, advertising and marketing, the politics of marketing and the role of techno-digital culture in the construction of market phenomena.

Dominic Medway is a professor who is based in the Institute of Place Management at Manchester Metropolitan University. His work examines the complex interactions between places, spaces and those who produce, manage and consume them, reflecting an academic background in geography. Recently completed studies have addressed issues such as stakeholder interaction in urban place partnerships, how litter affects people's perceptions of space and crime, and the potential role of smell in the marketing of places. Dominic is the Academic Editor of the *Journal of Place Management and Development*. He is currently engaged in research projects with some key external partners in the North West of England, and with colleagues at Alliance Manchester Business School and the Higher School of Economics in Moscow and St Petersburg, where he is a Visiting Professor.

Åsa Thelander, PhD, is Associate Professor and Senior Lecturer at the Department of Strategic Communication, Lund University, Sweden. Her research interests include visual studies, consumer research and qualitative methodology.

Anette Therkelsen, PhD, is Associate Professor at the Department of Culture and Global Studies, Aalborg University, Denmark. Her main areas of research are place consumption, identity and branding mainly in a tourism context. She is currently working on a project on innovation in coastal tourism with a particular focus on the potentials of local food.

Gary Warnaby is Professor of Retailing and Marketing, based in the Institute of Place Management at Manchester Metropolitan University. His research interests focus on the marketing of places (particularly in an urban context), and retailing. Results of this research have been published in various academic journals in both the management and geography disciplines, including *Environment and Planning A, Journal of Business Research, Tourism Management, Marketing Theory, Consumption Markets and Culture, European Journal of Marketing, International Journal of Management Reviews, Area, Cities* and *Local Economy*. He is co-author of *Relationship Marketing: A Consumer Experience Approach* (Sage, 2010), co-editor of *Rethinking Place Branding: Comprehensive Brand Development for Cities and Regions* (Springer, 2015), and has contributed to numerous edited books.

Staci M. Zavattaro, PhD, is Associate Professor of Public Administration at the University of Central Florida. Her research interests include place branding, social media in government and administrative theory. She also serves as a research associate for the School of Public Administration's Center for Public and Nonprofit Management. Her research appears in *Tourism Management, Journal of Place Management and Development* and *Public Administration Review*.

Foreword

The politics of event-led urban image construction – notes from Beijing and Rio de Janeiro

Anne-Marie Broudehoux

In our contemporary society of spectacle, the image of the city has gained a strategic importance for policy-makers as a formidable asset in the marketing of localities to tourists, investors and potential residents. Over the last few decades, practices of urban image construction have become increasingly sophisticated and cities have devised numerous strategies to transform their image in ways that appeal to a host of players in the new global economy. This foreword examines the diverse mechanisms of urban image construction that are commonly used to transform the way cities are imagined, experienced and designed. It is especially interested in the politics of representations behind such initiatives and their impacts on different population groups. Observations draw upon nearly twenty years of empirical research on the process of urban image construction, in the context of mega-event preparations, those global scale spectacles that are both powerful engines in the contemporary production of urban images while being themselves driven by an image imperative. I draw more particularly on the examples of Beijing, host of the 2008 Summer Olympics, and Rio de Janeiro, host of the 2014 FIFA World Cup and 2016 Olympic Games, with which I am most familiar.

Selective manipulations in the construction of place images

At a time when the economic survival of cities increasingly depends on their capacity to attract capital, visitors, wealthy taxpayers and members of the 'creative class', the production, marketing and visual control of a competitive urban image has taken centre stage in urban policy, becoming one of the hallmarks of contemporary urban governance. As aesthetic considerations and imaging strategies become primary generators of symbolic capital, the late capitalist city has witnessed the emergence of new design strategies and planning practices where decisions are increasingly made on visual terms, to the point where we can talk of a dictatorship of the visual.

The practice of urban image construction is deeply rooted in a politics of visibility, where selective visualizations of place and space increasingly shape urban policy interventions. However, these purpose-driven representations, aimed at attracting certain categories of people and interests, can yield decisions that are both exclusive and highly divisive. For Rosalyn Deutsche (1996), the construction of a unified, coherent and cohesive urban image is an exclusionary process that can only be achieved by expelling differences and conflicts. It entails the reduction of a rich, complex, heterogeneous urban reality into a simplified, homogenous, one-dimensional marketable commodity (Deutsche, 1996). Healy (2002) likens urban image construction to the creative projection of a fictional yet totalizing image of society, which undermines more plural, multidimensional and progressive visions.

Power is a determining factor deciding who and what should be included in official urban representations. The resulting image generally embodies the desires and aspirations of those who have the power to shape the urban environment and becomes the concretization of their cultural imaginings and visual fantasies (Smith, 2005). Based on an elitist conceptualization of what is deemed desirable, respectable or attractive, cities are expected to be at once 'vibrant, exciting and reassuringly safe, while providing a complete package of assets linked to status, quality of life, and business opportunities. For Healy (2002), the process of giving a city what elites believe is a 'modern' face often depends upon silencing the politically weak and making poverty purposely invisible. Usually left out from representations are the ordinary landscapes of the poor, the black, the homeless, and the 'unmodern', considered to be 'out of place' in the city's public space (Wright, 1997). Deutsche (1996, 173) talks of a 'politics of erasure', where undesirable groups are physically expelled from physical space while their absence is discursively inscribed in representations of the city.

Urban images essentially represent a compromise between an objective reality and a projected ideal. In the production of urban images, two complementary processes are at play: a process of *seduction*, and a process of *repulsion*. Seduction entails a desire to tempt, please or attract, and a willingness to manipulate reality, to deceive and mystify in order to succeed in this enticement. Architectural critique Neil Leach (1999) views seduction as a last recourse used when all substance or meaningful discourse is gone. In the process of urban image construction, seduction is used to create a *space of illusion*, where the best assets the city has to offer are pushed to the fore and celebrated as a utopian, picture perfect vision of reality. Seduction thus relies upon illusionism, theatricality, artifice and spectacle, with the construction of a spectacular front stage, upon which reality is embellished, manipulated, and glorified. In the context of pre-Olympic Beijing, I use the notion of Potemkinism, a 'fake it till you make it' approach to modernization, where re-engineering reality helped project a highly controlled and overly positive image of the city. In more vulgar terms, one could talk of 'pimping the city' for maximum effect.

This process of seduction in the construction of place images is complemented by a process of *repulsion,* which covers up social divisions and deliberately omits, silences and denies realities that could be detrimental to the city's reputation, relegating them to a hidden backstage, which we can call a *space of exclusion.* It is a vision from which aspects of the urban landscape that may cause prejudice to the city's image are cropped out of the picture, both symbolically and literally. In a form of visual eugenics, the existence of the poor, the ugly and the un-photogenic is negated, while the plain, banal, mundane and not so quaint are simply swept under the rug.

Three dimensions in the production of the city's image

The production of the city's image rests upon different modes of intervention, which can be categorized based upon three dimensions of the city's image: the conceived, the built and the lived image of the city. This categorization borrows from Henri Lefebvre's distinction, in *The Production of Space* (1991), between conceived space (or the *representation of space*) and lived space (what he calls *spaces of representation*). Conceived space is a theoretical representation of the city, as imagined and imposed, from a distance, by city officials, planners, and other imagineers. Lived space is the actual physical city, as it is experienced at street level on a daily basis, and used by diverse social groups for self-representation. I understand this lived space as having both a social and a material dimension, thus resulting in a triangular conceptualization of the city's image: the *conceived* (discursive or imagined) image of the city, the *built* (physical, material or concrete) image of the city and the *lived* (experienced or social) image of the city.

In this typology, the discursive image of the city corresponds to rhetorical place images promoted through media-based advertising and city marketing campaigns for both internal and external consumption. This is the city found on glossy magazine covers, tourism literature and boosterist discourse. The second aspect of the city's image focuses on the concrete image of the city, built through architecture and landscape interventions. It is concerned with the city's actual physical landscape, in its materiality, composed of the city's existing assets, inherited from the past, and of newly built edifices and spaces, created as beautification projects and image-improving investments. The third dimension of urban image presented in this foreword is the social image of the city, shaped through initiatives that seek to transform both the bodies and the minds of the local population. It corresponds to the social landscape of the city, in its multiple expressions. Each of these three levels of intervention in the practice of urban construction practices is further discussed in what follows.

The conceived image of the city

The first level of intervention in the process of urban image construction lies in the symbolic realm. It consists of the production of an intangible, mental place image and the projection of an abstract idea of the city upon collective consciousness through discursive means and virtual representations. Such rhetorical image construction aims to instil a cognitive representation of place that is attractive to people and will help anticipate their experience of the city. Playing on an affective level, it draws upon emotions and subjective feelings of attachment to place. These mental representations are either controlled products, purposely formatted by professional image-makers, or they can be uncontrolled, produced by autonomous agents, for example in popular culture.

As a controlled process, discursive image construction is the product of specialists in advertising, place marketing and destination branding, sponsored by local governments, tourism organizations or local interest groups, and diffused through mass media. Destination branding, which consists of the constitution a coherent representation that will attract, rally, inspire and stimulate a target audience, remains one of the principal instruments in the concerted construction of a mental place image. Turning the city into a distinctive brand and a consumable product with its trademark logo and unified look requires an explicit positioning, with a consistent message that will guide all marketing efforts.

In its desire to draw a favourable, flattering portrait of the city, destination branding requires a simplification of reality. City-brand construction generally rests upon a consensual, easily digestible and stereotyped interpretation of local identity and generally includes a part of fiction. In fact, the most successful marketing campaigns rest upon great story telling and myth making. No matter how fabricated, these fictional representations can have a real influence upon local identity formation, as populations internalize this vision, adopt it as their own and reproduce it for their own purpose. For example, Quebec City's brand identity, historically constructed to promote winter tourism at the turn of the twentieth century, was internalized in the collective consciousness and became part of the invented traditions that later defined the city's cultural practices and its residents' self-representation. Similarly, idealized portrayals of Rio de Janeiro found Olympic propaganda, which depict the city's landscape without its favelas, comfort local elites in their unspoken desire to eradicate such 'eyesores' and help legitimate the destruction of these settlements, where a large proportion of the urban poor resides.

Today, the use of mass media forms of communication for the diffusion of urban representations facilitates the production of deceitful mental place images. Sophisticated imaging technologies allow the construction of computer-generated images to project a photoshopped vision of the city where flaws are corrected and eyesores erased. As seen in televisual portrayals of Beijing during the 2008 Olympics, carefully chosen elements of the landscape were juxtaposed and space was contracted and recomposed into a seamless, if improbable, geography. In such broadcasted representations, as well as in tourism promotion and event advertising, the poor, the uncivilized, the unsightedly, the dangerous, and the unmodern were unashamedly left out and made invisible, in a process I call *symbolic erasure*.

The construction of a positive mental place image can also be the work of autonomous agents, who cannot be controlled by image producers. Independent news coverage or popular culture products like literature, theatre, film, songs, visual arts and television represent powerful image construction agents, often perceived as more reliable and unbiased than carefully planned advertising campaigns. Films and television programs that are not concerned with tourism promotions have been shown to have a greater impact than purpose-made advertising because they lack the perceptual bias of promotional material. They cast a wider net than magazines and newspapers advertisement. They give exposure to vast audiences that could never be reached by traditional advertising and targeted tourism promotion. Films also have a longer shelf-life and persist for decades in providing publicity, with less investment than place marketing campaigns. On-screen 'imaging' of cities do not only make these locations more desirable as places to visit, but as places to live as well, as testified by the ever-growing number of people moving to New York or Los Angeles.

Today, films are increasingly seen as effective marketing tools, which play up the image of a city and turn it into a fashionable destination. As powerful myth-makers, films have the power to inscribe emotions and desire onto place, and help create seductive fantasy worlds that attract visitors in search of specific experiences. A film that portrays a destination in a favourable light is seen as the ultimate in place-based product placement. In recent years, cities have become proactive in leveraging their film potential, targeting filmmakers in the preproduction stage, offering grants, tax credits and free scouting trips to encourage producers to film in their city. Rio de Janeiro's mayor recently claimed he would give whatever Woody Allen wanted to get him to film in his city. Some local governments go as far as dictating the way their city should be portrayed and censoring negative depictions. In 2015, Mexico City major offered an extra six million dollars to the fourteen million already granted to the James Bond movie franchise for his city to be shown as a booming modern metropolis rather than a decaying, ancient capital. Another condition was that the Bond girl be Mexican, while the villain should not.

The physical image of the city

If mental urban image construction sought to communicate ideas about places through advertising strategies and the creation of a brand image, physical image construction focuses on improving the product itself, that is, the actual city, in its material, three-dimensional reality. The city's physical landscape, both natural and man-made, is thus subjected to a transformation process in order to conform, as much as possible, to the picture-perfect vision conjured up by urban imagineers and city marketers.

Architecture and urban design are the raw material of such urban image construction programs and their principal means of expression. The built environment communicates a host of information about the society who created it, in terms of history, wealth, character, and values. Through the ages, power holders have time and again used their cityscape to convey ideas about a regime, an ideology, or a vision. Architecture similarly served as an instrument of mass communication, a kind of word in stone, which could manifest civic values and shared ideals.

Physical image construction through spatial illusionism

Landscape-based urban image construction strategies act upon the city's existing physical assets, which are renovated, improved upon and turned into positive urban amenities and factors of attraction. This includes diverse public infrastructure and services, but more importantly, natural and heritage resources, whose value is enhanced and creatively exploited. As a valued element of place image that is positively connoted, history conveys a sense of stability and continuity, and suggests deeply rooted cultural practices and traditions.

Many cities, especially those lacking rich historical landmarks or striking scenery, also invest in the creation of new assets in the hope of boosting their profile. Cultural amenities like opera houses, theatres and museums, shiny new transportation projects like light rail systems, business infrastructure such as convention centres and other leisure, shopping and entertainment venues, including aquariums and urban stadia, have become part of what Kaika (2005) calls the 'urban dowry', or the ever-growing list of must-have amenities that cities must be equipped with in order to attain the elusive 'world-class' status. In their fear to lose out in the global inter-urban competitions, cities are compelled to follow the same trends and fashions and to emulate one another's success by reproducing tried and true solutions. Yet, seeking distinction within a spectrum of conformity often proves counter-productive: rather than reinforcing their unique place identity, these initiatives often make cities increasingly similar.

The marketing literature talks profusely of the construction of flagship projects, or newsworthy buildings that generally house cultural or state institutions. Cultural amenities are valued because they can supplement the local cultural offer and dynamize the city's creative credentials. Conceived by so-called starchitects, these signature buildings are instrumentalized as part of a marketing strategy for the creation of a city brand. The 'iconic' label confirms their image function, while their striking architecture acts as a logotype that is widely exploited for its advertising power. The main mode of communication of this material form of advertising is seduction, which draws upon the magnetic appeal of novelty architecture to entice visitors to the city.

A prime example of such architectural branding was Beijing's grand Olympic projects, whose arresting design served as powerful instruments of persuasion to attract global interest. In these spectacular projects, technological prowess, glittering surfaces and monumentalism conspired to connote stability, boldness, might, and prosperity, qualities that deeply resonate with those valued by wealthy investors and business leaders. These brand-name buildings, bearing the signature of some of the world's most renowned architects, conveyed a mix of cultural sophistication, discriminating taste and distinction that bespoke self-confidence and modernity.

The use of mega-events as city marketing opportunities epitomizes architecture's new role as a media object in the service of the spectacle. Event-related architectural production is often reduced to a matter of superficial appearance, subsumed into a visual marker and an iconic emblem carried around in the popular imagination to help 'envision' the city and place it on the world's cognitive map. Designed for a global audience, event venues are conceived to be seen from afar, from a broadcast helicopter and on large television screens, rather than experienced spatially and tactically in their third dimension at street level. Their design prioritizes appearance over substance and visual impact over functionality. Their conspicuous nature also suggests a vane desire to eclipse other sensational projects, contributing to the hyperinflation of self-conscious exceptionalism in an increasingly fragmented urban landscape. Gaffney (2016) refers to such expensive, sparkling structures whose 'wow' factor trumps their durability as elements of 'urban bling', which glorify consumerism and wealth ostentation in order to stimulate capital accumulation. The contemporary emphasis on surface and readable imagery has thus deeply transformed architectural production, generating two-dimensional buildings designed for their photogenic effect rather than their experiential potential.

Urban design is similarly deployed as an image construction strategy, with the creation of signature districts and the branding of neighbourhoods. These single-purpose sectors, specialized in business, leisure, or the arts, are transformed through the use of a visual form of urbanism, with a uniform look, distinct signage, remarkable architecture and sleek urban design. Here again, a shortlist of widely copied must-have amenities have become a standard fare of the globally hopeful city: museum and entertainment districts, waterfront redevelopment, festival marketplaces, creative clusters, artist colonies, international business district, ethnic neighbourhoods, gay village, nightlife quarter, etc.

Physical image construction through spatial exclusion

As mentioned earlier, the construction of a material image of the city relies as much on the production of *spaces of illusion*, through spectacular urban projects, as they require the creation of *spaces of exclusion,* where less savoury aspects of the urban environment are relegated. Cities have developed sophisticated means to limit what is to be shown to the world, hiding what is deemed irrelevant or detrimental to their image, and concealing those aspects that could cause reputational damage. Urban features that suggest poverty, backwardness or decline are often hidden, on account that they risk tarnishing the city's carefully constructed image. Four invisibilization strategies are detailed in what follows. They include *displacement*, with the bulldozing of material landscapes of poverty and the eviction of their population; *concealment*, with the use of screens or walls to hide the blight that cannot be displaced; *anesthetization*, which seeks to beautify poverty and make it more visually acceptable; and *denied access*, with the creation of territories of exceptions and a complex filtering system that limit access to urban spaces.

Displacement

The most common response to the excessive visibility of an embarrassing urban poverty is slum clearance, through forced evictions and population displacements. Mega-events often require the clearing of vast swaths of land around event venues to create safety perimeters and protect visitors from a potentially dangerous and visually offensive urbanity. The violent dislocation of the poor is justified by a rhetorical association between urban decay and crime, which helps conceal deeper economic motives. The poor and their physical manifestations are seen as liabilities in real-estate valuation, and their eviction as an opportunity for capital to expand into new territories. Over 1.5 million people were displaced in pre-Olympic Beijing, in what is largely seen as the worst event-led displacement in history.

Concealment

A second means of making urban poverty invisible that is commonly used, especially but not exclusively in mega-event host cities from the Global South, involves the erection of screen walls along the roads linking event sites to the city centre and the airport in order to hide squatter settlements and slums, like the so-called 'acoustic barriers' built in Rio de Janeiro in 2009, a few weeks after the city was chosen as host of the 2016 Olympic Games. If the use of walls remains common, it is also highly controversial and highly contested, because of its strong ideological charge and negative connotations, linked to notions of separation, isolation and exclusion. Visual filters thus increasingly take the form of large structures conveniently positioned to block the view of poor neighbourhoods.

Anesthetization

A third approach to minimize the visibility of poverty combines several tactics of anesthetization and urban camouflage to tame images of destitution and limit their negative impact, with a visual discourse that is both neutralizing and pacifying. Rather than being hidden or destroyed, landscapes of poverty are embellished so as to become visually acceptable. This aestheticizing often takes the form of landscaping interventions near the point of contact with the formal city or of façadist projects that beautify the most visible portion of a neighbourhood, as was vastly seen in many of Rio de Janeiro's *favelas* before the World Cup and the Olympics, where quaint colourization projects anesthetized the political power of these settlements.

Denied access

A last strategy to conceal the presence of the poor in the urban landscape consists in the intentional design of public space so as to make it inhospitable for the poor, thereby limiting their appropriation. Garnier (2004) talks of a 'preventive architecture of fear' to describe the design and landscaping of public spaces in ways that eliminate dark corners, shady spots, setbacks, and screens where indigents could find refuge. The festive redesign of urban spaces as playful and convivial leisure places for people 'of the right kind' also facilitates the expulsion of the poor from the public eye and the planned gentrification of city districts. In this substitution process, the poor and the marginal are expelled from urban sectors, which are re-appropriated by a more deserving elite. Mega-event sites are similarly designed to exclude undesirables, with the use of a defensive, fortress-like architecture complete with moats, checkpoints, security perimeter, and fences that filter access and control admission.

The social image of the city

The third and last dimension of image construction discussed in this foreword is concerned with the city's human environment, through the deployment of vast social engineering programs that seek to reform public behaviour and civilize bodies. If some population groups are warranted privileged access to urban spaces, other, more marginalized users are targeted by social reform state programs. High-visibility global-scale mega-events play a major role in fostering state interventions for the planned management of human activity and the regulation and normalization of social behaviour. Beijing was famous for its multiple campaigns to improve the demeanour of the city's fifteen million inhabitants. The way people spoke, dressed, their manners and personal hygiene, the way they moved, waited in line, cheered at events, and behaved in public were all considered important issues for the success of the Games. Focusing on hygiene, civility, morality, sports ethics, and respect for law and order, public interest messages in the press, on television and on public billboards across the city instructed citizens on the proper use of public toilets, urged them to speak proper mandarin or learn English, to smile more, and to keep their shirts on in the summer. Specifically, targeted behaviours included spitting, queue jumping, jaywalking, hawking, swearing, and smoking.

Other social reform initiatives follow a more legal approach with the banning of certain behaviours and their criminalization and seek to impose a new disciplinary landscape by conflating disarray and indiscipline with crime. Public policies display a blanket intolerance for all forms of disorder and so-called 'quality of life' crimes associated with poverty and informality. Initiatives range from anti-homeless and anti-mendicity laws, to repressive measures of social control that criminalize the poor and purge the city of informal commerce, upon which so many urban dwellers depend for their survival. They target specific classes of people who have themselves become markers of disorder, including vagrants, prostitutes, street children, panhandlers, drug users, the homeless, and certain classes of youth. Urban space is also increasingly policed and regulated against visual pollution and other forms of nuisance from the poor and marginal. Weeks after Rio de Janeiro was selected as host of the Olympics in 2009, Mayor Eduardo Paes initiated his 'Shock of Order' initiative to crack down on urban disorder and small crime. Modelled on the zero-tolerance campaign perfected by Rudolf Giuliani in 1990s New York, the program was influenced by the 'broken windows' theory, which rests upon the assumption that minor disorder and small-scale incivilities, if not taken seriously, will escalate into uncontrollable crime and chaos. Giuliani himself was hired in 2010 as a security consultant for the Rio de Janeiro Olympic Games.

These repressive measures are generally justified by a need for increased security. Mega-events are greatly infused by the spectacle of public order and security, and seek to make the state presence more visible in the urban landscape, with the proliferation of police patrols and the multiplication of public interest messages. This conspicuous visibility of law and order helps normalize intrusive security measures, thereby concealing their discriminatory nature and making it acceptable for people to be arrested for the crime of being undesirable. These actions often stem from an image construction imperative rather than from a real security threat and are meant to ensure that undesirable social elements will not ruin image construction efforts. Security thus serves as a code word for social beautification initiatives, used to justify the imposition of a strict public order and the targeting of vagrancy, begging, prostitution and other illicit activities.

Conclusion: the impacts of urban image construction

This survey of image construction strategies suggest that such initiatives are neither harmless nor innocuous, but can have very real and profound social implications. By impacting the way the city is conceived, experienced and designed, they not only foster the socio-spatial reorganization of urban space and transform the cityscape in its very materiality but they also redefine the terms of belonging to society and allow for the construction of certain members of the citizenry as structurally irrelevant and unworthy of equal rights.

Far from being politically neutral, urban image construction practices are instruments in the exercise and consolidation of power. They enable ruling coalitions to impose a particular worldview upon society, shaped by the interests of local economic and political elites, and external stakeholders. By contributing to the crystallization of a partial, exclusive, and reductive representation of the city, where the poor, the black, the marginal, and the informal have no legitimate place, they reinforce power disparities and perpetuate patterns of stratification, thereby posing a sizable threat for social justice.

In its desire to stand out in the global competition for visitors and capital, the late capitalist entrepreneurial city has turned to the event spectacle and the manipulation of images to both seduce and manufacture consent. The resulting socio-aesthetic transformation of the city promotes the construction of a consensual image, hostile to conflict and difference, and the depoliticization of the urban landscape, reduced to a mere object of consumption and speculation. The spaces of illusion and exclusion that result from such image construction processes function as instruments of deception that conceal the rising contradictions and social inequalities of the neo-liberal city. However, multiple examples included in this volume suggest that other, alternative and inclusive place branding practices that convey a more complex, transparent and diversified portrait of urban reality are emerging and contributing to the creation of more expansive urban representations.

References

Deutsche, Rosalyn. (1996) *Eviction: Art and Spatial Politics*. Cambridge and London: MIT Press.

Gaffney, C. (2016) 'Geo-porn: Selling the city through mediated spectacle', Urban Transformation Processes: The role of Flagship Architecture as Urban Generator (American Association of Geographers Conference). San Francisco.

Garnier, J.-P. (2008) 'Scénographies pour un simulacre: L'espace public réenchanté'. *Espace et Société*, 3(134), pp. 67–81.

Healey, P. (2002) 'On creating the "city" as a collective resource'. *Urban Studies*, 39, pp. 1777–1792.

Kaika, M. (2005) *City of Flows: Modernity, Nature, and the City*. London: Routledge.

Leach, N. (1999) *The Anaesthetics of Architecture*. Boston: MIT Press.

Lefebvre, H. (1991) *The Production of Space*. Oxford: Blackwell.

Smith, A. (2005) 'Reimaging the city: the value of sport initiatives'. *Annals of Tourism Research*, 32(1), pp. 217–236.

Wright, T. (1997) *Out of Place: Homeless Mobilizations, Subcities and Contested Landscapes*. Albany, NY: State University of New York Press.

1 Introduction

Maria Lichrou, Mihalis Kavaratzis and Massimo Giovanardi

Tensions, intentions and pretentions

Places are of vital significance for all of us. And yet, do we understand them well? Do we attempt to examine them in adequate detail before we engage in projects that influence the identity of a place, its history and heritage, its population, their attachment to their place and their future prospects in it? Significant tensions arise when, for the sake of branding, authorities, politicians or consultants interfere with the processes of place development, place attachment, place identity and so on. A series of significant risks are taken, often without consideration of the consequences. In the Foreword that precedes this Introduction, Anne Marie Broudehoux gives an account of everything that is wrong with current understandings and misunderstandings, uses and misuses of place branding. Her typology of interventions for the production of a place's image (i.e. the conceived, the physical and the social) allows her to critically comment on both theory and practice across the world. In doing so, she highlights the existing and potential tensions created by the 'who', the 'what for' and the 'how' of place branding projects. Who, what for and how conceives, designs and implements place branding projects? What are the intended and unintended, planned and unplanned, explicit and implicit aims and consequences? How do they fit in the political and ideological agenda? Place branding is not as innocent as some like to think of it and observations on the current state of the discipline make any critical researcher engage in serious wonderings around place brands and their effects on places and the people that live in them. As Vanolo (2017, 1) puts it, 'the construction and manipulation of urban images triggers a complex politics of representation, modifying the visibility and the invisibility of spaces, subjects, problems and discourses'. Place branding produces, reproduces, circulates and, perhaps, imposes place imaginaries that affect the lives of real people, reconstructing and reinforcing narratives of power. Such wonderings have provided the motivation and inspiration for this edited volume. It is the intention of both editors and contributors to consider the evident tensions around place branding in an attempt to shed light on them and make them more approachable as political phenomena. And, thus, perhaps identify ways to resolve them. It is for the readers to judge whether this intention is achieved or remains a pretention.

Background

Behind the notions of place marketing and place branding usually lies the assumption that, not too differently from products and services, cities, countries and other spatially extended 'products' can be managed, developed and promoted following a marketing business philosophy. In this view, place managers can orient their policymaking activities towards the needs of different targets. How did such a view develop historically? Alarmed by the pressure of the socio-economic changes begun in the mid-1970s and the unprecedented globalizing tendencies weakening national state's traditional role, places approached the 'marketing discourse' voraciously. This was coupled with a crisis in public sector planning from the 1970s onwards. There was an onset of disillusionment with the effectiveness of traditional urban planning regulatory instruments that seemed to have lost their efficacy, together with changes in fashionable political approaches (Ashworth and Voogd, 1990). Furthermore, with the increased mobility of capital, the ability of states to control multinational economic flows was almost eliminated, which increased competition among places for the attraction of capital investment (Harvey, 1989). Competition is thus a key concept in this respect. The notion of competitiveness has been unfolded as a hegemonic discourse not only in economics and economic geography (see Sheppard, 2000) but also as the aspect that enabled (and legitimized) the quick marketing-arms race pursued by many places. This perspective sees place marketing as a pragmatic, objective, and apolitical activity. In essence, what is suggested is that the place-product can be marketed with the same logic, tools and methods as most other products. The above described dominant view of place marketing is problematic in many ways, two of which are particularly important and serve as starting points here. First, it seems to 'naturalize' the ideas of competition and competitiveness, which are understood in absolute terms – in other words, these are 'given' and cities are thought to operate in a 'playground of competition'. Second, this is reinforced by the prescriptive managerial perspectives offered in the literature and in practice. These become the two indissolubly and mutually reinforcing facets of what we might term the 'conventional wisdom' of place marketing and branding, which we problematize in this book.

The conception of the 'place-product' entails certain challenges, because it is characterized by increased complexity and intangibility. This complexity calls for a collaborative effort, which acknowledges and brings together the wishes of all stakeholders involved in the process. Moreover, places are not simply physical settings with tangible attributes; the 'reality' of place is largely mental and perceived based on subjective experiences of place. Due to these challenges, more recent developments in the place marketing field have engendered a shift of terminology from place marketing to place branding, something that has generated both a newly found enthusiasm (e.g. Kavaratzis, 2004) and an increased mistrust (e.g. Greenberg, 2009). For Eshuis and Klijn (2012), the use of branding and its application by policymakers and public managers can be explained by the nature of current governance processes (which, for instance, are more image and perception based) and by wider societal changes such as mediatization and information overload. These have led municipalities to practice 'many of the same promotional and image-generation techniques as private-sector PR firms use' (Zavattaro, 2010: 191) and with the same goals. Place branding integrates functional and representational elements (Giovanardi *et al.*, 2013), but, similarly to other forms of branding, relies heavily on representations. As the Foreword to this book has already indicated, the discipline has developed a set of methods (e.g. catchy slogans, colourful logos, presumptuous identity claims, hiring 'starchitects', bidding for 'city of culture' status etc.) that are applied as quick-fix solutions in very different geographical and socio-political contexts. These strategies have almost uniformly been adopted by various cities and locales in the hope of creating distinctive images that will help them differentiate themselves from other places. However, this has led cities across the world to dubious results and to a serial reproduction of very similar logos, campaigns and attractions across places. One of the main reasons for this, is that in the same logic as place marketing, very often place branding is suggested as a response to inter-place competition and is discussed as if it operates in vacuum only addressing the needs of external audiences, regardless of the needs of local communities. The external orientation of these strategies overlooks key dimensions of places, such as the people constituting place, and – ironically – erodes the distinctiveness of places.

Critical views of place branding have been raised in cognate disciplines such as human geography and sociology, focusing on its unexplored consequences on the physical and, in particular, the social fabric of places. These more critical approaches reveal place branding as an essentially political activity and, accordingly, condemn it as a purely commercial practice that serves hidden agendas and marginalizes particular social groups. The most common criticism sees place branding as an instrument used by urban elites to legitimize their own strategic decision-making. Elsewhere, we have described two generations of critique against place branding (Giovanardi *et al.*, forthcoming). The first generation of critique (e.g. Harvey, 1989; Philo and Kearns, 1993; Paddison, 1993; Holcomb, 1994; Griffiths, 1998; Morgan and Pritchard, 1998; Evans, 2003) revolves around the following main arguments: (1) place marketing and branding ignore the complexity of place and culture; (2) place branding serves the interests of elites and is socially regressive; (3) place branding misinterprets place competition; (4) place marketing and branding produce 'sameness'. The second generation of critique (e.g. Broudehoux, 2007; Colomb, 2011; Gotham, 2007; Greenberg, 2009; Lichrou *et al.*, 2008; Pasquinelli, 2010; Johansson, 2012; Lucarelli and Giovanardi, 2014) starts from a similar point as the first generation: place branding is an instrument used by urban elites to legitimize their own strategic decision-making in the wider context of the hegemonic project of neo-liberal urban governance (see Colomb, 2011). However, this second generation is also marked by the emergence of novel elements such as more applied and empirical perspectives, which investigate an increasingly wider array of place branding campaigns and the emergence of new methodological approaches and research themes.

Advancements in the critical marketing literature (partly also made through the book series in which this book is published) have also boosted motivation and confidence of place marketing and branding researchers in their efforts to question the taken-for-granted pillars of place marketing as usually portrayed by the managerial marketing management literature. It is in this background that this book attempts to make its contribution.

Inclusive place branding

This book aims at consolidating the above critical perspectives on place banding and at laying the foundations for a more responsible development of the place branding discipline. It identifies novel, inclusive alternatives for theory and practice and it explores the preconditions necessary for a constructive turn towards more socially responsible practices. As an alternative approach to the mainstream place branding practice and an idea that might tie together the criticism, we propose the idea of inclusive place branding, which is also what binds together the contributions included in this book. Inclusive place branding is critical both in the sense that it goes against dominant understandings and narratives but also in the sense that, as Akbar and Higgins-Desbiolles (this volume) put it, it attempts to historicize, politicize and contextualize the topic under study. It is alternative in the sense that it does not focus on the usual motivations for and aims of place branding projects. It is political in the sense that it is inspired by an ideology of justice and inclusion. It is socially sensitive in the sense that it caters for the less powerful; for those whose voices are not heard often. Inclusive place branding is made inclusive by adopting the idea of participation, enhancing it and facilitating stakeholder engagement.

Although inclusive place branding is certainly not mainstream, traces of it are evident in academic commentary, scholarly research and, importantly, in practice. One of the intentions of this book is to bring together such instances, examples and ideas and try to figure out what they mean collectively and how they might be used to further advance inclusive place branding. That is why we have tried to include a wide array of contributions. We wanted to include theoretical contributions on the foundations of inclusive and participatory place branding as well as empirical contributions on specific projects or aspects. We wanted to include contributions covering the political/ideological aspects as well as the social consequences of place branding. We wanted to include contributions on the idealistic nature of participation as well as its pragmatic challenges. Finally, we wanted to include contributions on different parts of the world to highlight the different cultural contexts in which inclusive place branding might develop.

We will not endeavour to define here inclusive place branding in a precise manner. We are exploring and delineating inclusive place branding as a form of place branding that a) goes beyond economic interests and goals; b) focuses on the residents; c) integrates the voices of many stakeholders through participatory methods; and d) 'listens' to the non-powerful. For the moment, however, there is no clear form of such branding to observe in practice or define in theory.

This book is about scrutinising the various forms that such inclusive place branding might take and we feel it important to examine several aspects before we can say with any certainty what inclusive place branding looks or should look like. This book sets out to explore the different faces that inclusive place branding might assume, the various aims it might potentially serve, the forms and shapes it already takes in practice, the possible methods it might use, the potential futures it might have. Only then will we be able to say what inclusive place branding means and what it might mean, and assess what is already being done and what more needs to be done.

The chapters of this book

As already stated above, the Foreword by Anne-Marie Broudehoux provides a detailed description of the background against which our proposition of inclusive place branding is made. The Foreword, then, and this introductory chapter by the editors set the scene for everything that follows.

The second chapter by Eva Maria Jernsand and Helena Kraff is an attempt to identify the democratic foundations of place branding. The authors make an important observation about the role of consensus. Consensus is commonly sought in order to legitimize the aims, processes and outcomes of place branding projects and to give an aura of participation and openness to the place branding endeavour. However, the authors argue, consensus-seeking through representative democracy might be more of an obstacle rather than a tool. A particularly interesting aspect of their chapter is the discussion of the inherent contradictions between complexity and consensus. If we accept places and place brands as multiple, dynamic, complex entities, then how is it possible and why is it desirable to seek consensus? Consensus tends to conceal the complexity of the place so doesn't this process ignore (in the best case) and ruin (in the worst) the fascinating complexity of place identity? The authors argue that differing views and even conflicting aims need to be accommodated and offer a range of methods that can assist in this, which leads them to a discussion of power inequalities in participatory projects.

In the first case-based chapter, Skye Akbar and Freya Higgins-Desbiolles take us to Australia in order to explore the extent to which indigenous-led approaches to place branding offer higher inclusiveness. Tourism has been indicated as a major opportunity for both income generation as well as socio-cultural revival for Aboriginals and Torres Strait Islanders. At the same time, the Olympic Games of Sydney in 2000 have used them and their culture, as the authors argue, as anchor for the marketing and promotion of the Games and the country. Yet, the effort has always been top-down and this has resulted in significant resistance from indigenous people themselves leading to alternative bottom-up initiatives that go against the official ones. The authors' insightful analysis concludes that the inclusion of Indigenous people in tourism promotion does not offer inclusiveness because post-colonial Australia has actually failed to resolve its historical tensions. Interestingly, the authors manage to go beyond highlighting once again the complexity of place branding and offer a set of practical recommendations as to how this inclusiveness can be 'restored' and facilitated.

Aram Eisenschitz bases his chapter on an attack on the neo-liberal transformation of society that underpins much of place branding. His motivation is to contribute towards the plea made and shared by the participants in this book that we need to find forms of place promotion that genuinely foster inclusion. 'Genuinely' is the key word here. He uses a series of examples from London's Docklands via Baltimore's regenerated and tourist-beehive Inner Harbour to the skyscrapers in Caracas, Venezuela to criticize the 'politics of the spectacular' that mainstream place branding forms part of, reinforces and legitimizes. Asking whether any of this actually serves in any way the needs and desires of residents, he goes on to wonder whether this extreme focus on the symbolic might be turned into a step towards a more inclusive form of decision making. The possibilities for such a reversal are – he argues – nowhere more apparent than in Baltimore's depiction in the TV series *The Wire*, which centres on a depiction of life physically adjacent to the Inner Harbour but socially many miles away. The chapter identifies and exemplifies many ways to enhance democracy in the local context (e.g. participatory budgeting in Porto Alegre or Boston's Dudley Street Neighbourhood Initiative) while utilizing participation for place marketing and branding.

A very useful examination of mainstream marketing theories is undertaken in the next chapter by Jan Brown, which advances our understanding of the theoretical underpinnings of a marketing view of places. She proposes and develops the idea of a service ecosystem, which puts humans and their diverse interactions at its core. To increase inclusiveness, she argues, we need to search for the uniqueness of the place and its brand in the unique ways in which resources are integrated through networks and institutional arrangements. The chapter's mission is to understand, include and celebrate processes that put people first and include a much wider range of representations than are currently common. She adopts a service ecosystem perspective of Service Dominant Logic and proposes a typology of six types of place actors with different stakes in the value co-creation process. Her analysis shows the need for representations of place to be communicated in different ways in order to capture the ecosystem and its subsystems in a process of convergence. This opens several possibilities for novel understandings of place representations and their role in place branding.

Cecillia Cassinger and Åsa Thelander use Lefebvre's production of space triad to ground their processual view of place identity and the ways in which place branding influences it. Their empirical investigation of a collective, participatory place branding project on the Instagram account of the Swedish city of Landskrona, leads to very interesting findings. First amongst those is the mutual influence of internal and external views of the city; an idea that provides substantial evidence for much of place branding's recent theorization. They show that the tourist gaze is as much a mirror that shows what we want changed and their analysis demonstrates that the city's residents explicitly use tourist photography as a point of reference, thus relying on the practice of tourists to re-imagine their own city. Another interesting finding relates to a painfully relevant and 'hot' issue at the moment, namely immigrants. As they find, while immigrants were mentioned in their interviews, they never featured in the Instagram posts. Their chapter is very illustrative of the complexities of participation in place branding. When one of the participants (participant 6) posted photos in order to highlight issues he thought were crucial (such as deprived areas, the poor, immigration etc.) he didn't get 'likes' on Instagram and he was told that he was not in the spirit of the participatory project. As the authors state, 'in effect, the inclusiveness of the project became excluding'.

In their chapter, Kevin Fox Gotham and Cate Irvin offer a fascinating account of the many phases, aspects and faces of branding New Orleans since hurricane Katrina hit the city in 2005 followed by a series of image-damaging disasters. Participation and inclusion are covered indirectly and rather implicitly here. On the one hand, participation, especially of the residents, is striking in its absence making a powerful comment on the current state of place branding practice. Yet, the chapter does bring to the foreground the need for participation and cooperation between several stakeholders (from the authorities to Airbnb hosts and even celebrities like Brad Pitt). At the same time, the authors evaluate what the opportunities and challenges provided by the blurring between tourism and everyday life might mean for branding in New Orleans. Finally, the authors remind us something very important for this book: place branding is done by many people at many points and times. It is as much a practice and set of activities by officials and authorities who actually call what they do 'branding' as it is a practice and set of activities by people who don't call what they do 'branding' but many other things, including 'everyday life'.

In their chapter, Gary Warnaby, Richard Koek and Dominic Medway utilize de Certeau's conception of maps and tours. They argue that the common top-down approaches to place brands and place branding are rooted in a visual understanding of place, captured by the map metaphor. They favour instead a more bottom-up approach based on the wider, actual experience of the place, which is captured effectively by the tour metaphor. The authors combine these metaphors with other place-related theories to ask and answer their three central questions, namely 'what is being represented?', 'how does the representation occur?' and 'who is implementing representational activities?' In doing so, they actually discuss many of the current misapprehensions of place branding and, at the same time, they offer alternative routes for the future. They suggest a move of focus from materiality (in other words the static views of place representations) towards storytelling and movement (in other words the more fluid and open views of place representations), which allows them to find ways forward in developing more overt performative dimensions of place branding. They argue that such a development (particularly as it can be facilitated by information technology and web 2.0 applications) is very likely to increase individual engagement with a collective narrative of the place.

The popular topic of food in place branding is the main topic of the next chapter by Anette Therkelsen. Her examination of four Danish destinations actively profiling themselves as food places for tourists allows her to identify food narratives developed in the effort to achieve distinct food-based place brands. However, these are shown to point towards conformity and indicate an undifferentiated approach to place branding. Furthermore, the generic food place brands generated give very little substance to local food, particularly missing out on its territorial and temporal construction. This leads to what the author describes as the conformity paradox, whereby the effort to create differentiation is based on the same motives and very similar claims; something often noted in place branding practice as we have seen above. This promotional 'monologue' as the author calls it instead of a 'relationship building dialogue' hinders the development of authentic, local food-based place brands. In this sense, food extends beyond a mere focus of this chapter, actually offering a perspective of place branding efforts and how they so often lead to generic brands. Alternative promotional efforts aiming at a broader approach to local cultural capital are discussed in the chapter as a way forward.

In the next chapter, Johan Gromark takes us to Stockholm to critically examine from an inclusiveness point of view a campaign that has raised significant commentary (both praise and criticism): 'Stockholm – The Capital of Scandinavia'. He combines two central concepts, namely the idea of a projective brand orientation and the concept of organizational narcissism to provide a critical analysis of what he sees as a soft form of trademarked imperialism exhibited by the Swedish capital. His analysis illuminates the risk of organizational narcissism that comes with a projective form of brand orientation in a place branding setting. The case study examines in detail both the intentions behind the development of the brand and the logotype as well as the resistance it has generated. The diagnosis, as the title of the chapter suggests, is that Stockholm does suffer from narcissism. Evidence is found of all four traits of narcissism in Stockholm's brand: self-aggrandizement, entitlement, denial and rationalization. The chapter suggests the alternative of a relational brand orientation as the solution and a way forward both for Stockholm and for place branding in general.

The contribution by Staci Zavattaro and Daniel Fay brings us to Florida to examine the rather strange case of how an orange tie derailed the state's branding effort. In an attempt to go beyond the state's well-established tourism brand and emphasize the business aspects, they replaced the 'I' in the word Florida with an orange tie. However, the design was thought to be gendered, given that men wear ties and women usually don't. The chapter examines this case utilizing Zavattaro's own conceptualization of place branding through the phases of the image, which is inspired by the work of Jean Baudrillard and describes what might happen after places try to develop branding and marketing strategies. The analysis shows that the brand slides into the four phases of the image sometimes intentionally and sometimes not and that it can slide back and forth from one phase to the next or the previous. Interestingly, a major drawback of the campaign is found in the fact that local communities were not consulted and that local knowledge and local talent were left unused. The authors show how branding can go amiss when the focus is on the images rather than the content and various stakeholder groups are not included.

Andrea Lucarelli, in his chapter explores the political dimensions and the political consequences of place branding. He criticizes the lack of a deep-rooted political examination in the literature and scrutinizes the main ideas, the wider narrative and the vocabulary of the neo-liberal, economic approach to place branding. His analysis is based on the three dimensions of place branding as a policy process, place branding as an ideology and place branding as the politics of power. The integration of these three allows him to delve deep into the political nature of place branding and give us a framework that can be used as the basis for more politically-rooted and critical studies of place branding. A particularly helpful suggestion is the breaking of the dichotomy 'production vs consumption', which, he argues, hinders integration and restricts the chances for wider inclusiveness. Furthermore, and very interestingly, using David Harvey's relevant idea, this chapter expresses a major premise of this book as a whole: place branding is a policy contested and shaped both in the street and in the planning office.

The concluding chapter by the editors brings everything together identifying the main lines of arguments made in this book and extracting valuable lessons for the future of inclusive place branding.

Finally, in her invited closing commentary, Nadia Kaneva uses the exciting example of the Day of the Dead Parade in Mexico to bring our attention to the many and various questions that place branding efforts raise and the unintended effects of place branding decisions. A parade that never actually formed part of a famous and culturally important celebration now features as a major place branding and tourism marketing tool simply because it was conceived by a film maker. Is it that simple to mark a place's identity and add to it? Is it that simple to invite the residents to rethink their heritage? But, equally, is it simple to ignore the callings of a global market and a significant source of income? Is it simple to dismiss what actually might really be an identity-forming activity? The author also contributes to this book – and we think to the place branding discipline – a clear, well-articulated and specific research agenda for the future giving us the four main areas of focus.

It is the desire of both editors and contributors of this volume to move the discipline towards a better future and we are certain beyond any doubt that the readers of this volume share our sentiment. As editors, we would like to thank all the contributors for their time, effort, passion and hard work. The readers of this book will have the chance to engage in a series of thorough discussions and read about a range of examples stemming from diverse places. We hope you will find the book inspiring and it might serve as the springboard and a point of reference for more critical, more socially responsible and, indeed, more inclusive place branding.

References

Ashworth, G. J. and Voogd, H. (1990) *Selling the City: Marketing Approaches in Public Sector Urban Planning*. London: Belhaven Press.

Broudehoux, A. (2007) 'Spectacular Beijing: the conspicuous construction of an Olympic metropolis'. *Journal of Urban Affairs*, 29(4), pp. 383–399.

Colomb, C. (2011) *Staging the New Berlin*. London: Routledge.

Eshuis, J. and Klijn, E. H. (2012) *Branding in Governance and Public Management*. London: Routledge.

Evans, G. (2003) 'Hard-branding the cultural city–from Prado to Prada'. *International Journal of Urban and Regional Research*, 27(2), pp. 417–440.

Giovanardi, M., Lucarelli, A. and Pasquinelli, C. (2013) 'Towards brand ecology. An analytical semiotic framework for interpreting the emergence of place brands'. *Marketing Theory*, 13(3), pp. 365–383.

Giovanardi, M., Lichrou, M. and Kavaratzis, M. (forthcoming) 'Critical Perspectives on Place Marketing', in Tadajewski, M., Higgins, M., Denegri-Knott, J. and Varman, R. (eds), *The Routledge Companion to Critical Marketing*. London: Routledge.

Gotham, K. F. (2007) '(Re)Branding the Big Easy Tourism Rebuilding in Post-Katrina New Orleans'. *Urban Affairs Review*, 42(6), pp. 823–850.

Greenberg, M. (2009) *Branding New York: how a city in crisis was sold to the world*. London: Routledge.

Griffiths, R. (1998) 'Making sameness: Place marketing and the new urban entrepreneurialism', in Oatley, N. (ed.) *Cities Economic Competition and Urban Policy*. London: Paul Chapman.

Harvey, D. (1989). 'From Managerialism to entrepreneurialism: The Transformation in urban governance in late capitalism'. *Geografiska Annaler*, 71B.

Holcomb, B. (1994) 'City make-overs: marketing the post-industrial city', in J. R. Gold and S. V. Ward (eds), *Place Promotion*. Chichester: John Wiley and Sons, pp. 115–131.

Johansson, M. (2012) 'Place branding and the imaginary: The politics of re-imagining a garden city'. *Urban Studies*, 49(16), pp. 3611–3626.

Kavaratzis, M. (2004) 'From city marketing to city branding: Towards a theoretical framework for developing city brands'. *Place Branding*, 1(1), pp. 58–73.

Lichrou, M., O'Malley, L. and Patterson, M. (2008) 'Place product or place narrative(s)? Perspectives in the Marketing of Tourism Destinations'. *Journal of Strategic Marketing*, 16(1), pp. 27–39.

Lucarelli, A. and Giovanardi, M. (2014) 'The political nature of brand governance: a discourse analysis approach to a regional brand building process'. *Journal of Public Affairs*, 16(1), pp. 16–27.

Morgan, N. and Pritchard, A. (1998) *Tourism Promotion and Power: Creating Images, Creating Identities*. New York: John Wiley & Sons Ltd.

Paddison, R. (1993) 'City marketing, image reconstruction and urban regeneration'. *Urban Studies*, 30(2), pp. 339–349.

Pasquinelli, C. (2010) 'The limits of place branding for local development: The case of Tuscany and the Arnovalley brand'. *Local Economy*, 25(7), pp. 558–572.

Philo, C., and Kearns, G. (Eds.). (1993) *Selling Places: The City As Cultural Capital, Past And Present*. London: Pergamon Press.

Sheppard, E. (2000) 'Competition in space and between places'. *A Companion to Economic Geography*, pp. 169–186.

Vanolo, A. (2017) *City Branding*. Oxon: Routledge.

Zavattaro, S. (2010) 'Municipalities as public relations and marketing firms', *Administrative Theory and Praxis*, 32(2), pp. 191–211.

2 Democracy in participatory place branding

A critical approach

Eva Maria Jernsand and Helena Kraff

Introduction

This chapter follows the growing stream of research that acknowledges multiple stakeholder participation in place branding, in particular the emergent literature on residents as central participants (Baker, 2007; Braun *et al.*, 2013; Hanna and Rowley, 2011; Kavaratzis, 2012). Residents are strongly affected by place branding initiatives and therefore have the right to be deeply engaged throughout the entire process, rather than only being consulted in the start-up phase or at smaller events (Kavaratzis, 2012; Zenker and Beckmann, 2013; Zenker and Erfgen, 2014). Thus, residents need to be seen as one of many stakeholder groups who together own and co-create the place brand (Kavaratzis and Hatch, 2013). This participatory view resonates largely with how theories of public governance have developed, where participatory and deliberative democracy has become means to promote political renewal (Barnes *et al.*, 2004). As Giovanardi, Lucarelli and Pasquinielli (2013, p. 366) state, place branding is moving 'from the business context in which it was born' towards the 'public and spatial'. Place branding is thereby becoming a political tool, and as such needs to gain democratic legitimacy (Kalandides, 2011b).

However, there are aspects that need to be considered when dealing with participation. Otherwise, the risk is that place branding will fall under the same type of critique as fields such as design, architecture, planning and development studies, where participation has been practised for a long time. For example, in design it is argued that even though participation is seen as crucial, it is treated as unproblematic (Bødker, 2006) and 'the ideas behind it are rarely discussed critically' (Steen, 2011, p. 16). In architecture, participation is accused of having become a buzzword, described in a romantic way as being about inclusion and democracy, but 'if you scratch the surface, critical interrogations of what is at stake are strikingly absent' (Miessen, 2010, p. 33). There is a risk that participation is reduced to a form where residents are treated merely as informants, or are involved for educational purposes or for the justification of decisions already taken, under the veil of being participatory (Arnstein, 1969). As Kavaratzis (2012, p. 8) put it concerning place branding, residents should be seen as a main stakeholder group, not only be consulted or paid 'lip service'.

A critical aspect with participatory processes is that of consensus thinking, however, this discussion seems to have been absent from the place branding literature. Coherency and the formulation of a common vision are generally highlighted as central, but the question needs to be posed as to whether this corresponds with the inclusion of multiple stakeholders. In architecture and development studies, scholars claim that aiming for general consensus leads to reductive processes that fail to show disparities (Hamdi, 2009), and crucial matters risk falling under the rule of majority (Miessen, 2010). Rather, an inclusive process must acknowledge diverging views where conflict and power issues are allowed to come forth. This resonates with Kavaratzis and Hatch's (2013, p. 82) description of place branding as an ongoing 'dialogue, debate and contestation'. This chapter therefore aims to encourage a critical discussion on how the notion of participatory place branding is to be understood and practised, as a crucial foundation for the future of place branding. The purpose is to problematize the connection between inclusion and consensus in place branding, since there seems to be a romantic view that these two notions are somehow compatible.

Democratic legitimacy is discussed in relation to places, place identity, place branding and governance. Further, we question the view of consensus as a goal in place branding on the basis of how it is acknowledged as problematic in other fields. This in turn opens up the concept of participation for problematizing. The chapter ends with a conclusion and discussion on how democratic place branding through participation could be understood and performed in the future.

Democratic legitimacy

Places are not only geographical locations with physical attributes; they are settings for social relations, experiences and interpretations (Agnew, 1987; Insch and Florek, 2010; Lichrou *et al.*, 2014; Warnaby and Medway, 2013). The 'subjective dimension' (Agnew, 1987, p. 231) makes place identity something emergent, fluid and changeable, formatted through ongoing and sometimes contesting dialogues (Kalandides, 2011a; Kavaratzis and Hatch, 2013; Warnaby and Medway, 2013). There are, for instance, materiality and functionality, emotions and imagination, and individualism and collectivism (Kavaratzis and Hatch, 2013). Kavaratzis and Hatch (2013) propose that this perspective on place identity downplays the role of place branding to the facilitation of the identity process, where place brand authorities are one of many stakeholder groups in a system of interactions.

Similarly, in 1972, the American diplomat Harlan Cleveland foresaw that the hierarchical pyramids of governance will be replaced by 'interlaced webs of tension in which control is loose, power diffused, and centers of decision plural', where 'multilateral brokerage' will take place (Cleveland, 1972, p. 13). His prediction corresponds with a description of place branding as multiple systems of interaction between the internal and the external, the organized and the random, and the individual and the collective (Kavaratzis and Hatch, 2013). Both also emphasize a collaborative view through the inclusion of multiple stakeholders, which could be seen as a way of democratizing the processes.

Democratic legitimacy is a crucial foundation for political processes, of which place branding has increasingly become part (Giovanardi *et al.*, 2013; Kalandides, 2011b). However, it is argued that the electoral component of democracy, where citizens vote for representatives, is not always sufficient since those who are elected may use their power for self-interest, and thereby marginalize others (Lindberg *et al.*, 2014). Different forms of active citizenship are seen as alternative ways to renew and enhance democracy and to increase efficiency by putting pressure on public service organizations (Barnes *et al.*, 2004). Thus, the participatory component of democracy emphasizes values and mechanisms of direct rule (Coppedge *et al.*, 2011; Lindberg *et al.*, 2014). Another conception that is closely related to participatory democracy is deliberative democracy, which means that judgements are made by a process of logic and reason (Gutmann and Thompson, 2004; Ryfe, 2005). It returns to the classical idea that the democratic government should embody the people's will (Henneberg *et al.*, 2009). Political decisions should 'be informed by respectful and reasonable dialogue at all levels rather than by emotional appeals, solidary attachments, parochial interests, or coercion' (Lindberg *et al.*, 2014, p. 160). Successful deliberation helps people to evaluate alternative choices as well as providing engaging 'cultural glue' (Ryfe, 2005). Deliberative democracy is thus considered participative and legitimate. However, as will be examined below, it can also be questioned.

Complexity and consensus: contradictory notions

Public participation and deliberative democracy have come to be used as means to promote political renewal in governments all over the world (Barnes *et al.*, 2004). However, there is a contradiction between inclusion of diverse stakeholders and the goal of consensus. For example, Cleveland's (1972, p. 13) description of future governance, as a system of complicated processes and 'interlaced webs of tension', clashes with his desire for it to be 'collegial, consensual, and consultative'. As Henneberg *et al.* (2009, p. 176) point out, deliberative theorists seem to believe that there exists a unified will of the people, 'a rational consensus of public opinion'. It is suggested, for example, that conflict can be managed by continuous discussion and mutual respect, with the aim of reaching common ground (Gutmann and Thompson, 2004). Mouffe (2013), however, argues that too much focus on consensus leads to the avoidance of confrontation and suppression of controversial issues, which in turn leads to apathy and disaffection. It is to treat the process as rational led by an authoritarian order, which misses the whole point of what democracy needs to be: dialogic and pluralistic (Mouffe, 2013). Democracy should rather be a space where difference and even conflict is permitted and where multiple and heterogeneous voices are allowed to be heard. Also, reaching consensus does not mean that alternative views are not there or that they will disappear. Not allowing views that are seen as irrational can 'backfire into an explosion of antagonisms unmanageable by the democratic process' (Mouffe, 2013, p. 159). Further, in participatory planning, architecture and development studies, criticisms have been raised against a heavy focus on consensus. It is argued that consensus thinking leads to reductive processes that merely seek out commonalities but fail to see differences (Hamdi, 2009). Critical issues will fall under majority rule (Miessen, 2010), and the 'complexity of social relationships' will go unnoticed (Shah and Kaul Shah, 1995, p. 48). Consensus, especially during the early stages of a project, is not considered to be beneficial in the long run. In order to move forward and to reach longstanding results, diverging opinions need to be allowed and conflicts must be given room to be played out (Gujit and Cornwall, 1995; Miessen, 2010).

The consensus phenomenon, as well as its critique, can also be found in place branding; however, the critique is not as explicit and widespread as in the fields stated above. Rather, as wide a consensus as possible is regarded as important, in order to create a shared vision (Stubbs and Warnaby, 2015; Warnaby and Medway, 2015; Warnaby *et al.*, 2015). The aim is to create a coherent brand, which captures the essence of the place. This superficial view reduces place identity to something static, easily tapped and defined, (Kavaratzis and Hatch, 2013) and branding to a monologic, reductive and fully controllable type of communication where all actors are transformed into one unified voice (Marsh and Fawcett, 2011; Zenker and Beckmann, 2013). As Kalandides (2006) points out, this will ruin the complexity that makes places intriguing.

To counter this, a constant re-examination of places needs to be made; about culture, history, who lives and works there, and about inequalities and meanings (Philo and Kearns, 1993). Giovanardi *et al.* (2013, p. 368), drawing on the work of Lury (2004) and Pasquinelli (2010), similarly point out that the place brand needs to be understood as a 'relationship-builder', as an 'active interface' between the place and its actors, rather than as a 'promotional vehicle'. Further, if the complexity and heterogeneity of the place is to be respected, decision-making has to be spread out (Kalandides, 2006). This resonates with a process-based model of identity, where branding is the facilitator and where several interwoven processes take place at the same time (Kavaratzis and Hatch, 2013). As Kalandides (2006) suggests, a fragmented, non-coherent identity of a place is a more authentic picture than trying to squeeze identity down to standard formulas. In the case of Berlin, Kalandides (2006, p. 7) points out that the city can rest on its heritage from the Second World War, but it can also be a 'city of creativity, or a city of sustainability, a city of immigration, a city of sciences, a city of diversity and a lot more'. Different stakeholders can, and should, have their own perceptions of and relationships to the city. The complexity that this leads to is what makes the place alive, unique and interesting for present and future residents, investors, industry and tourists. As an example, Jernsand *et al.* (2015) refer to a participatory place branding project in Kisumu, Kenya, of which one part was to develop a packaged tour in collaboration with a local tour guide group. Earlier, a resident had expressed concerns about tourists only visiting the beautiful and sanitized parts of Kenya, such as the scenery of the Masai Mara.

He exclaimed that 'this is not Kenya!'. This consideration was taken into account in the development of the tour, where the exposition of challenges and social issues that residents face in their daily life was included, as well as more traditional activities such as a game ride and tasting local food. When the tour was tested on a group of tourists, the participants said that it was emotionally challenging, but that they appreciated the opportunity to experience it. The example shows that a permissive view of place branding includes diverse meanings. It also confirms that residents' involvement in the development of place is important, and shows that visitors want to (and should be able to) get a diverse experience, including both positive and problematic aspects of a place.

Participation: complex in practice

Participation generally has positive connotations due to its focus on empowerment and people-led procedures (Hickey and Mohan, 2004). However, in practice, arriving at a socially feasible process is extremely complex (Wall and Mathieson, 2006), since it involves issues of power dynamics (Cleaver, 2001). The authors agree with a view of place branding as participatory, with the inclusion of multiple stakeholders, especially residents, being seen as important. Residents need to be prioritized as participants throughout the entire place branding process (Kavaratzis, 2012; Kavaratzis and Ashworth, 2008), although, as several scholars have pointed out (e.g. Aitken and Campelo, 2011; Bennett and Savani, 2003; Kavaratzis, 2012), this is generally not the case. If residents are involved, they are predominantly represented by a few individuals, and only in selected parts of the process (Bennett and Savani, 2003; Eshuis *et al.*, 2014; Zenker and Erfgen, 2014).

Zenker and Erfgen (2014) state that when the participatory approach encounters the place authorities in public governance, a demanding and uncomfortable situation arises, in which some of the power of decision-making must be given up. This is far from the comfort zones of politicians, officials and consultants, and is the reason why there are significant deficiencies when it comes to implementation (Zenker and Erfgen, 2014). Kavaratzis (2012) points to the difference from general management, where project managers usually prioritize stakeholders who are powerful and interested. Such an approach is not suitable in a place branding context, since it 'leads to elitism, lack of inclusiveness and ultimately to a brand alien to the place' (p. 13). Stubbs and Warnaby (2015, p. 105) also acknowledge the risk of distorted stakeholder representations where only certain groups are heard, and that decisions are made easy by the avoidance of 'hard choices that may prove divisive'. An example is given by Kraff and Jernsand (2014), who refer to a process in Kenya that was not straightforward, not always rational and constantly affected by issues of power among stakeholders from both outside and inside the project. The focus was on residents' participation throughout, for example through workshops, open presentations and an available project space. However, despite the goal of being as inclusive as possible, it proved to be difficult to reach an equal gender distribution amongst participants. For example, women found it hard to participate in workshops, since they were too busy working and taking care of their families. The women also felt that the location for the project space was not available for them. This shows the importance of not taking for granted that the representations of participants will naturally be fair, of actively looking for groups that may not be represented, and of taking the duration of activities, timing and setting into account.

In other fields, scholars have raised similar concerns regarding power inequalities in participatory work. In the public sector, it is argued that participation has become a 'technology' to control citizens (Eshuis and Edwards, 2013). For example, in cases in the UK where consultation with residents was mandatory, people were 'presented with a narrow range of options' and asked to decide which one they preferred (Martin, 2009, p. 285). Since it is governments that set the rules of such arrangements and thereby shape citizen behaviour, participation becomes a tool to realize policies rather than giving people power (Eshuis and Edwards, 2013). Further, the groups that are represented are often narrowly defined and 'over-consulted', while others' views are not heard, especially those who are 'hard to reach' or have opinions that conflict with the policy-makers' opinions (Martin, 2009). It is also acknowledged that people are often consulted when decisions have already been made, and that public agencies 'fail to provide adequate feedback to consultees' (Martin, 2009, p. 285).

In design, it is claimed that it is easy for project leaders to interpret projects too narrowly and give priority to their own concerns rather than those of the users (Steen, 2011). In geography, Philo and Kearns (1993) state that powerful groups manipulate cultural and historical resources to further their own private interests, which leads to unresponsive commodification of places. Similarly, in development studies, it is recognized that participation is sensitive to being hijacked by hidden agendas (Kothari, 2001; McGee, 2002). There is a risk that participation goes no further than being a mark-up in policy documents (Chambers, 1997), that participants are given responsibility but not authority, and that they thereby act merely as a means to project workers' own decision-making (Hamdi, 2010). Another issue that is often raised regarding development projects is that communities are described in a simplistic manner, treated as homogeneous and harmonious entities. This is in sharp contrast with reality (Chambers, 1997; McGee, 2002), since it ignores divisions and differences. The focus on a single entity is easy to turn to when the situation gets 'difficult to pin down', since it makes the circumstances understandable and thereby also manageable (Hamdi, 2010, p. 54). Similarly, in place branding, Braun *et al.* (2013) point to the challenge of residents having different and even conflicting preferences and attitudes.

Participatory methods and tools

Participation manifests itself in various ways in different fields and contexts. In public management, the use of public meetings, panels, opinion polls, surveys and focus groups are common, as well as community appraisals and exercises to develop visions (Martin, 2009). In the UK, video booths and free phone lines have been utilized for people to record messages, and health authorities use citizens' juries to reflect on suggestions from experts (Martin, 2009). A growing interest in user-driven innovation to improve public services can also be noted (Sørensen and Torfing, 2011). For example, service and transformation design projects have gained prominent positions, especially in the health sector (see e.g. Swedish Design Research Journal, 2012; Burns *et al.*, 2006), with specific collaborative tools and the view that the users are the experts.

Further, new interactive technologies are claimed to have democratic potential for the inclusion of residents in public governance (Paganoni, 2012). Message boards, discussions with policymakers and consultations in budgeting are carried out online (Martin, 2009). However, as Evans and Campos (2013, p. 172) point out, 'current initiatives must be re-evaluated and new approaches explored'. Residents have difficulties in assessing the relevance and reliability of the information on websites since information on why and how this material was collected and what it should be used for is often lacking (Evans and Campos, 2013). Paganoni (2012, p. 23) stresses that social inclusion today is mainly about public consultation, where people get a chance to 'have their say' by filling in online forms that are rigidly structured with fixed alternatives, which leaves no room for closer engagement. She also points out that if citizens get feedback it is on a very basic level, or only if the results are positive.

In place branding, participation consists of similar tools to those stated above (see e.g. Kalandides, 2006; Kalandides, 2011b). Stubbs and Warnaby (2015) suggest the workshop format as a viable way to engage stakeholders in formatting a vision. These workshops are described as 'short, fun and highly engaging', including educational elements as well as stakeholders working and presenting together 'to provide feedback on a particular area of interest' (Stubbs and Warnaby, 2015, p. 112). Collaborative workshops are also commonly used in participatory design, where it is argued that stronger ideation and co-creative learning can occur when a number of people come together at the same time (Westerlund, 2009). Regarding action research, creative and non-verbal approaches are said to integrate both sides of the brain, which creates high levels of energy (Mackewn, 2008). Similarly, Greenwood and Levin (2007) propose that humour and playfulness are vital tools since they evoke tacit knowledge. However, scholars from development studies have found that workshops in themselves are not viable tools for dealing with conflicting views that may arise in a participatory process. For example, the workshop format, often built around an open discussion, makes it hard to reach beyond the safe topics and deal with the complex and contested (Pottier and Orone, 1995). Reaching a general agreement may be easy; however, the risk is that it will mask internal divisions and tensions. It should therefore be noted that the participatory methods described above must not work alone. Martin (2009) points out that each exercise needs objectives in order to 'ensure that the right tools and techniques are used and the right groups are involved' (p. 286) and 'to clarify what level of influence is being offered' (p. 287). This helps the participants in understanding what kinds of results they can expect to get, and thereby reduces disappointments (Martin, 2009).

Again, referring to the process in Kenya (Jernsand and Kraff, 2015; Kraff and Jernsand, 2014), the negotiation of problematic issues and concerns did not always take place during organized events such as workshops, but emerged in the spaces in between, during informal encounters and more private discussions. These situations gave crucial input to the overall process, for example with regard to what types of activities were suitable or not. It was also here that tensions between groups came to the surface. This shows that place branding must include knowledge of how to deal with issues, tensions and conflicts that may appear. Further, it shows that it takes time to form more open relationships and thereby build trust between people (Reason, 1994); discussing sensitive matters is easier after people have been working together for a longer period of time.

Concluding discussion

This chapter contributes to the current academic conversation on how the notion of participatory place branding is to be understood and practised. When place branding enters the public sphere, the democratic legitimacy of its initiatives is open for contestation. However, there seems to be a belief that the way to achieve legitimacy is to steer participating stakeholders' views towards consensus. The purpose of this work is therefore to problematize the connection between inclusion and consensus in place branding.

A critical reading shows that the notion of consensus is in contrast to the multifaceted nature of places. A place is not only a geographical location but a constantly changing 'lived concept' (Cresswell and Hoskins, 2008, p. 394). Trying to capture this complexity in one single and overarching vision is both impossible and inappropriate since it would water it down to nothing. Consensus thinking is also in contradiction to democracy. If democracy is a space where multiple and heterogeneous voices are allowed to be heard (Coppedge *et al.*, 2011; Mouffe, 2013), then place branding needs to be perceived as a relationship-builder (Giovanardi *et al.*, 2013) that allows several interwoven processes to take place at the same time (Kavaratzis and Hatch, 2013). Further, consensus as a consultative and once for all project is in contradiction with the notion of participation as an ongoing and profound process. The risk with a consensus-driven participatory process is that the pluralistic point of democracy is overruled by the majority (Miessen, 2010) and that strong groups will marginalize others (Eshuis and Edwards, 2013; Kothari, 2001). Rather, differing views and conflicts need to be allowed (Gujit and Cornwall, 1995; Miessen, 2010; Mouffe, 2013), since it is diversity that makes places worth living in, working in, investing in and visiting. Moreover, since consensus has the tendency to hide complex matters, it makes it hard to see and therefore also to deal with the challenges that often arise in participatory work.

Place brand authorities should take the opportunity to learn from other fields that have long standing experience of facing the challenges of participation.

Participatory events are not to be seen only as fun or consultative. Rather, they need to be adapted so that critical issues and internal divisions can be brought to the surface (Pottier and Orone, 1995). Approaches, methods and tools are needed that suit processes where residents and other stakeholders are involved on a long-term and regular basis. Participation in place branding is not like general management, where you work with those who are interested and have the power (Kavaratzis, 2012). It is an exercise of public authority (Zenker and Erfgen, 2014), which makes it important for the actors involved learn how to deal with conflicts and tensions, not only during planned events but also in the spaces in between and in a holistic manner. Decision-makers need to let go of some of their power, or place branding will become another tool for realising policies (Eshuis and Edwards, 2013) or may even serve hidden agendas (Kothari, 2001; McGee, 2002).

Further, to achieve democratic legitimacy, the connection must be strengthened between place branding and other governance processes, departments or functions that deal with related aspects, such as planning, public transport, the business sector and public health. Although some actors may have an interest in place branding remaining an isolated and independent area of practice, it is necessary to bring in multiple disciplines to be able to understand it in a holistic way (Ashworth *et al.*, 2015), both in practice and research. Place branding is not a solitary strategy that is detached from public authority, but 'part of policy making at different levels and in different contexts' (Kalandides, 2011b, p. 289).

In this chapter, participatory place branding has been discussed in relation to democratic legitimacy. However, the discussion is only exploratory, and the relations between participation, democracy, consensus and place branding need to be further developed. Another interesting continuation would be to explore how stakeholders perceive place branding and what they think about their current and future roles in a participatory context, for example by interviewing officials from different departments, as well as politicians, residents and consultants.

References

Agnew, J. A. (1987) *Place and Politics: The Geographical Mediation Of State and Society*. Boston: Allen & Unwin.

Aitken, R. and Campelo, A. (2011) 'The four Rs of place branding'. *Journal of Marketing Management*, 28(9–10), pp. 913–933.

Arnstein, S. R. (1969) 'A ladder of participation'. *Journal of American Institute of Planners*, 35(4), pp. 216–224.

Ashworth, G.J., Kavaratzis, M. and Warnaby, G. (2015) 'The need to rethink place branding', in Kavaratzis, M., Warnaby, G. and Ashworth, G. J. (eds.), *Rethinking Place Branding: Comprehensive Brand Development for Cities and Regions*. Switzerland: Springer, pp. 1–12.

Baker, B. (2007) *Destination Branding for Small Cities: The Essentials for Successful Place Branding*. Portland: Creative Leap Books.

Barnes, M., Newman, J. and Sullivan, H. (2004) 'Power, participation and political renewal'. *Social Politics*, 11(2), pp. 267–279.

Bennett, R. and Savani, S. (2003) 'The rebranding of city places: an international comparative investigation'. *International Public Management Review*, 4(2), pp. 70–87.

Bødker, S. (2006) 'When Second Wave HCI meets Third Wave Challenges', Keynote paper in Proceedings of the 4th Nordic conference on Human-computer interaction: changing roles. 14–18 October, Oslo, pp. 1–8.

Braun, E., Kavaratzis, M. and Zenker, S. (2013) 'My city – my brand: the different roles of residents in place branding'. *Journal of Place Management and Development*, 6(1), pp. 18–28.

Burns, C., Cottam, H., Vanstone, C. and Winhall, J. (2006) *Transformation Design Red Paper 02*. London: Design Council.

Chambers, R. (1997) *Whose Reality Counts?: Putting the First Last*. London: Intermediate Technology Productions.

Cleaver, F. (2001) 'Institutions, agency and the limitations of participatory approaches to development', in Cooke, B. and Kothari, U. (eds.), *Participation: The New Tyranny?* London: Zed Books, pp. 36–55.

Cleveland, H. (1972) *The Future Executive: A Guide for Tomorrow's Managers*. New York: Harper & Row.

Coppedge, M., Gerring, J., Altman, D., Bernhard, M., Fish, S., Hicken, A., Krenig, M., Linberg, S. I., McMann, K., Paxton, P., Semetko, H. A., Skaanig, S.-V., Staton, J., and Toerll, J. (2011) 'Conceptualizing and measuring democracy – a new approach'. *Perspectives on Politics*, 9(2), pp. 247–267.

Cresswell, T. and Hoskins, G. (2008) 'Places, persistence and practice: Evaluating historical significance at Angel Island, San Francisco, and Maxwell Street, Chicago'. *Annals of the Association of American Geographers*, 98(2), pp. 392–413.

Eshuis, J. and Edwards, A. (2013) 'Branding the city: the democratic legitimacy of a new mode of governance'. *Urban Studies*, 50(5), pp. 1066–1082.

Eshuis, J., Klijn, E.-H. and Braun, E. (2014) 'Place marketing and citizen participation: branding as strategy to address the emotional dimension of policy making?'. *International Review of Administrative Sciences*, 80(1), pp. 151–171.

Evans, A. M. and Campos, A. (2013) 'Open government initiatives: challenges of citizen participation'. *Journal of Policy Analysis and Management*, 32(1), pp. 172–203.

Giovanardi, M., Lucarelli, A. and Pasquinelli, C. (2013) 'Towards brand ecology: An analytical semiotic framework for interpreting the emergence of place brands'. *Marketing Theory*, 13(3), pp. 365–383.

Greenwood, D. J. and Levin, M. (2007) *Introduction to Action Research: Social Research for Social Change*. 2nd edn. Thousand Oaks, CA: SAGE.

Gujit, I. and Cornwall, A. (1995) 'Critical reflections on the practice of PRA'. *PLA Notes*, 24, pp. 1–5.

Gutmann, A. and Thompson, D. F. (2004) *Why Deliberative Democracy?* Princeton, NJ: Princeton University Press.

Hamdi, N. (2009) *Small Change: About the Art of Practice and the Limits of Planning in Cities*. London: Earthscan.

Hamdi, N. (2010) *The Placemakers Guide to Building Community*. London: Earthscan.

Hanna, S. and Rowley, J. (2011) 'Towards a strategic place brand-management model'. *Journal of Marketing Management*, 27(5–6), pp. 458–476.

Henneberg, S., Scammell, M. and O'Shaughnessy, N. (2009) 'Political marketing management and theories of democracy'. *Marketing Theory*, 9(2), pp. 165–188.

Hickey, S. and Mohan, G. (2004) 'Towards participation as transformation: Critical themes and challenges', in S. Hickey and G. Mohan (eds.), *Participation: From*

Tyranny to Transformation?: Exploring New Approaches to Participation in Development. London: ZED Books, pp. 3–24.

Insch, A. and Florek, M. (2010) 'Place satisfaction of city residents: findings and implications for city branding', in Ashworth, G. J. and Kavaratzis, M. (eds.), *Towards Effective Place Brand Management: Branding European Cities and Regions*. Cheltenham, UK: Edward Elgar, pp. 191–204.

Jernsand, E. M. and Kraff, H. (2015) 'Participatory place branding through design: the case of Dunga beach in Kisumu, Kenya'. *Place Branding and Public Diplomacy*, 11(3), pp. 226–242.

Jernsand, E. M., Kraff, H. and Mossberg, L. (2015) 'Tourism experience innovation through design'. *Scandinavian Journal of Tourism and Hospitality*, 15(1), pp. 98–119.

Kalandides, A. (2006) 'Fragmented branding for a fragmented city: Marketing Berlin'. Paper presented at the 6th European Urban and Regional Studies Conference, Roskilde, September.

Kalandides, A. (2011a) 'The problem with spatial identity: Revisiting the "sense of place"'. *Journal of Place Management and Development*, 4(1), pp. 28–39.

Kalandides, A. (2011b) 'City marketing for Bogotá: A case study in integrated place branding'. *Journal of Place Management and Development*, 4(3), pp. 282–291.

Kavaratzis, M. (2012) 'From "necessary evil" to necessity: stakeholders involvement in place branding'. *Journal of Place Management and Development*, 5(1), pp. 7–19.

Kavaratzis, M. and Ashworth, G. (2008) 'Place marketing: How did we get here and where are we going?'. *Journal of Place Management and Development*, 1(2), pp. 150–167.

Kavaratzis, M. and Hatch, M. J. (2013) 'The dynamics of place brands: an identity-based approach to place branding theory'. *Marketing Theory*, 13(1), pp. 69–86.

Kothari, U. (2001) 'Power, knowledge and social control in participatory development', in Cooke, B and Kothari, U. (eds.), *Participation: The New Tyranny?* London: Zed Books, pp. 139–154.

Kraff, H. and Jernsand, E. M. (2014) 'Designing for or designing with?' In Bohemia, E., Rieple, A., Liedtka, J. and Cooper, R. (eds.), *Proceedings of the 19th DMI Academic Design Management Conference: Design Management in an Era of Disruption*. Boston: The Design Management Institute, pp. 1596–1611.

Lichrou, M., O'Malley, L. and Patterson, M. (2014) 'On the marketing implications of place narratives'. *Journal of Marketing Management*, 30(9–10), 832–856.

Lindberg, S. I., Coppedge, M., Gerring, J., Teorell, J. *et al.* (2014) 'V-Dem – a new way to measure democracy'. *Journal of Democracy*, 25(3), pp. 159–169.

Lury, C. (2004) *Brands: The Logos of the Global Economy*. London, UK: Routledge.

Mackewn, J. (2008) 'Facilitation as action research in the moment', in Reason, P. and Bradbury, H. (eds.), *The Sage Handbook of Action Research: Participatory Inquiry and Practice*. 2nd edn. Los Angeles: SAGE, pp. 615–628.

Marsh, D. and Fawcett, P. (2011) 'Branding, politics and democracy'. *Policy Studies*, 32(5), pp. 515–530.

Martin, S. (2009) 'Engaging with citizens and other stakeholders', in Bovaird, T. and Löffler, E. (eds.), *Public Management and Governance*. 2nd edn. Abingdon: Routledge, pp. 279–296.

McGee, R. (2002) 'Participating in development', in Kothari, U. and Minogue, M. (eds.), *Development Theory and Practice – Critical Perspectives*. Palgrave Macmillan, pp. 92–116.

Miessen, M. (2010) *The Nightmare of Participation: [(Crossbench Practice as a Mode of Criticality)]*. New York, Berlin: Sternberg Press.

Mouffe, C. (2013) *Hegemony, Radical Democracy and the Political*. Abingdon, Oxon: Routledge.
Paganoni, M. C. (2012) 'City branding and social inclusion in the glocal city'. *Mobilities*, 7(1), pp. 13–31.
Pasquinelli, C. (2010) 'The limits of place branding for local development: The case of Tuscany and the Arnovalley Brand'. *Local Economy*, 25(7), pp. 558–572.
Philo, C. and Kearns, G. (1993) 'Culture, history, capital: A critical introduction to the selling of places', in Kearns, G. and Philo, C. (eds.), *Selling Places: The City as Cultural Capital, Past and Present*. Oxford: Pergamon Press, pp. 1–32.
Pottier, J. and Orone, P. (1995) 'Consensus or cover-up? The limitations of group meetings', *PLA Notes*, 24, pp. 38–42.
Reason, P. (1994) 'Inquiry and alienation', in P. Reason (ed.), *Participation in Human Inquiry*. London, UK: SAGE, pp. 9–15.
Ryfe, D. M (2005) 'Does deliberative democracy work?'. *Annual Review of Political Science*, 8, pp. 49–71.
Shah, P. and Kaul Shah, M. (1995) 'Participatory methods: precipitating or avoiding conflict?'. *PLA Notes*, 24, pp. 48–51.
Sørensen, E. and Torfing, J. (2011) 'Enhancing Collaborative Innovation in the Public Sector'. *Administration and Society*, 43(8), pp. 842–868.
Steen, M. (2011) 'Tensions in human-centred design'. *CoDesign: International Journal of CoCreation in Design and the Arts*, 7(1), pp. 16–28.
Stubbs, J. and Warnaby, G. (2015) 'Rethinking place branding from a practice perspective: working with stakeholders', in Kavaratzis, M., Warnaby, G. and Ashworth, G. J. (eds.), *Rethinking Place Branding: Comprehensive Brand Development for Cities and Regions*. Switzerland: Springer, pp. 101–118.
Swedish Design Research Journal, 2012, 'Better health with more design' No. 1. Available at: www.svid.se/upload/Forskning/Design_Research_Journal/Design_Research_Journal_nr_1_2012/Design_Research_Journal_no_1_2012_English.pdf (Accessed: 15 May 2015).
Wall, G. and Mathieson, A. (2006) *Tourism: Changes, Impacts, and Opportunities*. 2nd edn. Harlow, UK: Pearson Prentice Hall.
Warnaby, G. and Medway, D. (2013) 'What about the "place" in place marketing?'. *Marketing Theory*, 13(3), pp. 345–363.
Warnaby, G. and Medway, D. (2015) 'Rethinking the place product from the perspective of the service-dominant logic of marketing', in Kavaratzis, M., Warnaby, G. and Ashworth, G. J. (eds.), *Rethinking Place Branding: Comprehensive Brand Development for Cities and Regions*. Switzerland: Springer, pp. 33–50.
Warnaby, G., Ashworth, G. J. and Kavaratzis, M. (2015) 'Sketching futures for place branding', in Kavaratzis, M., Warnaby, G. and Ashworth, G. J. (eds.), *Rethinking Place Branding: Comprehensive Brand Development for Cities and Regions*. Switzerland: Springer, pp. 241–248.
Westerlund, B. (2009) 'Design space exploration: Co-operative creation of proposals for desired interactions with future artefacts'. Dissertation. Stockholm: Kungliga Tekniska Högskolan.
Zenker, S. and Beckmann, S. C. (2013) 'My place is not your place – different place brand knowledge by different target groups'. *Journal of Place Management and Development*, 6(1), pp. 6–17.
Zenker, S. and Erfgen, C. (2014) 'Let them do the work: A participatory place branding approach'. *Journal of Place Management and Development*, 7(3), pp. 225–234.

3 Critical perspectives on Aboriginal and Torres Strait Islander tourism

Towards Indigenous-led approaches

Skye Akbar and Freya Higgins-Desbiolles

Introduction

> Critical indigenous inquiry begins with the concerns of indigenous people. It is assessed in terms of the benefits it creates for them. The work must represent indigenous persons honestly, without distortion or stereotypes, and the research should honour indigenous knowledge, customs and rituals.
>
> (Denzin and Lincoln, 2008, p. 2)

Critical perspectives call on us to historicize, politicize and contextualize topics under study. A cursory glance might indicate that the promotion of Aboriginal and Torres Strait Islander tourism presents an ideal opportunity to share Aboriginal and Torres Strait Islander cultures and engage non-Indigenous people. However, our critical analysis indicates that such potential is not currently fulfilled as postcolonial Australia has failed to resolve historical tensions. Consecutive policy approaches have sought to involve Aboriginal and Torres Strait Islander people in tourism and use Aboriginal and Torres Strait Islander imagery in marketing campaigns which has brought a number of difficulties. However, there is opportunity for those supporting the industry to learn from Indigenous-led initiatives.

Aboriginal and Torres Strait Islander involvement in commercial tourism began with a duality that set its context to date. First, concerns with Aboriginal and Torres Strait Islander disadvantage as articulated in the Report of the Royal Commission into Aboriginal Deaths in Custody (1991) identified tourism as one means for economic opportunity and socio-cultural revival and connection. Simultaneously, the desire to use the 2000 Olympics to generate a tourism bonanza saw Aboriginal and Torres Strait Islander tourism positioned as a panacea and led to policy development, training programmes and resourcing to encourage Aboriginal and Torres Strait Islander people to enter tourism, as Aboriginal and Torres Strait Islander people and cultures were viewed as a marketing tool for branding and attraction. This has resulted in incompatible expectations of Aboriginal and Torres Strait Islander tourism between operators, consumers and governments, as it is promoted as an asset for place branding by some, while others see it as a tool for community development and others as a mechanism for self-determination.

What followed were top-down approaches to marketing Aboriginal and Torres Strait Islander tourism as Australian governments of all levels tried to leverage Aboriginal and Torres Strait Islander tourism products as their 'unique selling point'. However, such 'products' can fail to meet consumer demand as consumers hold unrealistic expectations that Aboriginal and Torres Strait Islander tourism operators could not or would not meet. These operators have asserted their agency by resisting inappropriate top-down approaches through a variety of strategies including: lobbying governments, developing their own approaches of bottom-up tourism development based on Indigenous ways and knowledge, developing codes and guidelines and creating organizations such as the Western Australian Indigenous Tourism Operators Council.

Following an analysis of these developments through an Indigenist lens, we assert Indigenous Peoples have a right to be involved in representing themselves in any place branding activity. We also offer a set of recommendations on how marketers and stakeholders can approach place marketing from a more responsible, collaborative and just approach as a result of the insights this Indigenous tourism case study offers.

Literature Review

Critical tourism studies

Until recently, the tourism discipline has been dominated by views of tourism as an industry (Higgins-Desbiolles, 2006) and a preference for positivist research methodologies to gain insights into the value of tourism (Tribe, 2005). However, as Tribe asserts, some tourism scholars have recently broken through such shackles and are embarking on more 'postmodern' explorations characterized by greater reflexivity and 'innovative and radical lines of enquiry' (2005, p. 376). A key feature of this work is the 'critical turn' which challenges conventional ways of knowing tourism, doing tourism research and relating to tourism stakeholders (Ateljevic *et al.*, 2007). Bianchi describes it as a 'product of the "cultural turn"' in the social sciences and the increased influence of post-structuralist [critical] theory in Leisure and Tourism Studies (2009, p. 486).

According to Wilson, Harris and Small (2008, p. 16):

> those employing a critical approach would generally be concerned with resisting positivist modes of enquiry, unmasking power relations, seeking emancipation, addressing inequalities, or calling for change or action within the field they are exploring (Brookfield 2005; Hooks 2003). Critical tourism and hospitality scholars are also drawn to these ideals.

Tribe (2007, p. 30) asserted that in critical scholarship:

> the current ordering of things is deliberately foregrounded. Power is a key issue to be researched and a critical approach to tourism would seek to

> expose whose interests are served and the exercise of power and the influence of ideology in the researched situation and the research itself.

A number of tourism analyses have outlined the key features of critical theory and paid tribute to its influence of the emerging critical tourism paradigm (e.g. Chambers, 2007; Tribe, 2008; Bianchi, 2009). Tribe asserted that 'critical research is uniquely placed to contribute to better management and governance of tourism' because it foregrounds the roles of ideology and power relations (2008, p. 253).

Indigenous standpoints in critical tourism studies

An emerging feature of critical tourism studies is an interest in Indigenous knowledge and methodologies and how these might inform a critical engagement with tourism disciplinary knowledges. This is inspired by the work of critical theorists such as Denzin *et al.* (2008) and McLaren and Jaramillo (2012). The challenges that critical theory and Indigenous methodologies raise pressure tourism scholars to engage with issues of power, voice, representation and agency in a way that invites radically new ways of understanding, managing and even overturning tourism and its practice.

However, it must be acknowledged that the interface between academia, Indigenous knowledge and tourism is not a 'smooth' space. There are tensions for the academy in engaging with Indigenous standpoints, there are challenges for Indigenous people to trust tourism and the tourism academy and Indigenous scholars bring new interactions to the area. As Martin Nakata has noted, negotiating the requirements and procedures of the academy and 'Indigenous knowledge, standpoints or perspectives' is profoundly challenging (2004, p. 14).

Universities are implicated in the colonial project and this tarnished history must be addressed and overcome for Indigenous research to be embraced by Indigenous Peoples. As Maori Professor Linda Tuhiwai Smith has demonstrated in her pioneering work *Decolonizing Methodologies* (2003) the Western-centric dominance of research theory and praxis makes the university an inhospitable environment for Indigenous communities and their knowledge. Additionally, Smith argues '… scientific research is implicated in the worst excesses of colonialism…the word itself, "research", is probably one of the dirtiest words in the indigenous world's vocabulary' (2003, p. 1).

The place of Indigenous standpoints in academic disciplines is contested due in part to the political disputes that underpin considerations of Indigenous and non-Indigenous relations in a post-colonizing context. Termed the 'history wars', disputes have raged about the shameful episodes in national histories, impacts resulting from previous polices and how current generations should address these. In Australia, during the tenure of the conservative government from the mid-1990s these history wars were fought with the conservatives calling revisionist history a 'black-arm band view' (Macintyre, 2003). As a result, disciplines such as marketing and tourism have made little engagement with the troubled colonial history of Australia with its legacies from invasion, dispossession and attempted cultural genocide. This may be a key barrier to inclusive marketing of tourism and Aboriginal and Torres Strait Islander tourism in Australia. As Cowlishaw (2004) has suggested, non-Indigenous Australians are generally unaware of Indigenous experiences, viewpoints and discourses and therefore are less accepting of them – unless they are situated in an accepted and recognized (Western) arena (Peters and Higgins-Desbiolles, 2012, p. 77). This chapter has given a context from which to understand the current circumstances of marketing tourism using Aboriginal and Torres Strait Islander imagery in Australian tourism.

Methodology

This chapter is a conceptual analysis of the interface between marketing, tourism and Indigenous Peoples based on the emerging critical, Indigenist paradigm. This chapter's insights are derived from the analysis of primary and secondary literature and applying a critical methodology to develop understandings of this interface.

First, it is essential to recognize the difficult context of research about, on and with Indigenous Peoples as a result of the problematic nature of relations between Indigenous and non-Indigenous Australians at the cultural interface. Trust is difficult when the context is recovering from invasion, dispossession and marginalization in settler-colonial societies such as Australia. This is perpetuated by the frequent refusal to acknowledge the history of colonial settlement factually. As Maori Indigenous scholar Linda Tuhiwai Smith has stated, '... scientific research is implicated in the worst excesses of colonialism ... the word itself, "research", is probably one of the dirtiest words in the indigenous world's vocabulary' (2003, p. 1).

This work was developed from a critical, Indigenist standpoint which engages with Indigenous communities from a position of solidarity. Critical theory contends that 'claims to truth are always discursively situated and implicated in relations of power' (Kincheloe and McLaren, 2005, p. 327). Denzin (2005, p. 950) advocated academic work that respects and follows an Indigenous research ethic and that aims to support Indigenous self-determination; Denzin described it as a:

> collaborative social science research model that makes the researcher responsible not to a removed discipline ... but to those studied ... it forcefully aligns the ethics of research with a politics of the oppressed, with a politics of resistance, hope, and freedom.
>
> (2005, p. 952)

Following the guidance of this critical, Indigenist approach, this work is able to illuminate an Indigenous-led approach to marketing that offers effective, ethical and empowered approaches and outcomes.

Background: Aboriginal and Torres Strait Islander tourism

It is important to remember that interest in Aboriginal and Torres Strait Islander tourism promotion was ignited from a social agenda for positive change for Aboriginal and Torres Strait Islander communities. In particular, the 1991 report of the Royal Commission into Aboriginal Deaths in Custody (RCIADIC) made the suggestion to explore tourism as a promising source for Aboriginal and Torres Strait Islander community development where it was seen as a promising source of self-esteem and economic opportunity (ATSIC and ONT, 1997). This report 'stressed the urgent need for the wider community to get to know Indigenous Australians, to learn about the shared history and to plan an inclusive future that respects and values Indigenous culture and heritage' (Universities Australia, 2011, p. 18).

The profile of Aboriginal and Torres Strait Islander Peoples is consistent in the marketing of Australia to international tourists undertaken by the government. In the past few decades, Aboriginal and Torres Strait Islander communities and individuals have entered the tourism industry with great hopes and some successes (e.g. Tjapukai Aboriginal Cultural Park in Cairns). The National Aboriginal and Torres Strait Islander Tourism Industry Strategy (NATSITIS) of 1997 established a national framework for organizing and planning Aboriginal and Torres Strait Islander tourism in order to meet the needs of all of the diverse stakeholders (ATSIC and ONT, 1997).

Aboriginal and Torres Strait Islander tourism has been promoted as a 'win-win situation' for all stakeholders in Aboriginal and Torres Strait Islander tourism: Tourists get a satisfying experience of the 'world's oldest living culture' while the tourism industry accesses Aboriginal and Torres Strait Islander tourism's power to 'brand' their destination as distinct from competing destinations around the world and attract new visitors. Aboriginal and Torres Strait Islander communities gain access to tourism's capacities to generate income and employment as well as many other benefits. Finally, governments make some advances in addressing the need for Aboriginal and Torres Strait Islander economic opportunities to alleviate Aboriginal and Torres Strait Islander disadvantage and thus enable governments to reduce spending and support for Aboriginal and Torres Strait Islander communities and individuals.

However, with some critical insights, Indigenous tourism is much more complex than this and in many circumstances the 'win-win' scenario appears overly optimistic. The opportunity to use Aboriginal and Torres Strait Islander imagery to market the 2000 Olympic Games was the major catalyst to promotion of Aboriginal and Torres Strait Islander tourism. This led to the development of Commonwealth and state level Indigenous tourism policies and marketing strategies such as NATSITIS.

This branding motivation is best exemplified by the statement made by Rod McGeogh, the Olympic bid convenor, who stated:

> We are always conscious of not overlooking the Aboriginality aspect of what we were doing. I was very aware that right through the early 90's

> there's actually an international fascination with the outback and our indigenous people. Their art is extremely popular overseas and their whole culture and so we wanted to show them, it was popular to show them, it helped our bid to show them. But without being crass about it, when you are marketing, you use the strengths of your community to bid and our Aboriginal culture, right now, is a major strength for Australia internationally.
>
> (McGeogh, 1995, p. 80)

The premise of this chapter is that this has resulted in incompatible expectations of Aboriginal and Torres Strait Islander tourism, as it is promoted as an asset for place branding by some, while others see it as a tool for community development.

Marketing Aboriginal and Torres Strait Islander Tourism and Branding Australia

Indigenous populations are frequently used in tourism promotion and marketing; knowledge of even remote Indigenous Peoples has been disseminated widely (Müller and Huuva, 2009). Opportunities to draw tourists to exotic cultures were established by colonizing governments and exploited for place branding purposes. These dynamics continue to this day and result in Indigenous tourism often presenting inappropriate stereotypes and inaccurate images of Indigenous Peoples and leading to ill will with Indigenous communities who are negatively impacted by such circumstances. This has been true globally and it is also very true for Australia, the focus of our chapter.

Since 1929, a Federal institution has managed the official marketing of Australia (Waitt, 1999). In the past, the government identified Aboriginal and Torres Strait Islander tourism as unique and utilized this to develop a distinctly Australian brand asset (Waitt, 1999). Initial Aboriginal and Torres Strait Islander tourism marketing depicted the people in a primitive state and from a Western perspective. Aboriginal and Torres Strait Islander people were not given the opportunity to define their own identity in the tourism context.

More recently, within both tourism and the broader Australian context, Australian governments have created depictions of Aboriginal and Torres Strait Islander people that have contrasted with the people's actual ways of living and self-perceptions, which Pomering (2010) proposed leads to reduced advertising effectiveness but more importantly leads to a dissonance and damaging of Aboriginal and Torres Strait Islander identity (Hollinshead, 1996). Waitt (1999) described the images created as 'noble savage and eco-angel syndrome', stating that the government's portrayals of Aboriginal and Torres Strait Islander people reflected hegemonic assumptions of the people, which in turn impacts consumer perceptions. This approach has denied Aboriginal and Torres Strait Islander people the opportunity to establish a protocol for presentations of cultural knowledge, with stereotyped imagery becoming engrained. This has extended to the marketing of Aboriginal and Torres Strait Islander tourism and negatively affected branding across the category. Over time consumers developed unrealistic expectations resulting in consumer product perceptions not matching tourism offerings developed by Aboriginal and Torres Strait Islander operators. More importantly for this analysis, this type of representation led to false measures of authenticity and stereotypes being imposed on Aboriginal and Torres Strait Islander tourism operators (Hollinshead, 1996). These stereotypes worked to cast Aboriginal and Torres Strait Islander people as traditional, thus negating engagement with the world and blending of old and new ways such as uptake of technology and interface with modern Australia. These stereotypes also negated the diversity of Aboriginal and Torres Strait Islander cultures and associated tourism products and experiences by portraying to consumers that there was just one type of Aboriginal and Torres Strait Islander tourism experience to have.

Renewed government focus continues to push for the development of the Aboriginal and Torres Strait Islander industry, particularly promoting participation by Aboriginal and Torres Strait Islander people in arts and crafts, the development of cultural tours and forging joint venture opportunities with non-Indigenous people (Altman and Finlayson, 2003). Altman and Finlayson (2003) argue that none of these options are easy for Aboriginal and Torres Strait Islander people, because employment in tourism-related industries requires a high level of literacy and communication skills and the adoption of cultural styles which may be foreign and daunting for some Aboriginal and Torres Strait Islander people. As common in small and medium enterprises, lower levels of marketing experience can impact abilities to develop branding. Marketing and branding are key skills required in the development of an emerging industry and competing brands. In addition, Aboriginal and Torres Strait Islander tourism operators were encouraged to enter the industry only to inherit a barrage of branding issues including misleading stereotypes and product expectations.

While, as discussed, initially Indigenous Peoples held little control over Indigenous tourism ventures to begin with, in recent decades Indigenous Peoples have taken active roles in developing this industry (Hinch and Butler, 2009). Progress towards Indigenous inclusion and control in the Indigenous tourism industry is supported by the United Nations Declaration on the Rights of Indigenous Peoples (UNDRIP), with tourism being one of the platforms Indigenous Peoples can use to argue for their human rights. While the UNDRIP does not address tourism directly, it does address rights to protection of cultural heritage and cultural practices. For instance, Article 15 states: 'Indigenous peoples have the right to the dignity and diversity of their cultures, traditions, histories and aspirations which shall be appropriately reflected in education and public information' (UN, 2007). As Indigenous rights permeate into multiple aspects of societies around the globe, they are beginning to have greater recognition and influence in business contexts and on business operations. This extends to tourism, with Indigenous Peoples working to apply UNDRIP principles to the tourism context and also asserting greater control over Indigenous tourism in some circumstances (see Johnston, 2003; Higgins-Desbiolles, 2007).

For instance, in acknowledgement of the progress of Indigenous rights in tourism, the Pacific Asia Travel Association, Tourism NT (Northern Territory) and the Australian Tourism Export Council supported a conference in 2012 convened in Darwin which saw the development of the Larrakia Declaration on the Development of Indigenous Tourism (PAITC, 2012). The Larrakia Declaration was adopted by the Pacific Asia Travel Association and endorsed by the United Nations World Tourism Organization in 2012. The Larrakia Declaration asserted that the United Nations Declaration on the Rights of Indigenous Peoples (UNDRIP) (UN, 2007) advocates control by Indigenous Peoples over developments affecting them, their lands and their resources.

The Larrakia Declaration recognizes the general marginalization of Indigenous Peoples from social, economic and political advancement and makes key observations on existing practices in Indigenous tourism with a view to empowering Indigenous tourism stakeholders. It begins by acknowledging that tourism can be a negative influence on culture, asserting that Indigenous Peoples have the right to protect their culture while pursuing their right to devising financial benefit from the same culture. Examples of the outcomes of these negative influences have been previously discussed, such as the misrepresentations of Aboriginal and Torres Strait Islander cultures through branding as one homogenized monoculture, featuring such accoutrements as boomerangs and didgeridoos, by early marketing campaigns.

The Larrakia Declaration astutely identifies that Indigenous cultures provide an opportunity for Indigenous Peoples to utilize their assets as sustainable unique selling points. This point is key; in a period of time where product imitation is rife and globalization has opened markets wider than ever before, Indigenous Peoples remain the only ones who can authentically represent their own culture, ways of knowing, being and interpretation of the world. This becomes increasingly important when considering Tourism Australia (2010) found that domestic consumers often perceived Aboriginal and Torres Strait Islander products to be contrived, lacking authenticity and developed for the international market. Key for enacting this will be the unique and distinctive branding of Indigenous People's tourism to authentically demonstrate the diversity of cultures and products available in the tourism marketplace.

Importantly, the Larrakia Declaration acknowledges that for Indigenous tourism to be successful and sustainable it needs to be based on traditional knowledge, cultures and practices. The great diversity of Indigenous Peoples and their cultures and their steadfast commitment to retain authenticity to tradition, means that organization and product identity should develop distinctively to be unique. This will further support the need for strong and independent brand offerings. Promotion of the diversity of opportunities available in Indigenous tourism and communication of product value to consumers (who may have previously thought that if they had one Indigenous tourism experience, they had satiated their needs for such experiences) will promote repeat patronage within the category.

The contributors to the drafting of the Larrakia Declaration expressed hope that the advancement of the Indigenous tourism industry promotes a cultural understanding, social interaction and peace between non-Indigenous and

Indigenous people. This sentiment denotes the particular opportunity that engagement with the tourism industry can offer; an experience that goes far beyond the sum of its parts. Enabling Indigenous Peoples to exercise further control over the development of their product offerings will lead to an increase in authentic product offerings and stronger brand identities, capable of attracting consumers who are a better fit for the product. This space provides an opportunity for improved customer experience and a genuine engagement between the knowledge holder and the learner; this creates a special and unique offering that may support understanding between these two worlds. It also may go some way in undoing the psychic violence that previous misrepresentations have done to Indigenous Peoples and their cultures.

The World Indigenous Tourism Alliance (WINTA) commenced in 2013 to give practical expression to the United Nations Declaration on the Rights of Indigenous Peoples and the Larrakia Declaration (WINTA, 2014). WINTA is an Indigenous-led global network of 170 Indigenous and non-Indigenous interests developing and implementing strategies for the advancement of Indigenous tourism in forty countries, including Australia. The organization works within the tourism industry in ways that promote partnerships and heightened respect for Indigenous wisdom, values and knowledge. The establishment of Indigenous networks provides an opportunity for sharing and developing marketing knowledge across the category of Indigenous tourism. This network of knowledge could support the advancement of Indigenous tourism by signalling the quality and authenticity standards within the industry.

Within Australia there is currently no organization of national scope representing the collaborations of Aboriginal and Torres Strait Islander tourism providers. However, tourism operators within the largest state of Australia, Western Australia (WA), have developed an industry-based association. The Western Australian Aboriginal Tourism Operators Council (WAITOC) is an association providing advice and information to all relevant State Government agencies as well as the tourism industry sector. WAITOC promotes Aboriginal tourism and provides a supportive network for Aboriginal tourism operators within Western Australia. WAITOC's annual conference shares knowledge with stakeholders from across Australia. To consumers, WAITOC provides a repository of information on potential tourism experiences. This is an important presentation of information as aligning with the WAITOC brand affords WA Aboriginal tourism operators a signal of quality which promotes Aboriginal tourism as a category and demonstrates the collective benefit of shared marketing efforts to operators and consumers. However, this configuration may cause disappointment for some international consumers who are unable to make it as far as WA and who would benefit from a similar organization being operative in other states and territories of Australia or even better representing the entire Aboriginal and Torres Strait Islander tourism sector of Australia.

Non-Indigenous organizations are also seeking to contribute to the development of Aboriginal and Torres Strait Islander tourism. One example of this is the Respecting Our Culture (ROC) (Ecotourism Australia, n.d.) programme. ROC is marketed as a tourism industry development tool which promotes national accreditation standards and encourages the industry to operate with respect for Aboriginal and Torres Strait Islander cultural heritage. ROC aims to use the power of co-branding to act as a quality signifier to potential consumers by licencing the ROC logo. However, a review of the ROC website shows that ROC accreditation is available to all operators who present products focused on culture, regardless of Aboriginal and Torres Strait Islander or non-Indigenous status. This becomes problematic where an organization's offering is based predominately on a cultural product, signalled accreditation by third parties, and yet provides no economic benefits to Aboriginal and Torres Strait Islander people or communities. Customers may mistakenly be under the impression that they will be purchasing an experience with Aboriginal and Torres Strait Islander people or one that supports Aboriginal and Torres Strait Islander development. It is in these contexts that the use of Aboriginal and Torres Strait Islander branding elements misrepresents the product to the consumer. It can be argued that third-party accreditation such as this removes the involvement of Aboriginal and Torres Strait Islander people, therefore negating Aboriginal and Torres Strait Islander people from the branding of their own cultural product and negating the recent progress on the inclusion of Aboriginal and Torres Strait Islander people.

Recommendations

Progress towards Indigenous ownership of Indigenous tourism has seen the strengthening of Indigenous voices within the industry. An inevitable development in the advancement of Indigenous rights will be the transition to Indigenous voices informing systems such as tourism and the demand that non-Indigenous stakeholders respect the right ways to engage with Indigenous issues and Indigenous Peoples. Indigenous Peoples have facilitated this engagement for non-Indigenous tourism stakeholders by developing guiding principles to make their respectful and ethical engagement easy and clear. Those in positions of marketing Aboriginal and Torres Strait Islander tourism can ensure they apply these principles so that their work supports appropriate Aboriginal and Torres Strait Islander inclusion in branding.

The Larrakia Declaration outlines six principles to support Indigenous rights in Indigenous tourism, providing Indigenous stakeholders with a unique opportunity for collaboration and non-Indigenous stakeholders with a model of best practice for this emerging aspect of Indigenous tourism.

The Larrakia Declaration asks for:

- Respect for customary law and lore, land and water, traditional knowledge, traditional cultural expressions, cultural heritage that will underpin all tourism decisions.
- Indigenous culture and the land and waters on which it is based, will be protected and promoted through well managed tourism practices and appropriate interpretation.

- Indigenous Peoples will determine the extent and nature and organizational arrangements for their participation in tourism and that governments and multilateral agencies will support the empowerment of Indigenous people.
- That governments have a duty to consult and accommodate Indigenous Peoples before undertaking decisions on public policy and programs designed to foster the development of Indigenous tourism.
- The tourism industry will respect Indigenous intellectual property rights, cultures and traditional practices, the need for sustainable and equitable business partnerships and the proper care of the environment and communities that support them.
- That equitable partnerships between the tourism industry and Indigenous people will include the sharing of cultural awareness and skills development which support the well-being of communities and enable enhancement of individual livelihoods.

(PAITC, 2012)

These principles are drawn from the UNDRIP (UN, 2007) to operationalize the progress of Indigenous rights in the tourism context. In our context of Australia, this is an essential process to right the wrongs of the past which saw Aboriginal and Torres Strait Islander people excluded from the development of Aboriginal and Torres Strait Islander tourism with consequences evident throughout the marketing and branding of the industry. These principles clearly outline how Aboriginal and Torres Strait Islander operators would like to be engaged with, how Aboriginal and Torres Strait Islander People's will seek to be included in Aboriginal and Torres Strait Islander tourism and how, moving forward, Aboriginal and Torres Strait Islander Peoples must be consulted and included in all aspects of developing the Aboriginal and Torres Strait Islander tourism industry. These principles must be considered in line with the wishes of localized Aboriginal and Torres Strait Islander tourism efforts to ensure improved inclusion of Aboriginal and Torres Strait Islander peoples in branding Aboriginal and Torres Strait Islander tourism.

Conclusion

In 2012, Peters and Higgins-Desbiolles brought attention to the lack of an engagement with Indigenous standpoints in the tourism academy and listed three reasons for a block to this important engagement: the narrow, commercial focus of the contemporary tourism industry under neoliberalism; the all-pervasive whiteness of contemporary Australian society; and a lack of Aboriginal and Torres Strait Islander researchers contributing to Aboriginal and Torres Strait Islander tourism analysis (2012, p. 79). This was intended to challenge the tourism discipline to rethink its engagement with Indigenous tourism topics. Simultaneously, the proponents of the Larrakia Declaration put the tourism industry and its stakeholders on notice that Indigenous rights must be respected.

But most importantly, change in Australia is being driven by Aboriginal and Torres Strait Islander tourism operators (and at the global level by Indigenous Peoples). Analysis of recent declarations and activities previously discussed, such as UNDRIP, the Larrakia Declaration, the formation of WINTA and the leadership of WAITOC demonstrate that Aboriginal and Torres Strait Islander tourism operators are taking charge of their engagement with tourism and are leading the way. Aboriginal and Torres Strait Islander tourism operators are working together to understand their shared challenges, learn from their models of best practice and identify cohesive approaches to re-orientating Aboriginal and Torres Strait Islander tourism to be Aboriginal and Torres Strait Islander controlled through opportunities offered by Aboriginal and Torres Strait Islander controlled bodies such as WAITOC. The progression of UNDRIP has provided a framework for Indigenous Peoples to assert their rights and demand their claims for self-determination and real autonomy be recognized. The Larrakia Declaration advances UNDRIP's principles into the tourism sphere and reclaims Indigenous tourism for Indigenous Peoples. And most importantly, forthright Indigenous tourism operators assert their own ways of doing things according to their particular cultural ways and provide their colleagues in their local tourism industry localized guiding principles and possibilities to work collaboratively on foundations of respect.

The principles propounded by Indigenous leadership based on Indigenous worldviews offer an exciting and unique opportunity for marketers; the opportunity to engage with a product that is unique and on a basis that is full of the positives of ethics, sustainability and fair exchange. Our chapter calls on the tourism industry and particularly its marketing professionals to appreciate the contributions of Aboriginal and Torres Strait Islander tourism operators and to recognize the unstoppable dynamics of self-determination and Indigenous rights in tourism. Recent Aboriginal and Torres Strait Islander initiatives provide tantalizing insights into the possibility to reframe this space and thereby develop a much more distinctive and attractive branding of Aboriginal and Torres Strait Islander tourism that benefits all stakeholders. This change allows an opportunity to overturn the exploitation and damage of the past and to turn marketing to more positive outcomes.

These changes also hold implications for communities beyond Australia. Under an Indigenous controlled approach to marketing and branding, marketing becomes a meaningful way for people to communicate their cultures to others. This invites positive engagement through tourism and also enhances marketing's capacities to support community building and enhancement rather than stereotyping and damage. This Indigenous-led approach offers a positive model worthy of further consideration and emulation as it demonstrates a way that marketing achieves much more than market building; it potentially can help strengthen people and foster people-to-people interactions and understanding.

References

Altman, J. and Finlayson, J. (2003) 'Aborigines, tourism and sustainable development'. *Journal of Tourism Studies*, 14(1), pp. 78–91.

Ateljevic, I., Morgan, N. and Pritchard, A. (2007) *The Critical Turn In Tourism Studies: Creating An Academy Of Hope*. New York: Routledge.

ATSIC and ONT (1997) 'National Aboriginal and Torres Strait Islander tourism industry strategy', Canberra: ATSIC. Available at: http://pandora.nla.gov.au/pan/41037/20050516/www.atsic.gov.au/programs/Industry_Strategies/tourism_industry_strategy/default.html. (Accessed: 6 October 2009).

Bianchi, R. (2009) 'The "critical turn" in tourism studies: A radical critique'. *Tourism Geographies*, 11(4), pp. 484–504.

Chambers, D. (2007) 'Interrogating the "critical" in critical approaches to tourism research', in Ateljevic, I., Pritchard, A. and Morgan, N. (eds), *The Critical Turn In Tourism Studies: Innovative Research Methodologies*. Amsterdam: Elsevier, pp. 105–119.

Cowlishaw, G. (2004) *Blackfellas, Whitefellas and the Hidden Injuries of Race*. Carlton, Victoria: Blackwell Publishing.

Denzin, N. K. (2005) 'Emancipatory discourses and the ethics and politics of participation', in Denzin, N. K. and Lincoln, Y. S. (eds), *The Sage Handbook of Qualitative Research*. 3rd edn. Thousand Oaks, CA: Sage Publications, pp. 933–958.

Denzin, N. K. and Lincoln, Y. S. (2008) 'Introduction', in Denzin, N. K., Lincoln, Y. S. and Smith, L. T. (eds), *Handbook of Critical and Indigenous Methodologies*. Los Angeles: Sage, pp. 2–20.

Denzin, N. K., Lincoln, Y. S. and Smith, L. T. (2008) *Handbook of Critical and Indigenous Methodologies*. Los Angeles: Sage.

Ecotourism Australia (n.d.) 'What is ROC certification?' Available at: www.ecotourism.org.au/our-certification-programs/eco-certification-4/. (Accessed: 31 January 2017).

Higgins-Desbiolles, F. (2006) 'More than an "industry": The forgotten power of tourism as a social force'. *Tourism Management*, 27(6), pp. 1192–1208.

Higgins-Desbiolles, F. (2007) 'Taming tourism: Indigenous rights as a check to unbridled tourism', in Burns, P. and Novelli, M. (eds), *Tourism and Politics: Global Frameworks and Local Realities*. Amsterdam: Elsevier, pp. 83–107.

Hinch, T. and Butler, R. (2009) 'Indigenous tourism'. *Tourism Analysis*, 14(1), pp. 15–27.

Hollinshead, K. (1996) 'Marketing and metaphysical realism: The disidentification of Aboriginal life and traditions through tourism', in Butler, R. and Hinch, T. (eds), *Tourism and Indigenous Peoples*. London: International Thomson Business Press, pp. 308–348.

Johnston, A. M. (2003) 'Self-determination: Exercising Indigenous rights in tourism', in Singh, S., Timothy, D. J. and Dowling, R. K. (eds), *Tourism in Destination Communities*. Oxon: CABI, pp. 115–134.

Kincheloe, J. L. and McLaren, P. (2005) 'Rethinking critical theory and qualitative research', in Denzin, N. K. and Lincoln, Y. S. (eds) *The Sage Handbook of Qualitative Research*. 3rd edn. Thousand Oaks, CA: Sage Publications, pp. 303–342.

'Larrakia Declaration on the Development of Indigenous Tourism' (2012) Inaugural Pacific Asia Indigenous Tourism Conference, Darwin, 28–30 March. Available at: ww.winta.org/wp-content/uploads/2012/08/The-Larrakia-Declaration.pdf. (Accessed: 3 September 2016).

Macintyre, S. (2003) 'The history wars', *The Sydney Papers*, Winter/Spring. Available at: www.kooriweb.org/foley/resources/pdfs/198.pdf. (Accessed: 10 December 2014).

McGeogh, R. (1995) 'Rod McGeogh: Social justice and Sydney 2000', interview by Christie, Suzanne and Maxwell, Britt. Polemic, 6(2), pp. 79–82.

McLaren, P. and Jaramillo, N. E. (2012) 'Dialectical thinking and critical pedagogy – towards a critical tourism studies', in Ateljevic, I., Morgan, N. and Pritchard, A. (eds), *The Critical Turn in Tourism Studies: Creating an Academy of Hope*. New York: Routledge, pp. xvii–xl.

Müller, D. K. and Huuva, S. K. (2009) 'Limits to Sami tourism development: the case of Jokkmokk, Sweden'. *Journal of Ecotourism*, 8(2), pp. 115–127.

Nakata, M. (2004) 'Aboriginal and Torres Strait Islandern studies and higher education' (Wentworth lecture), Australian Institute for Aboriginal and Torres Strait Islander Studies, Canberra. Available at: www.aiatsis.gov.au/events/wentworth.html. (Accessed: 12 December 2014).

PAITC (2012) 'The Larrakia Declaration on the Development of Indigenous Tourism', Darwin.

Peters, A. and Higgins-Desbiolles, F. (2012) 'De-marginalising tourism research: Indigenous Australians as tourists'. *Journal of Hospitality and Tourism Management*, 19(6), pp. 76–84.

Pomering, A. A. (2010) 'The portrayal of aboriginal spiritual identity in tourism advertising: creating an image of extraordinary reality or mere confusion?', in Timmermans, H. (eds), 17th International Conference on Recent Advances in Retailing and Services Science, European Regional Science Association, Belgium, pp. 1–15.

Royal Commission into Aboriginal Deaths in Custody (1998) 'Report of the Royal Commission into Aboriginal Deaths in Custody'. Available at: www.austlii.edu.au/au/other/IndigLRes/rciadic/. (Accessed: 3 September 2016).

Smith, L. T. (2003) *Decolonizing Methodologies: Research and Indigenous Peoples*. London: Zed Books.

Tourism Australia (2010) 'Selling Indigenous tourism experiences to the domestic market'. Sydney: Tourism Australia.

Tribe, J. (2005) 'The truth about tourism'. *Annals of Tourism Research*, 33(2), pp. 360–381.

Tribe, J. (2007) 'Critical tourism: Rules and resistance', in Ateljevic, I., Morgan, N. and Pritchard, A. (eds), *The Critical Turn in Tourism Studies: Innovative Research Methodologies*. Oxford: Elsevier, pp. 29–40.

Tribe, J. (2008) 'Tourism: A critical business'. *Journal of Travel Research*, 46(3), pp. 245–255 DOI: 10.1177/0047287507304051.

United Nations (2007) 'United Nations Declaration on the Rights of Indigenous Peoples'. *UN Wash*, 12, pp. 1–18.

Universities Australia (2011) 'National best practice framework for Indigenous cultural competency in Australian universities'. Available at: www.universitiesaustralia.edu.au/uni-participation-quality/Indigenous-Higher-Education/Indigenous-Cultural-Compet#.WFnw5JW7ptQ. (Accessed: 3 December 2016).

Waitt, G. (1999) 'Naturalizing the "primitive": A critique of marketing Australia's indigenous peoples as "hunter-gatherers"'. *Tourism Geographies*, 1(2), pp. 142–163.

Wilson, E., Harris, C., and Small, J. (2008) 'Furthering critical approaches in tourism and hospitality studies: Perspectives from Australia and New Zealand'. *Journal of Hospitality and Tourism Management*, 15, pp. 15–18. DOI 10.1375/jhtm.15.15.

WINTA (2014) World Indigenous Tourism Alliance Leadership Council to Promote Indigenous Human Rights in Tourism, World Indigenous Tourism Alliance, 25 June 2014.

4 Place marketing for social inclusion

Aram Eisenschitz

Introduction

As the introductory chapter to this book shows place marketing implemented within a neo-liberal polity has negative consequences for ordinary people. It has helped fashion a society characterized by enhanced insecurity in employment, housing, and indeed life in general. Place marketing is part of the shift in the mode of local governance that has seen the displacement of a local state concerned with the welfare of its population, by a business-friendly form, the entrepreneurial city. Yet while place marketing claims to bring prosperity to declining cities, it plays an active role in restructuring cities along class lines by making them attractive to the middle class and forcibly displacing the poor.

The emergence of the entrepreneurial city reflects the neo-liberal transformation of society that makes cities compete in the global economy. Corporate cities use image and spectacle to reposition themselves in the global hierarchy of consumption and production, on the assumption that cities will survive by becoming entrepreneurial. They subsequently are 'playing to the rules of capitalist accumulation rather than to the goals of meeting local needs or maximizing social welfare' (Harvey, 1989, p. 16). Moving production from traditional areas reflects the state of global class relations; the new service jobs in the former industrial cities reformulate those relations so as to return them to the position they had prior to dramatic increase in power achieved by labour forty years ago (Glyn, 2006).

Globalization helps achieve this new balance, overseeing an entirely different social and political infrastructure that depends upon the enhanced mobility of labour and capital. Place marketing is integral to these changes in the physical, political and economic environment of these cities, helping to construct a new type of consciousness. Places – and consequently people – are told to stand on their own feet without state support, expectations are lowered and collective social relations are replaced by unfettered competitive individualism. In short, this is a policy that is primarily oriented around changing class relations.

This politics makes the cities more attractive by developing culture, heritage, entertainment, and shopping, creating a class monopoly rent that supports landlords and tourists, and through gentrification, attracts inward investment

(Harvey, 2012, p. 90). Place marketing strengthens the implicit political assumptions of neo-liberal globalization that are used to interpret everyday life and that make it possible to create new class settlement. These ideas are so ingrained by constant repetition and exposure that they are barely recognized for the radical politics that they represent; they include low levels of democracy, a downsized local authority that no longer represents the interests of its constituency and the notion of the market as the organizing principle for society. Place marketing therefore obscures how it destabilizes and renews the working class. In this way, it has become a symbolic politics that employs physical propositions around localities and buildings to express wider ideas about society. It is a way of mediating and interpreting the narratives that are constructed by the dominant political values.

Place marketing, therefore, does not sell places; it sells politics through the built environment because of the Hegelian propositions, that what is real is rational, and that appearances conform to reality. Space has authority precisely because it makes political arguments real; it creates the lived experience that can be interpreted through ideological narratives such as that propagated by place marketing. Its concern with the changes that people and places must undergo to be competitive infuses each dimension of daily life with neo-liberal values. Its power derives from its class politics that paradoxically denies the relevance of class and proposes a consensual politics for economic success – it is a class politics that remains invisible. One of place marketing's beneficiaries is tourism, which reproduces many of the class characteristics of neo-liberalism albeit in a low-key manner (Eisenschitz, 2016).

Canary Wharf in London's Docklands expresses this narrative. It illustrates how the values of individualism and freedom liberated markets from the dead hand of the state, overcame a local government bureaucracy that had been working on a plan for over a decade, and freed enterprise to provide wealth for all. That story is constructed as a set of dualities that structure neo-liberalism's opposition to social democracy – enterprise versus welfare, redistribution versus growth, markets versus state, the deserving versus the undeserving poor, dependency versus self-help and finance versus industry. The common account, however, hides four decades of class struggle and the combination of co-option and economic violence that has tamed the cities and their populations. Place marketing puts forward interpretations that legitimate this class politics despite the fact that it has forced wages down, destroyed jobs, removed many institutions of working-class support, normalized insecurity and placed at least a quarter of the population in many advanced capitalist countries into the precariat (Standing, 2010, p. 24).

A firm of progressive architects in Venezuela describes Caracas as frozen politics (McGuirk, 2014, p. 144), with each building or district illustrating the politics under which it emerged. The argument here goes a step further – buildings, physical patterns and the iconic spectacle embody not simply politics but social relations (Debord, 1984). Place marketing comes into its own when those relations are precarious, when they need support, and when there is opposition.

Canary Wharf, for instance, makes a statement about the financialization of the economy, namely that goods and services are best bought individually rather than collectively shared, that debt is socially acceptable and that mortgages are superior to social renting. Finance's contemporary domination of the City skyline conveys powerful support for the politics of financialization. Not only does that have a 'shock and awe' effect but it confirms the permanence and legitimacy of Britain's unbalanced economy and the politics of de-industrialization that, among other things, normalizes social exclusion (Young, 1999).

Currently we, as citizens, have abdicated our right to manage our own environment and create cities that reflect our needs and desires; we have instead allowed developers, landlords and bankers to shape the city in their own interests (Harvey, 2006, p. 89). Planning for the public good has been replaced by landlord controls, typified by privatizing public land, or the state leasing shopping centres built on public land, to private firms (Minton, 2009). Divided cities are considered normal. Gentrification is confirmed as the solution to poor cities the world over (Smith, 2002, p. 439). In Britain, former industrial cities such as Glasgow, have abandoned their working-class populations and taken on entertainment and cultural attractions in order to attract tourists, the creative middle class and investors. This is place marketing's rationale, a narrative that tells a story from a particular political viewpoint in order to legitimate the politics of the day. Yet Glasgow's experience, where poverty has been exacerbated (Mooney, 2004), is not uncommon.

Neo-liberalism is an unstable settlement. The World Economic Forum sees inequality as the greatest threat to world economic health (Dorling, 2014, p. 69). If that is so, we need to develop alternative narratives of place marketing that look not to the inculcation of business values among the population, but that aspire to a fairer and more inclusive society. The new decentralized and entrepreneurial urban forms of governance do not necessarily support capital; they could use the focus on the symbolic as a step towards more democratic forms of decision-making (Harvey, 1989, p. 16). That is what this chapter explores.

In the following section, we examine neo-liberal place marketing as a class strategy that may occur 'naturally' without marketing organizations. That is followed by an examination of place marketing under more democratic forms of politics, while the final section looks at the potential for developing this activity for a more inclusive society.

Place marketing: a class strategy

Place marketing uses space symbolically to illustrate, legitimate and reproduce more abstract political ideas and arguments through its physical symptoms. This activity has always existed, but not always in an institutional capacity or even as a conscious practice to put forward the hegemonic politics of the time. Spatial form conveys a political message in ways that are not dissimilar from place marketing, during early industrial capitalism, imperialism and the social democratic settlement. It has also helped create the consensus around the recent renewal of capital's dominance, externalizing assumptions and arguments that are subsequently accepted by the population without any explicit place marketing. It substitutes a place-based consciousness over one of class, proclaiming a 'we are all in it together' that serves to underplay class antagonisms. Such arguments are often developed through the spectacle – the London Olympics has served in a similar capacity in the era of austerity, as did the Great Exhibition that was held three years after the European-wide uprisings of 1848. As Black (2007, p. 272), argues, sports mega-events always symbolize inclusion whether to heal internal division or conflict between countries; the language is always that of universality, using words like democracy, unity, coming together or multi-culturalism. Yet in practice they tend to increase the divisions within and between countries.

Architecture and urban morphology – from neo-classical architecture to council estates – are conduits for political discourse because they accommodate interpretations of the built environment that construct political narratives which subsequently diffuse throughout society (Cairns, 2012). Built forms create multiple discourses over time, which reinforce the relations of power that structure society; currently these are extremely unequal relations (Desiderio, 2013). Council estates, for instance, were once symbols of a socially progressive society, but in the last decades have become icons of a broken society, a breeding ground for the 'other'. Place marketing cannot, of course, accept this argument since it sits uneasily with its professional self-image. Yet its success in convincing people that the future of cities lies with neo-liberal politics makes it imperative to articulate a political alternative.

If conventional place marketing is more than changing the image of places in order to encourage economic prosperity, then one may legitimately argue that any instance of urban design and morphology that uses imagery to represent political argument qualifies as place marketing. Even if that process 'just happens', it nonetheless reflects the temper of the times. That may be seen by that most potent of images, St Paul's Cathedral dominating the city during the Blitz, which spoke volumes about national identity, tradition, political stability and social democracy's common bonds between the classes in the face of adversity (Kerr, 2002, p. 78). While that image was carefully selected it nonetheless had an impact on class similar to that of contemporary place marketing campaigns. 'Occupy', equally, used symbolic locations, its choice of St Paul's reflecting the Church's significance as a political institution with a history of support to social inclusion.

The politics of municipal socialism at the turn of the nineteenth century represented a progressive non-conformism (Hunt, 2005, p. 321), a radical break with the past that was competing for hearts and minds. It was branded by a spectacular public architecture, epitomized by the town halls of Manchester and Glasgow, which were represented as belonging to the people themselves. The extent of the power concentrated in the local authorities led to a century of conflict with central government, culminating in the near 30 per cent cut in their budgets in the five years since 2010. Place marketing has been involved in the rise, maintenance and fall of this politics. As Sue Townsend (2005), the cartoonist, reminisces, 'I'm a child of the municipal. Everything good had this word carved above its grand entrance'. This alternative met people's basic needs with collective rather than individual consumption, its political significance emphasized by the imposing architectural appearance of the buildings. Place marketing was thus enrolled as a means of signifying the importance of prioritizing need over ability to pay that defined citizenship and social inclusion. It was no less political than place marketing is now, but it was achieved in a different manner.

Baltimore is place marketing's poster boy illustrating the virtues of market-based regeneration that has successfully regenerated the docks, creating a major tourist attraction that currently sees around twenty-five million tourists annually. It has, however, been subject to another equally political form of place marketing that demonstrates why Baltimore's sustainability requires an inclusive approach to urban politics. That is the television serial *The Wire* that portrays a fourth-world country physically adjacent to the Inner Harbour, but socially many miles away. As Zizek (2013) argues, the five series connect the abstract process capital's self-expansion to the actual reality of society. Furthermore, he suggests (2013, p. 235) that its demonstration of the impossibility of real change within the political system opens spaces for radical change.

The series creates powerful imagery to motivate an engagement with political alternatives, particularly as for many it is a true representation of the realities of life for large sections of the population in many US cities (Levine, 2000). It successfully undermines place marketing's deeply reactionary proposition that 'a city can do well (in terms of capital accumulation) while its people (apart from a privileged class) and the environment do badly ...' Harvey (2012, p. 29). A city's health can only be measured by the quality of life of its population, yet as the series demonstrates, the relevant institutions – police, education, media, unions, and local government's regeneration strategy – are unable to improve it at a time of disappearing manual working-class jobs.

Whereas the Inner Harbour is an effective symbol of success that is falsely applied to the entire city, *The Wire* offers an incomparably richer set of symbols and political analysis that need imaginative application. While the narrative veers between radicalism and social democratic reformism, its Dickensian antecedents offer possibilities for the churches, trade unions and non-governmental organizations (NGOs) to employ symbolic resources to demonstrate how the USA creates exclusion, why the gentrification-led model of development is irrelevant, and why trickle-down effects cannot lead to social inclusion, a central claim of neo-liberalism. How then can cities be fashioned that allow growth to be more equitably shared and for place promotion to foster inclusion?

Social democracy and municipal socialism

In this section, we look at instances of inclusive place marketing during the long century of social reform. These are social democratic and democratic socialist strategies that promoted social inclusion through meeting basic needs by collective action and a degree of democratic control. Chamberlain's Birmingham with its promise of a New Jerusalem introduced strategies for inclusion and citizenship, represented by the concept of the civic. The policies were branded often on a spectacular scale because the underlying politics required legitimation in order to gain public support, particularly from rate payers. Many social institutions – schools, universities, libraries, baths, town halls, museums – gained support through the symbolism of their architecture. The importance of this symbolism was reflected by vituperative debates over the styles most suitable for public buildings. To Ruskin, for instance, the gothic symbolized the skill of the craftsman in opposition to the tyranny of the machine that emasculated its workers (Hunt, 2005, p. 121). Given the disruption that industrialism represented and its transformation of working-class lives, the gothic provided some 'ethical certainties' from a more remote period that was seen in ecclesiastical architecture (Hunt, 2005, p. 127). Civic buildings and the architecture of civil society, on the other hand tended to take an Athenian form, since Greece epitomized the values of reform that the emerging industrial bourgeoisie identified with: rationality, liberalism, democratic government, civic mindedness and the flowering of the arts and humanities (Hunt, 2005, p. 198). Place marketing's equation of industrial capitalism with these idealist values constituted an early version of laissez faire citizenship (Faulks, 1999).

A century later during that era's post-war zenith, the New Towns, Green Belts and the house-building and slum clearance programmes symbolized this politics through its liberation from the stultifying impacts of class relations. Social reform was branded by modernist architecture (Beech, 2014, p. 196). The shift in the balance of power towards people and greater democratic accountability was reflected by lack of unnecessary ornamentation, openness, light, space, simplicity and by prioritizing function over form, and human need over aesthetic dogma. These values were aptly represented by the Festival of Britain, as well as such icons as the Finsbury Health Centre, Bexhill's De La Warr Pavilion, (funded by the socialist ninth Earl), and London Zoo's Penguin Pool. Throughout Europe council housing adopted that style because its association with both democratic socialism and social democracy gave those political streams wider recognition. Showpieces such as Islington's Highbury Quadrant explicitly illustrated the state's potential to effect political change. East London's Balfron Tower, the creation of Erno Goldfinger, is a classic instance of a building symbolizing the politics of social inclusion.

> Like it or loathe it, this was intended to be heroic architecture that offered the best of design to the masses, freed people from condemned slum housing, and elevated them – literally – to a better life. Balfron Tower is the welfare state in concrete. It deserves, nay demands, our attention.
>
> (Municipal Dreams, 2014)

Place marketing therefore is always aligned to a particular politics that employs demonstration projects to diffuse awareness of successful initiatives. However, such marketing may remove the progressive element of welfare programmes.

The Garden City model behind the New Towns was a class politics that threatened private land ownership and symbolized the benefits of communally-owned property. It may be marketed by different paradigms, as an instance of either the freedoms of consumption, or the politics of social justice, democracy and the moral economy. Place marketing may then take a particular policy, but allow its own universalism – a politics that we have seen is demonstrably false – to conceal and distort a radical politics. That is a strong reason why any attempt to construct place marketing for inclusion must be careful of how such policies are marketed.

Place marketing for social inclusion

Demonstrating alternatives

Place marketing provides a class framework for interpreting society. The profession constructs place images of consensus but these obscure the oppressive class relations that underlies it. One starting point for inclusive strategies must be to demonstrate the mechanisms whereby these status quo strategies operate. Baltimore illustrates how policy statements and place promotion act as pedagogic schemes to socialize both citizenry and tourist into the neo-liberal interpretation of the world through the conventional dualities of who counts and who does not, of wage earners and the demonized welfare dependents (Silk and Andrews, 2011). Place marketing operates through discourses that make tourists feel safe, discourses that justify measures to contain the working class, to concentrate socialized investment and state power and to signal to capital the spaces where investment is secure. The anti-democratic nature of the spectacle, the sporting mega-event and the large-scale renewal project benefits capital (Colomb, 2012), prevents individuals from expressing and developing their own autonomy, and clearly demonstrates how place marketing furthers social exclusion.

Identifying how place marketing reproduces existing relations of power lets one investigate alternative politics and processes that benefit the disadvantaged: resistance by the poor, reformist capital concerned about neo-liberalism's inefficiencies and instabilities, or the possibilities of moralistic critiques. One must choose the agents able to articulate these processes, whether civil society or the state, and one must decide on the criteria that would define greater inclusivity such as democracy, community, the de-commodification of public goods, redistribution or welfare. Inclusive approaches could inspire more bottom-up forms of decision-making by empowering ordinary people to conceptualize their needs. For this they must to learn to think politically about society and themselves, as this relationship is mediated through the built environment. In this way people would be able to collapse the personal and the political and stimulate individual reflexivity so as to let people gain an understanding and influence over the forces that mould their lives and the many different elements that make up their inclusion into society.

Multiple possibilities arise if one looks at how examples of place marketing could be examined for enhancing social inclusion. For instance, citizenship, the rights that markets fail to provide and needs that are frozen by the operation of markets, yield interesting ideas. London's transport system is a major element in its branding. Yet its distinctiveness and the non-profit element, its association with high quality art and design arose out of notions of citizenship; that ordinary people deserved the best that society could offer. That provides an entirely different orientation to place marketing and one closer to the Moscow metro. Second, markets often fail to satisfy human need – one of the most important is the right to feel secure in all spheres of life. This is a composite good made up of individual and communal circumstances but it is absent among those groups that need it most as a consequence of neo-liberal individualism, welfare cuts, and a lack of concern over social capital and community. Third, the intensified emphasis on sport for place marketers creates spectacles for passive consumption (Nauright, 2004), yet this can damage society because it excludes participation in sport aimed at strengthening community bonds, personal development or the provision of identity in people's lives. Each example opens a different line of enquiry.

If one locates social inclusion in notions of enhancing individual and collective autonomy, if the tendency of policy making has been authoritarian and state-led, if one remembers the class basis of welfare, and if one rethinks health as a holistic phenomenon, then the Peckham Health Centre from the thirties is a good example of how place marketing could embrace a more inclusive stance. It located poor health in the totality of the environment that faced residents, and saw the solution in overcoming anomie by creating spaces for social interaction that strengthened the individual within the community. The approach impacted positively on health by enhancing social interaction and boosting working class self-esteem in many ways, including the introduction to the country of self-service throughout the centre (Pearse and Crocker, 1943, p. 74). This democratic socialist politics was branded by a modernist building that used light and space to break down traditional client-professional relations and create opportunities for autonomous activity by local residents. Whereas neo-liberal place marketing foregrounds wage cutting, competitiveness and efficiency, democratic socialism adopted real citizenship, personal autonomy and community engagement as its criteria. This was effective since the cause of most of their patient's symptoms lay in their class position.

The same criteria sees South America displays an architecture and urban politics that corresponds to Illich's ideas of autonomy for the excluded. Brazil has pioneered a form of participative democracy that invites citizens to determine part of their local authority's spending, thus giving voice to the marginalized (Avritzer, 2009). This has significantly changed the balance of class relations, giving the poor real benefits and including them as citizens for the first time. It originated in Porto Alegre, a town of over one million, and within a few years had thousands of participants including those in the poorest localities. Surprisingly, rich and poor worked together, with poor areas gaining facilities such as sewage and roads. It is a political movement that is to be judged by its re-distributional impact and its success in developing mass mobilization among the population so as to resist multinational power and fashion, and to create an environment suited to people's needs. Whereas re-distributional strategies can be easily countermanded, changing the political environment can have lasting impacts on social inclusion.

This politics has been widely disseminated with the support of the World Bank (Pateman, 2012) but what is being sold is participation rather than the development of a radical class consciousness. Effective place marketing would demonstrate under what conditions this could change the relationship between state and civil society, just as it could have focused on the unique politics of land that underlay the New Towns experiment.

In a similar vein Latin America provides examples of housing developments that have abandoned top-down practices in favour of embodying principles devised by the residents themselves. They may include developing physical connections to the rest of the city, cheap ways to provide community facilities and novel solutions to the provision of basics, such as dry toilets (McGuirk, 2014, p. 147). In Chile, for instance, one estate aimed at the poor managed to retain a central location unlike the usual schemes, but given the higher cost of land were only able to provide half a house, leaving the tenants to build the other half themselves, when they were able to (McGuirk, 2014, p. 80). Here are two initiatives that lend themselves to marketing using emotive symbols and language – direct democracy, empowering the poor – that constitute a politics with widespread appeal.

Localism and holistic political strategies

Community and locally focused policies aimed at the excluded such as training or physical regeneration appear attractive to those wishing to reduce inequality yet they are often zero-sum and move the poor around the poverty line but rarely change their class position. Local urban initiatives are limited because of their fragmentation, narrow focus and reliance on discretionary financing. Local policies are often treated apolitically because they appear to be so obviously 'good', that they fall victim to the class politics of the market (Sharzer, 2012). The British Transition Towns (Taylor, 2012), for instance, foreground place marketing for inclusion, but without a political motivation they do the opposite, since the middle class buy their way in and bid up house prices. Like so many local policies – community energy is a good example (Seyfang *et al.*, 2012) – they focus on sustainability and resilience and ignore the economic processes that cause exclusion and shun explicit political connections. That frustrates their social aims (Sharzer, 2012).

Challenging entrenched class power necessitates framing local initiatives through a political strategy. Community energy, for instance, could be organized so as to prioritize democracy, change workplace relations, reduce the power of the large energy companies and consider new means of distribution that support inclusion. If that is not done, then apparently progressive strategies will offer false hope to the poor since the aims of self-reliance and autonomy have been redefined in a 'politically regressive, individualized and competitive direction' (Mayer, 2012, p. 365). If policies do not explicitly resist that politics, they are likely to result in greater inequality because of the dominant political environment (Harvey, 2012, p. 83). Pro-poor tourism, for instance, is often thought to help inclusion but it is likely to increase overall levels of exclusion (Chok *et al.*, 2007). The social economy, similarly, promises workers greater autonomy but often leads to self-exploitation and co-option for similar reasons (Eisenschitz and Gough, 2011).

Social exclusion has multiple causes. Policies may fail because local and immediate gains are compromised. One area may benefit but the problems are exported. Advances in housing for the poor may be undermined in the longer term, by shifts in the location of employment. The situation is complicated because there is no simple dualism between 'in' and 'out', either socially or spatially. The poor are not physically or morally separated from the included but are integrated in society in many ways: they have internalized the values of consumption yet are excluded from the well-paid, meaningful and secure work that would allow access to that society (Young, 2003, p. 397). At the same time, the better off working class as well as the middle class can be subject to various forms of alienation and exclusion such as the absence of community and in London, the problems of housing. One cannot therefore focus on the very poorest but must take a class viewpoint.

Two instances of a more comprehensive approach, spring to mind. Coin Street in central London was born out of a seven-year battle by the community. Two planning enquiries and support from the socialist Greater London Council that placed conditions on the use of the privately-owned part of the site in order to reduce its market value, made it possible for the community to acquire it (Tuckett, 1988). As a social enterprise, it not only managed to build social housing and repay the loan, but uses commercial activities to support social housing and workshops that provide a degree of individual autonomy to residents within a collective framework.

The second example is Boston's Dudley Street Neighbourhood Initiative (DSNI). That community saw collective self-help that developed endogenously by strong political organization that was aimed at taking on both the state and capital (Medoff and Sklar, 1994). This poor and socially disorganized locality developed strategies of direct action that managed to create a working community in which nearly everyone participated. By combining direct democracy with grants from foundations it forced the state to grant it Eminent Domain legislation to buy out their slum landlords and form a Community Land Trust to keep that housing under local control. It developed a holistic programme of economic and social development that was focused on all the dimensions of community citizenship (Engelsman *et al.*, 2016). This experience could act as a demonstration project to poor communities the world over on how to improve the quality of life without succumbing to what conventional place marketing would describe as the realities of the global marketplace.

Where to intervene?

Intensified central government control over local authorities and civil society within a market-oriented political environment has reduced opportunities for representing spaces to promote for social inclusion. One has therefore to look beyond traditional institutional structures maybe to urban social movements that may occasionally have an effective politics of inclusion (Harvey, 2012, Chapter 5). Resistance to neo-liberalism increasingly lies in the interstices of society (Dinerstein, 2012). It may lie where there is resistance to the dominant urban politics, for instance action against the forces of dispossession that are blighting the lives of those who have become surplus to the upwards transfer of wealth (Harvey, 2006). Resistance may involve the protection of communities from the privatization of communal resources such as social housing or pensions. Tourism is a particularly good example of accumulation by dispossession, since it reduces cultures to stereotypes for consumption and sees firms dump their costs onto society and hotels enclose beaches as a consequence of their economic and political power. There has been little resistance because of tourism's benign image. Yet the narratives of place marketing are eventually being challenged by alternatives; Podemos' mayor of Barcelona, for instance, wishes to limit the sector's growth because of its impact upon exclusion (Gant, 2016).

Place marketing is narrowly focused upon a location's competitive edge and the money coming into it. This is mostly irrelevant since most of that money does not go to those who need to most. In fact, the richest locations often have the greatest inequalities and may enclose the poorest populations. Strategies for inclusion must deal with the reactions of the excluded in this situation and their attempts to regain control whether through drugs or crime, as collectives, such as family and community, fall apart. Initiatives may try to resist the spread of individualism by encouraging communal ways of social organization in order to increase security and enhance social capital. They may try to reclaim human rights that are embedded in subsistence necessities, such as affordable and healthy food and water, air, housing, healthcare and safety, but to be effective they would require transformed social relations, and new conceptions of citizenship. Inclusive place marketing would put forward an attractive vision of society that rests conceptually on the damage neo-liberalism does both to humans and capitalism itself (Wilkinson and Pickett, 2009). Wherever that is achieved, it should be branded into the very fabric of the location so as to demonstrate the significance of promoting values that are in opposition to the conventional wisdom of place marketing and neo-liberalism.

The difficulties of doing this should not be underestimated. Spaces that promote social inclusion require a politically educated citizenry schooled in reflexivity, able to read cities and conscious of how we internalize ideas as part of our socialization. Above all they must be able to link their personal situation to institutional processes. On the other hand, we should not underestimate the potential for real change that can be achieved since physical artefacts and patterns stir strong emotions and can generate movements in defence of communal rights.

A particularly striking example was achieved by Chris Searle a primary school teacher in East London who was able to engage schoolchildren to write poetry about their perceptions of their local environment, using a class framework corresponding to their own lived experience (Davis, 2009). By giving them a sense of autonomy he unleashed a vein of political creativity that led to their walking out of school when he was sacked for publishing their work. Similarly, the DSNI's success reflected the way that its political organization and its collective experience of exclusion inevitably led to particular model of society and politics. That in turn explained the nature of its strategy and its model of community citizenship. In both these instances the experience of social exclusion and their understanding of its underlying mechanisms in particular places, created solidarity between people and politicized them.

Conclusion

We have argued that place marketing strategies for social inclusion requires explicitly political approaches. Conventional place marketing uses the built environment to change and legitimate class relationships, but does so in the belief that this is a universal principle that provides benefits to everyone. Its lack of reflexivity ensures that its assumptions are unchallenged, while a rationale other than economic growth is deemed 'unrealistic'. There is accordingly little resistance to the global epidemic of dispossession by a place marketing that extols the virtues of the newly gentrified spaces or supports land grabs. Similarly, there is little resistance to the symbolic politics of sporting mega-event or iconic projects and the way they intensify the problems of deeply divided societies.

Promoting social inclusion is difficult, not least because it is a vague concept with differing criteria. Like motherhood it is rarely opposed, but since it can be implemented within a range of political positions there will be many ideas over what it means to define and achieve inclusion. Localist approaches that appear to be attractive tend to exacerbate the problems. Yet if one ceases to see place marketing just as a conscious activity, but a process in which spatial structure develops under a range of political, social and economic forces, there will be a congruence between the values of the dominant loci of power and the built environment, mediated in ways that are read by the population. This process can sometimes be captured by subordinate groups; that is particularly likely when the dominant politics is itself problematic. In this post-crisis age of austerity that is increasingly possible.

References

Avritzer, L. (2009) *Participatory Institutions in Democratic Brazil*. Baltimore: Johns Hopkins University Press.

Beech, N. (2014) 'Ground exploration; producing everyday life at the South Bank, 1948–1951', in L. Stanek, C. Schmid and A. Moravanszky, A. (eds.) *Urban Revolution Now*. Farnham: Ashgate, pp. 191–206.

Black, D. (2007) 'The symbolic politics of sport mega-events: 2010 in comparative perspective'. *Politikon*, 34(3), pp. 261–276.

Cairns, G. (2012) 'Architecture as political image: the perspective of advertising', Architecture – *MPS*, 1(1), pp. 1–13 Available at: www.ingentaconnect.com/contentone/uclpress/amps/2012/00000001/00000001/art00001 (Accessed: 2 August 2016).

Chok, S., Macbeth, J. and Warren, C. (2007) 'Tourism as a tool for poverty alleviation: A critical analysis of "pro-poor tourism" and implications for sustainability'. *Current Issues in Tourism*, 10(3), pp. 144–165.

Colomb, C. (2012) *Staging the New Berlin: Place Marketing and the Politics of Urban Re-invention Post-1989*. London: Routledge.

Davis, B. (2009) 'Teaching tough kids: Stepney and Searle'. *Race and Class*, 51(2), pp. 18–32.

Debord, G. (1984) *The Society of the Spectacle*. Detroit: Black and Red.

Desiderio, A. (2013) 'Branding Stratford: social representations and the re-making of place'. *Architecture_media_politics_society*, 2(3). Available at: http://architecturemps.com/wp-content/uploads/2012/07/amps-vol-2-no3-abstract-branding-stratford-social-representation-and-the-re-making-of-place.pdf.

Dinerstein, A. (2012) 'Interstitial revolution: on the explosive fusion of negativity and hope'. *Capital and Class*, 36(3), pp. 521–540.

Dorling, D. (2014) *Inequality and the 1%*. London: Verso.

Eisenschitz, A. (2016) 'Tourism class and crisis'. *Human Geography*, 16(3), pp. 110–124.

Eisenschitz, A. and Gough, J. (2011) 'Socialism and the social economy'. *Human Geography*, 4(2), pp. 1–15.

Engelsman, U., Rowe, M. and Southern, A. (2016) 'Narratives of urban resistance: The Community Land Trust'. *Architecture – MPS*, 9(1), pp. 1–22. Available at: www.ingentaconnect.com/contentone/uclpress/amps/2016/00000009/00000001/art00001;jsessionid=21vie38u6qe6e.alexandra (Accessed: 5 August 2016).

Faulks, N. (1999) *Citizenship in Contemporary Britain*. Edinburgh: Edinburgh University Press.

Gant, A. (2016) 'Holiday rentals: the new gentrification battlefront'. *Sociological Research Online*, 21(3), 10. Available at: www.socresonline.org.uk/21/3/10.html (Accessed: 21 March 2017).

Glyn, A. (2006) *Capitalism Unleashed*. Oxford: Oxford University Press.

Harvey, D. (1989) 'From managerialism to entrepreneurialism'. *Geografiska Annaler, Series B Human Geography*, 71(1), pp. 3–17.

Harvey, D. (2006) *Spaces of Global Capitalism*. London: Verso.

Harvey, D. (2012) *Rebel Cities: From the Right to the City to the Urban Revolution*. London: Verso.

Hunt, T. (2005) *Building Jerusalem*. London: Orion.

Kerr, (2002) 'The uncompleted monument: London, war, and the architecture of remembrance', in Borden, I., Kerr, J., Rendell, J. and Pivaro, A. (eds.) *The Unknown City*. Boston: MIT, pp. 69–90.

Levine, M. (2000) 'A third-world city in the first world; social exclusion, racial inequality and sustainable development in Baltimore', in Polese, M. and Stren, R. (eds.), *The Social Sustainability of Cities*. Toronto: Toronto University Press, pp. 123–156.

Mayer, M. (2012) 'The "Right to the City" in the context of shifting mottos of urban social movements'. *City*, 13(2–3), pp. 362–374.

McGuirk, J. (2014) *Radical Cities*. London: Verso.

Medoff, P. and Sklar, H. (1994) *Streets of Hope: The Fall and Rise of an Urban Neighborhood*. Boston: South End Press.

Minton, A. (2009) *Ground Control*. London: Penguin.

Mooney, G. (2004) 'Cultural policy as urban transformation? Critical reflections on Glasgow, European City of Culture 1990'. *Local Economy*, 19(4), pp. 327–340.

Municipal Dreams (2014) 'Social housing as heritage: thoughts on the National Trust and Balfron Tower'. Available at: https://municipaldreams.wordpress.com/3235-2/ (Accessed: 12 August 2016).

Nauright, J. (2004) 'Global games: Culture, political economy and sport in the globalised world of the 21st century'. *Third World Quarterly*, 25(7), pp. 1325–1336.

Pateman, C. (2012) 'Participatory democracy revisited'. *Perspectives on Politics*, 10(1), pp. 7–19.

Pearse, I. and Crocker, L. (1943) *The Peckham Experiment*. London: George Allen and Unwin.

Seyfang, G., Park, J. and Smith, A. (2012) 'A thousand flowers blooming? An examination of community energy in the UK'. *Community Energy*, 61, pp. 977–989.

Sharzer, G. (2012) *No Local: Why Small-scale Alternatives Won't Change the World*. Alresford, Hants: Zero Books.

Silk, M. and Andrews, D. (2011) '(Re)Presenting Baltimore: place, policy, politics, and cultural pedagogy'. *Review of Education, Pedagogy, and Cultural Studies*, 33(5), pp. 433–464.

Smith, N. (2002) 'New globalism, new urbanism; gentrification as global urban strategy'. *Antipode*, 34(3), pp. 427–450.

Standing, G. (2014) *The Precariat: The New Dangerous Class*. London: Bloomsbury.

Taylor, P. (2012) 'Transition towns and world cities: towards green networks of cities'. *Local Environment*, 17(4), pp. 495–508.

Townsend, S. (2005) 'My heartlands'. *Guardian*, 24 April, p. 25.

Tuckett, I. (1988) 'Coin St: there is another way'. *Community Development Journal*, 23(4), pp. 249–257.

Wilkinson, R. and Pickett, K. (2010) *The Spirit Level; Why Equality is Better For Everyone*. London: Penguin.

Young, J. (1999) *The Exclusive Society: Social Exclusion, Crime and Difference in Late Modernity*. London: Sage.

Young, J. (2003) 'Merton with energy, Katz with structure: The sociology of vindictiveness and the criminology of transgression'. *Theoretical Criminology*, 7(3), pp. 389–414.

Zizek, S. (2013) '*The Wire*, or, what to do in non-evental times', in Bzdak, D., Crosby, J. and Vannatta, S. (eds.) *The Wire and Philosophy*. Chicago: Open Court, pp. 217–236.

5 A service ecosystem approach to representing a place's unique brand

Jan Brown

Introduction

Understanding uniqueness is at the heart of modern marketing. The concept of uniqueness was proposed by advertising executive Rosser Reeves (1961) has now become a basic tenet in marketing and relates to how organizations could create unique offers for the market, a 'unique selling point' or USP, that makes what is offered by one organization different from the rest. Brands are representations of those unique offers. In order to help reduce the complexity of the real world conceptual models and frameworks for marketing have been devised, for example, 7 Ps, Porter's 5 Forces Model, Boston Consultancy Group (BCG) Matrix, Product Life Cycle Model, and continue to be devised to provide mental models for managers to navigate this complexity and guide the development of their own individual offers. These models were never meant to be straightjackets of thought or rigidly adhered to laws, rather mental models that added value to the user. As commerce evolves to face the challenges of providing offers in an increasingly global and connected world the mental models proposed are adapting to meet the changing market needs. As the use of mental models, originally devised to meet the needs of the commercial world, start to be transferred into new and more complex contexts, such as place; the models and frameworks used to guide thought must evolve to ensure that they remain fit for use and flexible enough to meet the needs of a wide and diverse audience. A 'one model fits all' approach will not meet the needs of all and is more likely to produce sameness rather than difference and uniqueness. As Ashworth and Kavaratzis (2014, p. 133) note 'the only lesson of global experience [relating to place branding] is that there is no universally applicable model, no set of reliable and predictable instruments and no certain successful outcome'.

One way forward, but not the only way, could be to use theoretical developments emanating from mainstream marketing to assist in the development of the place marketing and branding field. This chapter proposes the potential use of an overarching framework of thought, the service ecosystem, that has humans and their diverse interactions at its core and is based on systems thinking emanating from an emerging stream of research in mainstream marketing, service-dominant logic of marketing (S-D logic). The framework offers the potential to aid in the consolidation of the place marketing and branding corpus and provide a basis on which some innovative and novel mental modelling for place marketing and branding could be undertaken in the future. At the heart of this mindset (S-D logic) are humans, or actors, and how they form networks; institutions and institutional arrangements, in which resources are integrated and exchanged to create value. It is proposed in this chapter that the uniqueness of this integration, or elements of this uniqueness, could and should be reflected in the place marketing and branding campaigns and communications more effectively to increase inclusiveness. Putting people at the centre of place provides the potential to re-orientate many of the mental models developed in mainstream marketing that were devised to focus on a purely goods, or outputs objective, instead to include and celebrate processes and outcomes and therefore meet a broader set of needs. This reorientation has the potential to further demonstrate the usefulness of many of the current mental models in use but it may also provide the basis on which new and more appropriate models are developed in the future. The use of an S-D logic mindset provides just one way of doing this. This reorientation in mindset relating to place marketing and branding puts marketing *in service* to people rather than marketing viewing people purely as units of analysis on which outputs are measured. By viewing place marketing and branding as being in service to all people allows mental models to be applied or developed that provide greater opportunities for a wider range of actors and their networks to be acknowledged and represented in both official and unofficial place marketing and branding communications.

The evolution of marketing: marketing in service – an S-D logic perspective

Marketing thought was originally developed and has evolved to meet the needs of mainly goods based economies (Vargo *et al.*, 2008). This meant that it was the requirement of the discipline to aid in the development and the understanding of the needs and structures required by manufacturers to sell their goods effectively in the commercial marketplace. However, as many economies shifted towards a more service-orientated focus the marketing concept was broadened to include more complex frameworks of thought that investigate marketing from not only a goods perspective but also a service and experience perspective. This broadening of the discipline has included among others more balanced views of the organization and customer interactions, an understanding of how digital age is changing, or showing more clearly, interactions, and the rise in power and endurance of strong brands in the global and local marketplace and humans, previously only identified as customers and consumers, being acknowledged as actors with multiple roles in their life journeys.

This evolution in the mainstream marketing discipline offers the potential to develop the thinking about place marketing and branding using some of the emerging contributions and mindsets emanating from mainstream marketing. A mindset that is currently being developed in the mainstream marketing literature that is gaining increasing traction, but not without its critics, is one that is developing around systems thinking: the service-dominant logic of marketing (S-D logic). In this mindset, value is co-created by actors who employ, integrate and exchange various resources to create value and service (Vargo and Lusch, 2004, 2008, 2011, 2016). This co-creation occurs and is sustained by institutions that form open systems (service ecosystems) that interact with one another. S-D logic has already been identified as having some potential value in place marketing and branding. Warnaby (2009, p. 415) indicated that '… S-D logic of marketing could potentially offer a new perspective through which to view the existing canon of (urban) place marketing literature'. Recent developments in the S-D logic literature (Vargo and Lusch, 2011, 2016) further develop the premises of this new logic and recent evolutions in the branding and digital literature demonstrate some convergences in marketing thought with S-D logic that might prove useful for the development of the place marketing and branding literature with regards to understanding and representing the individual, unique and complex nature of places. From an S-D logic mindset marketing is seen as being *in service* to humans so that marketing and branding is not 'done to' but 'works with' individuals and groups to represent what is unique about their offer. For place marketing and branding this may allow some interesting ways forward particularly in relation to inclusiveness and the ability to incorporate a wider range of representations within their communications.

The evolving use and understanding of brands and branding

The use of brands and branding for commercial purposes is not a new phenomenon. As Hankinson (2014, p. 15) states 'branding's use as a modern business tool can be traced back to the end of the nineteenth century …'. However, the use of brands and how they are conceptualized has changed over time, and will continue to change, to suit the needs of those who believe it is a valid construct. Merz, He and Vargo (2009, p. 331) have identified four specific eras of brand conceptualizations (see Table 5.1) due to branding evolving to the current stakeholder-focus era in which brands are seen as dynamic and social processes. For place marketing and branding this provides potential opportunities for the application and development of conceptual models that have been informed by a comprehensive range of actors thus increasing inclusivity.

This stakeholder-focus era of branding offers those stakeholders interested in being represented in place marketing campaigns and being part of the place brand (and this should not be taken as a given) some potentially useful marketing and brand conceptualizations and models. The identification of brands being dynamic means that the models that view brands as static constructs may now be less useful or outdated and the social nature of the process means that the imposition of a brand (being branded) on actors and their place rather than representing it may offer limited long-term benefits or value. Within the place branding literature, the dynamic nature of place is clearly identified by Kavaratzis and Hatch (2013, p. 75–82) who state that 'cultural geographers and environmental

Table 5.1 Evolving brand eras

Timeline	*Era*	*Brand as...*	*Examples of relevant literature*
1900s–1930s	Individual goods-focus brand era	Brands as identifiers	Copeland (1923); Low and Fullerton (1994); Strasser (1989)
1930s–1990s	Value-focus brand era	Brands as functional images	*Functional Value-Focus*: Brown (1950); Jacoby and colleagues (1971, 1977); Park *et al.* (1986)
		Brands as symbolic images	*Symbolic Value-Focus*: Gardner and Levy (1955); Goffman (1959); Levy (1959)
1990s–2000	Relationship-focus brand era	Brands as knowledge	*Customer-Firm Relationship Focus*: Aaker (1996); Blattberg and Deighton (1996); Kapferer (1992); Keller (1993)
		Brands as relationship partners	*Customer-Brand Relationship Focus*: Aaker (1997); Fournier (1998); Gobe (2001)
		Brands as promise	*Firm-Brand Relationship Focus*: Berry (2000); de Chernatony (1999); Gilly and Wolfinbarger (1998); King (1991)
2000 onwards	stakeholder-focus brand era	Brands as dynamic and social processes	McAlexander *et al.* (2002); Muniz *et al.* (2001); Muniz *et al.* (2005); Ballantyne and Aitken (2007); Ind and Bjerke (2007); Jones (2005)

Source: Adapted from Merz *et al.* (2009, p. 331).

psychologists have repeatedly demonstrated the dynamic nature of places and place identities' and believe '... place branding is best understood as dialogue, debate, and conversation'.

The identification of a broad range of stakeholders, rather than just the customer and consumer, in marketing allows for the potential to examine the collective and dynamic processes that underlie brand consumption within society (Merz *et al.*, 2009). The increasing recognition of brand consumption being based on collective processes provides further opportunities in place branding to develop more inclusive conceptualizations that represent a broader range of stakeholders. Within the mainstream branding literature, a brand will have increasingly been conceptualized as a continuous social process (e.g. Muniz *et al.*, 2001; Jones, 2005; Gregory, 2007; Ind and Bjerke, 2007) whereby brand value is being co-created through stakeholder-based negotiations (e.g. Brodie, 2009; Brodie *et al.*, 2009). There is potentially great value in conceptualizing place marketing and branding as a continuous social process and the use of current and future brand frameworks, emanating from this new brand era, could potentially offer some exciting place brand representations that communicate the uniqueness of each place and increase inclusivity.

Current work being undertaken from within the place brand community has already identified the social process nature of brand formation (Campelo, 2014; Evans, 2014; Florek, 2014; Kerr and Oliver, 2014; Hankinson, 2014). However, an overarching framework in which to 'house', congregate or distil the wide diversity of thought is currently missing within the place branding literature. One potential overarching framework emanating from S-D logic is the ecosystem framework (Vargo and Lusch, 2016).

Service-dominant logic of marketing: the growth of systems thinking

The application of S-D logic to the place branding field has been developing over the past few years (Warnaby, 2009; Nilsson and Ballantyne, 2014; Warnaby and Medway, 2014). During this period, the theoretical development of S-D logic has continued and this chapter proposes that further contributions to place branding literature can be made from an S-D logic perspective. One area that has the potential to unify many of the place branding contributions to date, and allow for the potential of more inclusive models of place marketing and branding to be developed in the future, is the consideration of place as a service ecosystem while using an S-D logic mindset. By using a service ecosystems view, a framework for studying systems of service systems or the interaction and value co-creation among multiple service systems can be developed on which potentially multiple and varying place brand models can be developed to meet various stakeholder needs based on dynamic and social processes (Vargo and Lusch, 2011).

In order to develop a service ecosystem mindset from an S-D logic perspective the basic tenets on which the logic has been developed need to be first highlighted. Warnaby (2009, pp. 404–418) identified the main characteristics and foundational premises of S-D logic and stated that '...this paper can therefore perhaps be regarded as the first iteration of the process of applying the fundamental principles of service-dominant logic in the context of the marketing of places...'. In summary, Vargo and Lusch (2004, 2008, 2011, 2016) identify that marketing has evolved with a heavy focus on a goods-based understanding of markets. In this goods-dominant (G-D) logic:

> ... value is created (manufactured) by the firm and distributed in the market, usually through exchange of goods and money. From this perspective, the roles of "producers" and "consumers" are distinct, and value creation is often thought of as a series of activities performed by the firm.
>
> (Vargo *et al.*, 2008, p. 146)

However, Vargo and Lusch propose an:

> ... alternative view, service-dominant (S-D) logic, is tied to the value-in-use meaning of value (Vargo and Lusch, 2008). In S-D logic, the roles of

> producers and consumers are not distinct, meaning that value is always co-created, jointly and reciprocally, in interactions among providers and beneficiaries through the integration of resources and application of competences.
>
> (Vargo *et al.*, 2008, p. 146)

Fundamental to the development of S-D logic is the reconceptualization of services to service so that:

> … the traditional conceptualization of *services* (usually plural) as a *unit of output* (i.e., an intangible product) are reconceptualized as *service* (singular), defined as "the application of specialized knowledge skills … for the benefit of customers" (Vargo and Lusch 2004: 2) in a process of joint and reciprocal co-creation of value between providers, beneficiaries, and others (e.g., other market-facing, public, and private actors) … The benefit provided through service is *value*, that is, an increase in the viability of the system (e.g., individual, family, firm, customer, etc.) under consideration, which arises as actors in an exchange integrate their varied resources (Vargo and Lusch 2004, 2008, 2011).
>
> (Vargo *et al.*, 2008, p. 146)

In 2011 Vargo and Lusch introduced the service ecosystems perspective. This perspective was developed by working closely with service science theorists. Lusch and Spohrer (2012, p. 1497) state that 'we borrow from the recent work on the ecosystems concept (networks of individual actors) from ecology (networks of populations of actors) and how this thinking can be applied to organizations (Mars *et al.*, 2012)'. Development of this service ecosystem perspective has grown in importance since it was introduced and in 2016 Vargo and Lusch updated the foundational premises (FP) for S-D logic and added a further FP (see Table 5.2). The introduction of an eleventh FP based on institutions and institutional arrangements and its axiomatic status clearly reinforces the importance of understanding value co-creation from a service ecosystems perspective.

Using a S-D logic mindset, the term 'actor' is used rather than producer and consumer as '…all actors are engaged in the same, generic activities: resource-integration and service-for-service exchange' (Barrett *et al.*, 2015, p. 142). This identification of actors is a useful designation within place marketing and branding as it allows value to be represented from multiple perspectives as advocated by Stubbs and Warnaby (2014) who identified multiple stakeholder groups (residents, politicians, government organizations, promotion agencies, infrastructure and transport providers, cultural and sports organizations, businesses, academic organizations and schools, and religious organizations). These intra and actor-to-actor activities are '…coordinated and assisted through the creation of *institutions*: norms, meanings, symbols, and institutional arrangements (constellations of integrated institutions) that guide cognitive and behavioural activities to facilitate collaborative value cocreation' (Lusch and Vargo, 2014, p. 116). The proposal of the use of the term 'actor' within place marketing and branding is developed further later in this chapter.

Table 5.2 S-D logic foundational premises development

Foundational premise	*Description*	*Axiom*
FP1	Service is the fundamental basis of exchange	Axiom status
FP2	Indirect exchange masks the fundamental basis of exchange	
FP3	Goods are distribution mechanisms for service provision	
FP4	Operant resources are the fundamental source of strategic benefit	
FP5	All economies are service economies	
FP6	Value is co-created by multiple actors, always including the beneficiary	Axiom status
FP7	Actors cannot deliver value but can participate in the creation and offering of value propositions	
FP8	A service-centered view is inherently beneficiary oriented and relational	
FP9	All social and economic actors are resource integrators	Axiom status
FP10	Value is always uniquely and phenomenologically determined by the beneficiary	Axiom status
FP11	Value co-creation is coordinated through actor-generated institutions and institutional arrangements	Axiom status

Source: Adapted from Vargo and Lusch (2016, p. 8).

Service-dominant logic: a service ecosystem perspective

Warnaby and Medway (2014, p. 44) believe that '…the notion of "service systems" has much potential utility in conceptualising the nature of place products'. This chapter proposes further contributions to place marketing and branding from an S-D logic perspective by introducing and developing the conceptualization of place as seen as a service ecosystem in which value is co-created by actors within multiple sub-ecosystems. All of which converge to form one overall place service ecosystem. It is with a detailed understanding of this service ecosystem that a marketing campaign or brand can be formed and place represented. This representation could include past, present, desired or ideal service ecosystems and the mental models used, academic or otherwise, to devise marketing campaigns can be chosen based on what value and which service ecosystems are to be represented.

The importance of viewing value co-creation as occurring within a service ecosystem was clearly identified by Lusch and Vargo (2014, p. 161) who state that 'these resource-integrating service-exchange activities, coordinated through institutional arrangements for mutual value creation, establish *service ecosystems*, formally defined as "relatively self-contained, self-adjusting system[s] of resource-integrating actors connected by shared institutional logics and mutual value creation through service exchange" '. By viewing place as an eco-system in which multiple resource-integrating service-exchange activities are being undertaken by multiple actors and actor-to-actor networks, places can be represented from multiple perspectives. Identifying and accepting the complexity within a place does not mean however that place marketing and branding necessarily has to become more complicated. As Norman (2011, p. 3) states 'making sense of complex worlds is facilitated by developing a mind-set around which to view the world'. As Lusch and Spohrer (2012, p. 1492) reflect 'for Norman, complexity "describes the state of the world" and complicated "describes a state of mind". Complexity is thus inherent in the thing or the system …'. Thus, the ability to frame the complexity of a place within a place service ecosystem mindset when developing place marketing activities, representing the place as a brand or rebranding exercise(s), allows the complexity to be represented. At the same time reducing the complication of trying to understand how the broad range of place marketing and branding conceptual contributions relate to one another and the hierarchy within. By viewing place as the unit of analysis in marketing and branding (see Figure 5.1) and defining place as an adaptable open service ecosystem in which multiple actor sub-ecosystems operate, interact and change over time, decisions can be made by marketers and branders about which sub-ecosystems are important to represent the uniqueness of the whole ecosystem at any given time.

By moving the focus away from trying to force the great complexity inherent in a place into one or two mental models towards accepting and acknowledging that rich and dynamic diversity exists in sub-ecosystems forms; exploring where

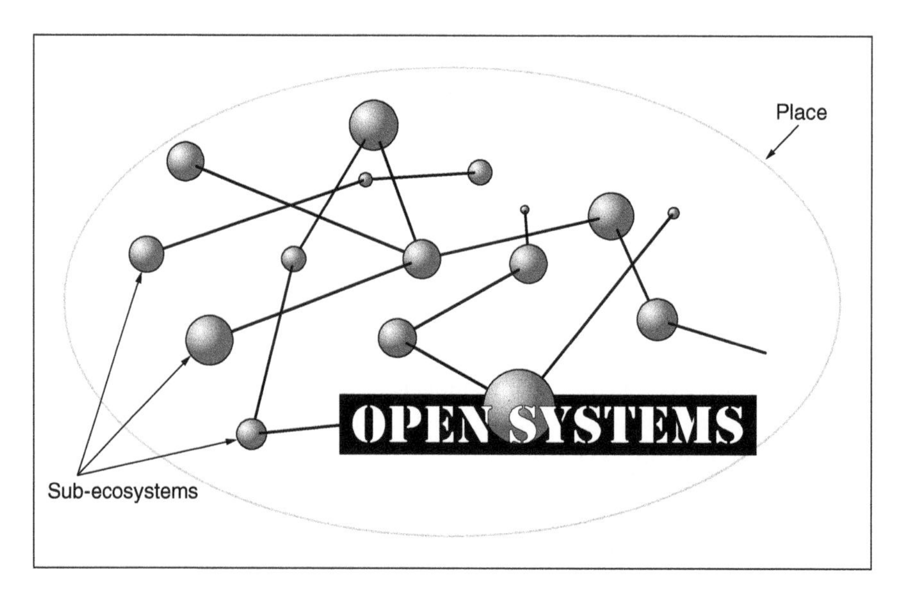

Figure 5.1 Place as a service ecosystem.

value is really being co-created; identifying and selecting the sub-ecosystems that are going to represent the whole ecosystem for that specific place marketing campaign or place brand offers greater opportunities to create more inclusive place brands. This provides a wide range of actors more flexibility in choosing the right conceptual models to suit their marketing and or branding objectives and needs. These choices can then be used within the overall service ecosystem's place marketing and branding activities.

By viewing place as service ecosystem all actors are seen to be part of an ecosystem (Spohrer and Maglio, 2010). This ecosystem of actors, with their rights and responsibilities, include people, organizations, and societal institutions. By placing actors at the heart of place marketing and representing the ecosystems and sub-ecosystems that they form means, by its very nature, each place marketing and branding campaign has to be based on the ecosystem's uniqueness and offers greater potential to be more inclusive.

As with other various theories on systems (Barile and Polese, 2010; Ng *et al.*, 2012) an S-D logic service ecosystem view '... considers service systems to be emergent, dynamic networks of actors and their interactions' (Vargo and Akaka, 2012, p. 208). The ecosystem metaphor is widely used by a number of disciplines to study social arrangement such as sociologists and organizational scientists (Mars *et al.*, 2012). The use of systems thinking in place marketing and branding could empower actors to understand and express the value being created in their own ecosystems and allow for wider participation in the choice and development of suitable marketing and branding conceptualizations that represent each individual ecosystem and their convergence into one whole place service ecosystem.

Putting humans at the centre of place: operant and operand resources

Using an S-D logic mindset broadens the focus of marketing to embrace processes and outcomes as well as outputs. Vargo and Lusch (2011, p. 184) conceptualize service provision as 'the ongoing combination of resources, through integration, and their application, driven by operant resources – the activities of actors'. An understanding of the distinction between operand and operant resources is fundamental to S-D logic where *operand resources* (e.g. natural resources) are usually tangible and static resources that require some action to make them valuable. *Operant resources* (e.g. human skills and knowledge), on the other hand, are usually intangible and dynamic resources that are capable of acting on operand and other operant resources to create value (Constantin and Lusch, 1994; Madhavaram and Hunt, 2007). The conceptualization of human actors being at the core of value creation is fundamental to S-D logic. This means that they (we) use a variety of resources, operand and operant, to create value (FP6). It therefore follows that humans and their value co-creation should be at the centre of all marketing and branding conceptualizations and representations. The fact that operant resources (FP4), human skills and knowledge, are the fundamental source of strategic benefit means that a detailed understanding of what humans are doing, the groups they form and the value they co-create is vital to successful marketing and branding. This human interaction and transformation puts complexity at the heart of all marketing and is leading to an evolution in the conceptualisations of marketing and branding.

In complex ecosystems, such as place, in which complexity is the very nature of the system, putting human actors at the heart of all conceptualizations of value co-creation could offer some very interesting developments of future place marketing and branding conceptualizations and representations. The use of systems thinking to communicate networks of operand resources is well established and common in place marketing communications, particularly when communications occur in a map format for example, tourist maps, railway systems, university campus maps etc. However, the representation of actors and the human resources (operant) they utilize to co-create value is often under-represented in formal marketing communications; whereas it is very apparent in unofficial and uncontrollable channels such as digital communications, for example YouTube, blogs, Twitter, TripAdvisor. The ability of actors to use varying combinations of operand and operant resources to co-create value offers some potentially interesting and novel opportunities for place actors when exploring and representing the place service ecosystem, whether they are in formal positions of marketing or not (e.g. Medway, 2014). As highlighted by Vargo and Lusch (2004) 'resources are not: they become', only when resources are used do they add value and these resources are used and transformed by humans.

We are all actors

The use of the term actor is not a new one in marketing and beyond. Bagozzi (1974, p. 78) identified marketing as an organized behavioural system of exchange, defined the exchange system as a 'set of social actors, their relationships to each other, and the endogenous and exogenous variables affecting the behavior of the social actors in those relationships'. It is also the convention of most Industrial Marketing and Purchasing (IMP) Group scholars to use this term (e.g. Håkansson and Snehota, 1995).

The proposed use of the term actors in place marketing and branding has the potential of bringing together multiple studies that might have previously been envisaged as providing very different perspectives. By understanding actor-to-actor interactions and the resources used in those interactions to add value, the resulting brands, and the conceptualizations used to represent those brands, could more easily be compared and contrasted and developed to meet actor needs more effectively. As Vargo and Lusch (2011, p. 184) state:

> much progress can be made rather quickly by the cross-fertilization implied in an A2A orientation. That is, in an A2A world, the insights into context, language, meaning, signs, symbols, experiences, rituals, etc. apply not just to what has traditionally been thought of as the 'consumers' world but

> equally to the 'producers.' Likewise, what has been learned about relationship, partnering, networks, and value, as studied in B2B, apply to the consumers' network. Much of this cross-fertilization has already begun.

As Vargo and Lusch (2011, p. 182) reflect:

> ... there is perhaps a certain irony in this position; it implies that we must move toward a more macro, systemic view of generic actors in order to see more clearly how a single, specific actor (e.g. a firm) can participate more effectively.

Within institutional studies Marti and Mari (2009, p. 95) identify that 'over the past fifteen years a new emphasis in institutional studies has emerged, which centers on understanding the role of actors in creating, maintaining, and transforming institutions and fields'. Who and what can be classified as an actor was clearly articulated by Scott (2014, p. 288) who stated that '...although they (we) are biological creatures, they (we) are also social constructions, possessing institutionally defined identities including capacities, rights, and responsibilities. These institutional elements at work are primarily cultural-cognitive, especially in their constitutive capacity, and normative'. Six types of actor are highlighted with examples from healthcare providing clear examples (Scott, 2014, p. 228). Examples of how these six categories of actors are easily transferrable to place have been provided in Table 5.3.

The use of the term actor is clearly stated in FP9 ('all social and economic actors are resource integrators') and is identified as having 'axiom' status in S-D

Table 5.3 Examples of types of place actors

Types of actors	*Examples provided by Scott*	*Example of place actors*
1 Individual	A specific doctor	Resident, tourist, business owner, employee
2 Association of Individuals	Medical Association e.g. American Medical Association	Housing association, travel group, unions
3 Populations of Individuals	Patients, physicians, nurses	Stakeboarders, musicians, parents
4 Organizations	Stanford University Hospital	Local independent business, medium-sized business, national business, international business
5 Associations of Organizations	Multi-hospital systems	Business associations, for example, Association of Small Business
6 Populations of Organizations	Hospitals or nursing homes	Tourism, manufacturing, construction, agriculture, creative, digital

Source: Adapted from Scott (2014, p. 228).

logic (Vargo and Lusch, 2008, 2016). The identification of different types of actors using a systems orientation is important to both academics and practitioners because it has different implications for understanding and applying principles of value co-creation, as is particularly essential in an increasingly interconnected, and thus increasingly dynamic, world (Vargo and Lusch, 2011, p. 182). From an S-D logic perspective '…all actors are fundamentally doing the same things, co-creating value through resource integration and service provision' (Vargo and Lusch, 2011, p. 182). It is proposed that the term actor be used in place marketing and branding to allow academics and practitioners to explore the multiple roles humans can play and how they can act in different ways depending on the role they play. From a practitioner perspective Stubbs and Warnaby (2014) clearly identified different stakeholder groups contributing to place brands and suggested that a standardization of the language within place marketing could allow the interactions and value co-creations occurring within and between actor groups which would allow for the complexity of the place ecosystem and its sub-ecosystems to be represented simply and effectively and thus reduce complication in mental modelling. There is a lot of valuable work being contributed to place marketing and branding that develops the role of a wide range of actors (e.g. Ashworth and Kavaratzis, 2014; Campelo, 2014; Kerr and Oliver, 2014; Therkelsen, 2014). An overarching framework, that is the S-D logic ecosystem and the actors within, may allow this body of literature to develop in new and exciting directions in the future whilst at the same time drawing on and encouraging the diverse contributions to date but allowing greater coherence between these contributions. By recognizing the roles that a diverse range of actors play in the collective and dynamic processes involved in brands and branding, a wide range of opportunities present themselves in which more participatory and inclusive place marketing and branding can be applied and developed.

The nested nature of ecosystems

The ability of 'actors' to vary from individuals to large groups of individuals allows marketing and brands to be constructed to represent service ecosystems using multiple scales that can highlight different sub-ecosystems; all of which are nested within the larger ecosystem, see Figure 5.2.

From a place perspective, and the resultant place marketing and branding, viewing place as being formed by multiple sub-ecosystems, all of which are nested in one whole ecosystem, allows for opportunities to represent different sub-ecosystems at different times in different ways. The acknowledgement of the different actor service ecosystems allows for the potential of marketing and brands to be constructed using different perspectives and increase the inclusion of actors being represented. Different place marketing and branding could select different combinations of sub-ecosystems to represent the brand and could be changed over time. This could, and should, acknowledge the official and unofficial versions of the brand and could represent existing, emerging or desired

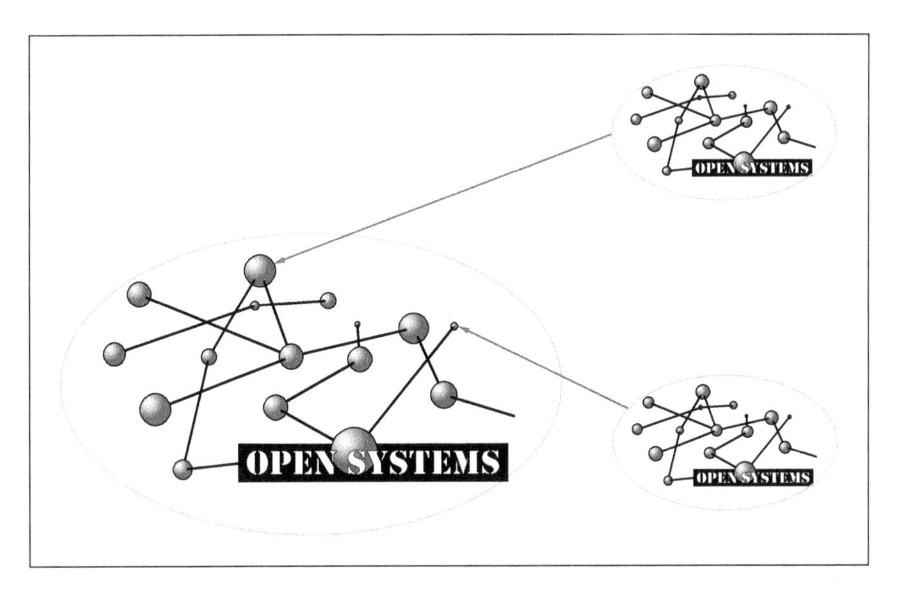

Figure 5.2 Place as a nested service ecosystem.

future representations. The choice of conceptual model(s) on which to develop place marketing and branding communications could either be based on deductive or inductive methods and is the decision of the service ecosystem and its actors to decide which of the conceptualizations and mental models suit their needs.

The acceptance of this systems thinking and the need to understand open systems and their nested nature is clearly seen in the digital technologies literature and its increasing influence on many disciplines such as marketing, sociology and psychology (Barrett *et al.*, 2015). This is also clearly represented in the place branding literature by Govers (2014, p. 73) who pondered whether '... one could pose the question whether not all place branding is to a certain extent virtual' and Hanna and Rowley (2014, p. 90) who identify that '...places of any size have a digital presence, and possibly multiple brand representations'.

The use of an oscillating focus

The identification of place as a nested service ecosystem acknowledges that these service ecosystems are open systems that are made up of multiple different sub-ecosystems. This means that an oscillating focus can be taken when representing the service ecosystem and its sub-ecosystems. Representations of the service ecosystem can be made at a micro, meso and macro level (Chandler and Vargo, 2011) and can include singular or multiple systems, see Figure 5.3.

The potential usefulness of this conceptualization to a place context was identified by Warnaby and Medway (2014, p. 45) who stated that 'given the inherent

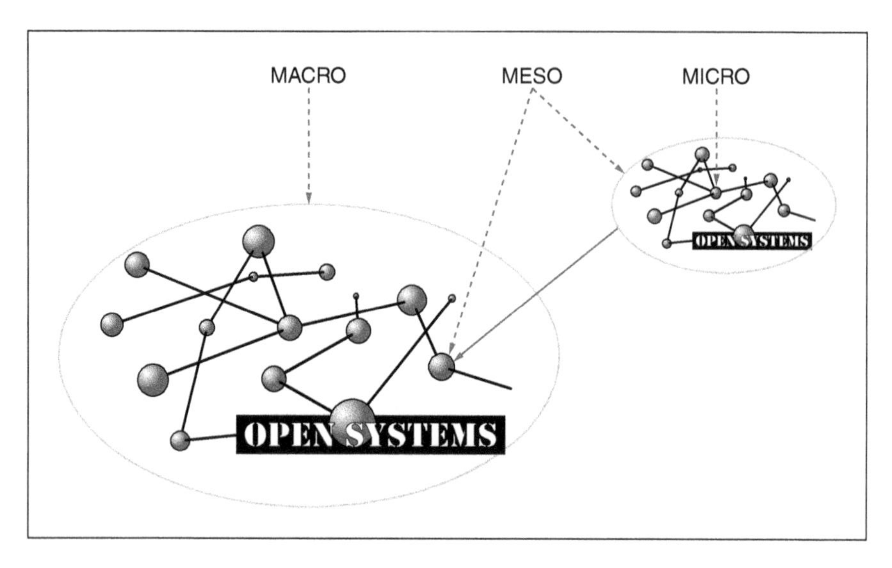

Figure 5.3 Place viewed as a nested service ecosystem.

complexity of organizational mechanisms for the marketing which, *inter alia*, creates the specific characteristics – or context – of place marketing, then these levels may be even more interrelated'. The importance to understand the institutions and the institutional arrangements formed, and the scale on which they have formed (micro, meso and macro) in the service ecosystem is clearly identified in the new foundational premise, FP11, introduced to S-D logic in 2016. Wieland *et al.*, (2015, p. 2) state that

> the existence of more complex and dynamic exchange systems of actors (i.e. service ecosystems) in which value creation practices are guided by institutions (i.e. rules, norms, meanings, symbols and similar aides to collaboration) and more generally institutional arrangements (i.e. interdependent sets of institutions)

are important to understanding the viability of the ecosystem. For place marketing and branding the ability to represent as small a unit as an 'individual-to-individual' sub-ecosystem whilst at the same time being able to scale up to represent populations of organizations provides marketers, official or unofficial, the ability to oscillate the focus between these very different sized sub-ecosystems within a single marketing or branding campaign. This provides the potential for communications to move quickly between sub-ecosystems and highlight the similarities and differences offered whilst at the same time increasing the opportunities to represent a wide range of actors and their sub-ecosystems. It should be noted that the most exciting and unique value co-creation may not always be being produced by the larger sub-systems and that a place brand's uniqueness may be emanating from small but perfectly formed or forming sub-ecosystems that represent *the* something that is unique about that place.

This view is supported by Vargo and Akaka (2012, p. 207) who state that '... to fully conceptualize how value is co-created and service systems are formed and reformed, a deeper understanding of the actions (resource integration practices) and institutions that shape them is needed ...'. It is the institutions that the actors form and the institutional arrangements that are created that should provide the reference base for value assessments (Edvardsson *et al.*, 2014; Lusch and Vargo, 2014). Investigating the actors and the value co-creating practices in a place that has been established, past and present, or is being established or envisaged may provide extremely powerful representations that can be used in place marketing and branding campaigns. They may also be used to challenge current communications that actors do not feel represent their place.

Unique place brand ecosystems and relevant representations

The use of an S-D logic mindset and a service ecosystem view of place may allow actors who are involved in marketing and branding of place, whether officially or unofficially, to explore in detail where value is being co-created in that place using one overall framework, see Figure 5.3. This value may include celebrating past or current successes or communicating future visions of place and will be from multiple perspectives. The acknowledgement of complexity and diversity puts the potential for greater inclusivity at the heart of a service ecosystem view of place as it allows actors to engage in debates around whether this diversity, or lack of it, is good, bad or indifferent from the perspective of multiple actors and allows sub-ecosystems big and small to engage in the debate using one overall framework. Representations of place may need to be communicated in different formats to effectively represent those sub-systems and some sub-systems may not want to be part of the convergence process. This is their human choice.

However, the conceptualization of marketing and branding being *in service* could allow for some very powerful inclusive debates about how place and its uniqueness should be represented. As Vargo and Lusch (2011, p. 184) comment:

> in our view, and apparently that of a growing number of scholars, the concept of service, at least as we define it, can provide the necessary common denominator. It identifies the reason that we have interaction in society – service-for-service exchange – and its corollary, value (i.e., benefit) (co)creation, is the glue (common goals of survivability and well-being) that holds social units (including economic units) and society in general together. That is, society is the result of the necessity of mutual value creation through mutual service provision, as implied by Plato (360 BCE/1930).

By establishing a clear understanding of the service ecosystem and its sub-ecosystems first and then reviewing the available alternative mental models available to represent the place in marketing and branding communications a wide range of actors can make more informed choices about the suitability of the mental models to meet their own needs and objectives. Rather than the models being imposed, because they were deemed to be useful in other campaigns or successful in the past, causing a place's uniqueness to be ineffectively communicated, a place's uniqueness can be represented and celebrated with inclusion potentially being increased.

Conclusions

The development of S-D logic and its rise in popularity within the mainstream marketing literature offers some potentially interesting contributions to the place marketing and branding literature, particularly in relation to representation and inclusion. This chapter proposes an overarching framework of place viewed as a service ecosystem from an S-D logic perspective, that could help consolidate a wide range of place marketing and branding contributions to date and develop the literature in new and innovative directions in the future. Viewing marketing as being *in service* puts humans at the centre of place marketing and branding; and this allows the diversity and uniqueness of various service ecosystems and sub-ecosystems to be represented and celebrated. With diversity and uniqueness at the heart of the S-D logic perspective greater opportunities to include and represent a wider range of actors and their sub-ecosystems in place marketing and branding activities are presented. Conceptual models and frameworks accommodating such inclusion provide great potential to aid academics and practitioners alike to communicate this inclusion and provide some exciting future research opportunities.

References

Ashworth, G. J. and Kavaratzis, M. (2014) 'Rethinking the roles of Culture in place branding', in Kavaratzis, M., Warnaby, G. and Ashworth, G. J. (eds), *Rethinking Place Branding: Comprehensive Brand Development for Cities and Regions*. Switzerland: Springer, pp. 119–134.

Bagozzi, R. P. (1974) 'Marketing as an organized behavioral system of exchange'. *Journal of Marketing*, 38, pp. 77–81.

Barile, S. and Polese, F. (2010) 'Smart service systems and viable service systems: Applying systems theory to service science'. *Service Science*, 2, pp. 21–40.

Barrett, M., Davidson, E., Prabhu, E. J. and Vargo, S. L. (2015) 'Service innovation in the digital age: Key contributions and future direction'. *MIS Quarterly*, pp. 39, 135–154.

Brodie, R. J. (2009) 'From goods to service branding: An integrative perspective'. *Marketing Theory*, 9, pp. 103–107.

Brodie, R. J., Whittome, J. R. M. and Brush, G. J. (2009) 'Investigating the service brand: A customer value perspective'. *Journal of Business Research*, 62, pp. 345–355.

Campelo, A. (2014) 'Rethinking sense of place: Sense of one and sense of many', in Kavaratzis, M., Warnaby, G. and Ashworth, G. J. (eds), *Rethinking Place Branding: Comprehensive Brand Development for Cities and Regions*. Switzerland: Springer, pp. 51–60.

Chandler, J. D. and Vargo, S. L. (2011) 'Contextualization and value-in-context: How context frames exchange'. *Marketing Theory*, 11, pp. 35–49.

Constantin, J. A. and Lusch, R. F. (1994) *Understanding Resource Management: How to Deploy Your People, Products, and Processes for Maximum Productivity*. New York, USA: University of Michigan Press.

Edvardsson, B., Tronvoll, B. and Gruber, T. (2011) 'Expanding understanding of service exchange and value co-creation: A social construction approach'. *Journal of the Academy of Marketing Science*, 39, pp. 327–339.

Edvardsson, B., Kleinaltenkamp, M., Tronvoll, B., McHugh, P. and Windahl, C. (2014) 'Institutional logics matter when coordinating resource integration'. *Marketing Theory*, 14, pp. 291–309.

Evans, G. (2014) 'Rethinking place branding and place making through creative and cultural quarters', in Kavaratzis, M., Warnaby, G. and Ashworth, G. J. (eds), (2014), *Rethinking Place Branding: Comprehensive Brand Development for Cities and Regions*. Switzerland: Springer, pp. 135–158.

Florek, M. (2014) 'Rethinking Brand Equity – Possibilities and Challenges of Application to Places', in Kavaratzis, M., Warnaby, G. and Ashworth, G. J. (eds), *Rethinking Place Branding: Comprehensive Brand Development for Cities and Regions*. Switzerland: Springer, pp. 225–240.

Gregory, A. (2007) 'Involving stakeholders in developing corporate brands: The communication dimension'. *Journal of Marketing Management*, 23, pp. 59–73.

Gobe, M. (2001) *Emotional Branding: The new Paradigm for Connecting Brands to People*. New York, N.Y.: Allworth Press.

Goffman, E. (1959) *The Presentation of Self in Everyday Life*. Garden City, N.Y.: Doubleday and Co., Inc.

Govers, R. (2014) 'Rethinking virtual and online place branding', in Kavaratzis, M., Warnaby, G. and Ashworth, G. J. (eds), *Rethinking Place Branding: Comprehensive Brand Development for Cities and Regions*. Switzerland: Springer, pp. 73–84.

Håkansson, H. and Snehota, I. (1995) 'The IMP perspective', in Sheth, J. and Parvatiyar, A. (eds), *Handbook of Relationship Marketing*. Thousand Oaks, CA: Sage.

Hankinson, G. (2014) 'Rethinking the place branding construct', in Kavaratzis, M. Warnaby, G. and Ashworth, G. J. (eds), *Rethinking Place Branding: Comprehensive Brand Development for Cities and Regions*. Switzerland: Springer, pp. 13–32.

Hanna, S. A. and Rowley, J. (2014) 'Rethinking strategic place branding in the digital age', in Kavaratzis, M., Warnaby, G. and Ashworth, G. J. (eds), *Rethinking Place Branding: Comprehensive Brand Development for Cities and Regions*. Switzerland: Springer, pp. 85–100.

Ind, N. and Bjerke, R. (2007) 'The concept of participatory market orientation: An organisation-wide approach to enhancing brand equity'. *Journal of Brand Management*, 15, pp. 135–145.

Jones, R. (2005) 'Finding sources of brand value: Developing a stakeholder model of brand equity'. *Brand Management*, 13, pp. 10–32.

Kavaratzis, M. and Hatch, M. J. (2013) 'The dynamics of place brands: An identity-based approach to place branding theory', *Marketing Theory*, 13, pp. 69–86.

Kerr, G. and Oliver, J. (2014) 'Rethinking Place Identities', in Kavaratzis, M., Warnaby, G. and Ashworth, G. J. (eds), *Rethinking Place Branding: Comprehensive Brand Development for Cities and Regions*. Switzerland: Springer, pp. 61–72.

Levy, S. J. (1959) 'Symbols for sale'. *Harvard Business Review*, 37, pp. 117–124.

Low, G. S. and Fullerton, R. A. (1994) 'Brands, brand management, and the brand managers system: A critical-historical evaluation'. *Journal of Marketing Research*, 31, pp. 173–190.

Lusch, R. F. and Spohrer, J. S. (2012) 'Evolving service for a complex resilient and sustainable world'. *Journal of Marketing Management*, 28, pp. 1491–1503.

Lusch, R. F. and Vargo, S. L. (2014) *Serivce-Dominant Logic: Premises, Perspectives, Possibilities*. New York, USA: Cambridge University Press.

Madhavaram, S. and Hunt, S. D. (2007) 'The service dominant logic and a hierarchy of operant resources: Developing masterful operant resources and implications for marketing strategy'. *Academy of Marketing Science*, 36, pp. 67–82.

Mars, M. M., Bronstein, J. L. and Lusch, R. F. (2012) 'The value of a metaphor: Organizations and ecosystems'. *Organizational Dynamics*, 41, pp. 271–280.

Marti, I. and Mair, J. (2009) 'Bringing change into the lives of the poor: Entrepreneurship outside traditional boundaries', in Lawrence, T. B., Suddaby, R. and Leca, B., *Institutional Work: Actors and Agency in Institutional Studies of Organizations*. New York, USA: Cambridge University Press.

Medway, D. (2014) 'Rethinking place branding and the "other" senses', in Kavaratzis, M., Warnaby, G. and Ashworth, G. J. (eds), *Rethinking Place Branding: Comprehensive Brand Development for Cities and Regions*. Switzerland: Springer, pp. 191–210.

Merz, M. A., Ye, H. and Vargo, S. L. (2009) 'The evolving brand logic: A service-dominant logic perspective'. *Journal of the Academy of Marketing Science*, 37, pp. 328–344.

Muniz, A. M. Jr, Albert, M. and O'Guinn, T. C. (2001) 'Brand community'. *The Journal of Consumer Research*, 27, pp. 412–432.

Muniz, A. M. Jr, Albert, M. and Schau, H. J. (2005) 'Religiosity in the abandoned Apple Newton brand community'. *The Journal of Consumer Research*, 31, pp. 737–747.

Nilsson, E. and Ballantyne, D. (2014) 'Reexamining the place of servicescape in marketing: A service-dominant logic perspective'. *Journal of Services Marketing*, 28, pp. 374–379.

Ng, I. C. L., Badinelli, R., Polese, F., Di Nauta, P., Löbler, H. and Halliday, S. (2012) 'S-D logic research directions and opportunities: The perspective of systems, complexity, and engineering'. *Marketing Theory*, 12, pp. 213–217.

Norman, D. A. (2011) *Living with Complexity*. Cambridge, MA: MIT Press.

Reeves, R. (1961) *The Reality of Advertising*. New York, USA: McGibbon and Kee.

Scott, W. R. (2014) *Institutions and Organizations: Ideas, Interests, and Identities*. 4th edn. California, USA: Sage.

Spohrer, J. C. and Maglio, P. P. (2010) 'Toward a science of service systems: Value and symbols', in Maglio, P., Kieliszewski, C, and Spohrer, J. (eds), *Handbook of Service Science*. New York, NY: Springer, pp. 157–195.

Stubbs, J. and Warnaby, G. (2014) 'Rethinking branding from the practice perspective: Working with stakeholders', in Kavaratzis, M., Warnaby, G. and Ashworth, G. J. (eds), *Rethinking Place Branding: Comprehensive Brand Development for Cities and Regions*. Switzerland: Springer, pp. 101–118.

Therkelsen, A. (2014) 'Rethinking place brand communication: From product-oriented monologue to consumer-engaging dialogue', in Kavaratzis, M. Warnaby, G. and

Ashworth, G. J. (eds), *Rethinking Place Branding: Comprehensive Brand Development for Cities and Regions*. Switzerland: Springer, pp. 159–174.

Vargo, S. L. and Lusch, R. F. (2004) 'Evolving to a new dominant logic for marketing'. *Journal of Marketing*, 68, pp. 1–17.

Vargo, S. L. and Lusch, R. F. (2008) 'Service-dominant logic: Continuing the evolution'. *Journal of the Academy of Marketing Science*, 36, pp. 1–10.

Vargo, S. L. and Lusch, R. F. (2011) 'It's all B2B … and beyond: Toward a system perspective of the market'. *Industrial Marketing Management*, 40, pp. 181–187.

Vargo, S. L. and Lusch, R. F. (2016) 'Institutions and axioms: An extension and update of service-dominant logic'. *Journal of the Academy of Marketing Science*, 44, pp. 5–23.

Vargo, S. L. and Akaka, M. A. (2012) 'Value co-creation and service systems (re)formation: A service ecosystems view'. *INFORMS Service Science*, 4, pp. 207–217.

Vargo, S. L., Maglio, P. P. and Akaka, A. A. (2008) 'On value and value co-creation: A service systems and service logic perspective'. *European Management Journal*, 26, pp. 145–152.

Warnaby, G. (2009) 'Towards a service-dominant place marketing logic'. *Marketing Theory*, 9, pp. 403–423.

Warnaby, G., Ashworth, G. J. and Kavaratzis, M. (2014) 'Sketching futures for place branding', in Kavaratzis, M., Warnaby, G. and Ashworth, G. J. (eds), *Rethinking Place Branding: Comprehensive Brand Development for Cities and Regions*. Switzerland: Springer, pp. 241–248.

Warnaby, G. and Medway, D. (2014) 'Rethinking the place product from the perspective of the service-dominant logic of marketing', in Kavaratzis, M. Warnaby, G. and Ashworth, G. J. (eds), *Rethinking Place Branding: Comprehensive Brand Development for Cities and Regions*. Switzerland: Springer, pp. 33–50.

Wieland, H., Koskela-Huotari, K. and Vargo, S. L. (2015) 'Extending Actor Participation in Value Creation: An Institutional View'. *Journal of Strategic Marketing*, DOI: 10.1080/0965254X.2015.1095225.

6 Spaces of identity in the city

Embracing the contradictions

Cecillia Cassinger and Åsa Thelander

Introduction

Participatory approaches to place branding have gained increased attention during the past decade (e.g. Zenker and Erfgen, 2014; Kavaratzis and Kalandides, 2015). Residents are considered to be key in giving place brands legitimacy and authenticity by enacting the identity of the place (Freire, 2009; Colomb and Kalandides, 2010). Contemporary place branding strategies often incorporate bottom-up communication and elements of co-creation in their campaign designs. Participatory place branding typically attempts to co-create the city's identity together with the residents by engaging them in meaning making activities through events or social media platforms (cf. Christensen, 2013). Residents' participation is regarded important for the production of meanings of the place in order to strengthen the brand. While several studies have demonstrated the value of residents' voices in the place branding process (Braun *et al.*, 2013; Zenker and Petersen, 2014), relatively little is known about how residents experience participating in place branding campaigns and what the consequences for place identity may be. Previous studies predominately concern more or less organized voices of opposition and research about the role of non-oppositional voices in the course of everyday life for negotiating place brands is currently missing. The incorporation of social media into place branding strategies makes it easier for non-oppositional voices to be heard and responded to. This chapter adopts a geographical approach to place identity and branding and analyses the representational spaces that emerge in residents' narratives. Drawing on Lefebvre's (1991) threefold dialectics of how social space is produced, the chapter explores the question of whether participatory branding strategies could potentially lead to novel and more inclusionary representational spaces in the city. Representational space refers to the passively experienced and symbolic use of space by inhabitants (Lefebvre, 1991). It originates in history and in the imagination of users. Representational space is constructed in relation to representations of space, which is the conceptualized space of planners and strategists (e.g. place brand managers), and spatial practice (or perceived space) defined as the routines and practices of an urban reality. More specifically, we examine how residents experience their engagement in participatory place branding and the implications for the construction and enactment of place identity. As a particular case in point, the study focuses on a social media initiative launched by a small post-industrial city in Sweden (medium size with Swedish standards) with the aim to reimagine the current identity of the city as more inclusive.

The chapter contributes insights regarding the construction process of place identity as resulting from the contradictions that arise in the overlap between the lived spatial experience and the place branding strategy. We argue that these contradictions are useful for understanding the construction of place brand identity as a dynamic process. Embracing contradictions in accounts of place identity could allow for a marginalized and silenced voice to be heard, and contribute to an awareness of what place branding strategies accomplishes in social life. The analysis of residents' narratives reveals the difficulties in opening up place brands to include a manifold of voices. Despite the initiative's good intention to increase engagement and inclusion in community life, participatory place branding became exclusionary due to its selective recruitment of participants and vague aim.

The chapter is organized in four parts that together demonstrate how representational spaces of place identity emerges in narratives of participatory place branding. First, we outline the mutual relation between place brand and place identity and how they unfold in time and space. Second, the spatial construction of place brand identity is examined in resident's narratives identifying three types of representational spaces. The different but sometimes overlapping spaces are labelled counter space, digital space, and absent space. We argue that knowledge about how these spaces are produced can inform the maintenance of place brand identity on the strategic level and how it may include the needs of the local community.

Place identity, branding, space

Geographical approaches to place branding typically find its roots in the disciplines of human and cultural geography (e.g. Colombino, 2009; Kalandides, 2011; Kavaratzis and Hatch, 2013; Kavaratzis and Kalandides, 2015). Human geography and place branding unite in the interest of how places are assigned identity and meaning. The construction of identity and meaning is also the construction of space; meaning is enacted in space. Spatial practices, however, differ from signifying practices in the sense that, in addition to representing the world, spatial practices also perform representations in the world. The particular mimetics of humans is a poetics of space in which meaning is central to orientation in space. Meaning is constructed because of the way that organisms are symbolic in a spatial sense (cf. Bachelard, 1994). Human geographical research concerning the production of space, often involves a critique of structuralism and representation. Instead, the goal is to investigate lived spaces from the viewpoint of everyday life (Lash, 2002). The early studies on place identity were influenced by the phenomenological tradition of humanistic geography (Relph, 1976; Tuan, 2001) and environmental psychology (Proshansky *et al.*, 1983; Knez,

2005). The psychological approach primarily focuses on how people identify with and form attachments to place and the congruency between individual identity and place identity.

The phenomenological approach to place identity focuses on the human experience or sense of place and feelings of belonging to a place. Places are understood as symbols, rooted in the past growing into the future (Tuan, 2001). People form different spatial relations to places that are developed over time and inscribed by meaning. Research in this tradition often conceives of place identity as an experienced 'sense of place' (Kalandides, 2011) and as a multiple construct. In particular, the work of Massey (1994) have been influential for conceptualizing place identity as a multiple construct in a continuous process of becoming within the field of place branding (e.g. Kalandides, 2011; Kavaratzis and Hatch, 2013; Kavaratzis and Kalandides, 2015). Massey (2001) argues that places are constructed in and through trajectories of stories-so-far, which warrants an examination of alternative place identities in the process of place branding. Informed by the works of Massey (1994, 2001), Kavaratzis and Hatch (2013) propose that the place identity and the place brand stand in a dialectical relation to one another and hence need to be studied in relational terms. If the place brand is too far from the place identities held by residents, the place brand is not likely to be accepted either by local or external audiences (Kavaratzis and Hatch, 2013). Geographical approaches are also concerned with urban sociology and the relationship between the city and its inhabitants (e.g. Harvey, 1989; Lefebvre, 1991). Within urban geography, increased attention is paid to the production of space in relation to questions of power and representation. Hayden (1995) shows how parallel place identities involving ethnicity, gender and class, are hidden in official accounts of place. While these spaces are absent in the official narratives, they exist in the histories and memories of the place. Identifying such narratives could lead to a more comprehensive place identity and the formulation of a more inclusive place branding. Along a similar line of thought, in the context of place marketing, Colombino (2009) rethinks Lefebvre's (1991) threefold dialectics by way of mobilizing a different conception of power to demonstrate that ordinary people, like the elite of planners, scientists, strategists and so on, construct conceived spaces (i.e. spaces of representation). She concludes that promotional images of the city do not necessarily – as previous research seems to suggest – misrepresent the place or foster opposition. Thus, there is a need to go beyond the binary of 'false images of real places' in the analysis of place promotion (Colombino, 2009: 294).

This study focuses on the construction of representational spaces in relation to the conceived space constructed by the apparatus of place branding and the lived space conjured by people's spatio-temporal rhythms (cf. Lefebvre, 1991). Place branding not only governs perceptions of the city, but also its spatial organization. The place brand serves as a strategic blueprint to how the city's identity is to be enacted, the boundaries between areas and neighbourhoods and possibilities of crossing them. For example, a single street may mark a mental boundary that cannot be transgressed. At the same time, the city is a lived mythological reality for those who live and work there who bring their memories and stories to play in the manifestation of the place in their lived experiences. Under such circumstances, it seems difficult to separate place identity from the space in and through which it is produced. The proposition that an identity is difficult to separate from the space in which it is produced, problematizes the modelling of identity on specified attributes of the place and the idea of that a place has an inherent identity. Instead, considering identity as space leaves open the question of what identities are modelled on open, and treats identity as meaning that emerges in practice. Participatory place branding campaigns are designed to engage residents in co-constructing meanings of a place, which can then be incorporated into the identity of the place brand. Participatory campaigns often rely on social media enabling residents to produce and circulate images of places to an unprecedented extent.

Participatory place branding: the case of Landskrona

The question of whether participatory branding strategies may lead to novel and more inclusionary representational spaces in the city is investigated by drawing on a qualitative study of residents' experiences of partaking in a participatory place branding initiative. The initiative was launched by the city Landskrona situated at the Swedish southwest coast. Landskrona corresponds with the characteristics of the post-industrial city (Bell, 1973). Since the closing down of the shipbuilding industry, which employed many of its residents, the city has searched for a new identity. The population has declined and unemployment is currently an urgent problem for the city. Social problems are well documented and several violent incidents (e.g. shootings, assaults, and honour crimes) have gained negative attention in the national media. Housing in Landskrona is highly segregated with the city centre being dominated by immigrants and economically disadvantaged populations, whereas the middle-class live in the coastal area in the outskirts of the city. A study carried out by the municipality in 2012, revealed that common associations of Landskrona, among those living and working there, were unemployment, criminality and multiculturalism (Landskrona City, 2013).

In order to improve the reputation, the municipality launched a participatory place branding initiative involving the social media platform, Instagram in December 2012. Landskrona's social media initiative aimed to create and encourage alternative imaginaries of the city that could counter the stereotypical conception of Landskrona. The project team anticipated that the representations in social media would provide an authentic image of the city, which in turn could serve as a positive contrast to the media's portrayal of the city as decaying (Personal communication, 2013). Residents were invited to participate in the construction of a new place identity by way of curating the city's official Instagram account for one week. During the week, the residents could freely upload posts about the city. Participants were recruited on a voluntary basis. The official requirement for partaking in the initiative was that participants should have a personal Instagram account, which could be linked to the official one. For the most part, the participants were politicians, local celebrities and entrepreneurs, municipal employees, and friends of those working at the city's communication department. Hence, the participants belonged to a relatively homogenous group of people identified by the project team to be opinion leaders in Landskrona.

Qualitative interviews were carried out with fifteen participants in the project. At the time for the interviews, the project had been running for eight months and almost thirty citizens had participated. Half of this group were selected for an interview. The criteria used for the selection were time for participation and the character of the posts. We selected interviewees who participated in the very beginning of the project and those who participated in the later stage, since their interpretation of the task were expected to differ. The participants were between 25 and 54 years of age and had high profile occupations. On average, participants published between one and five posts per day during the week.

The photographs that the participants had published on Instagram served as input to the interviews. The procedure can be defined as an interview over photographs implying that the photographs were important to structure the conversation between the interviewer and the informant, but they were not analysed per se (Harper, 2002). The analysis was directed towards the participants' experience of participating in the project. The analysis was conducted in three steps: categorization, comparison, and dimensionalization (Spiggle, 1994). Lefebvre's (1991) spatial imagination guided the analysis and was used for identifying chunks of texts that belonged to the different steps. Based on the codes dimensionalization was made. The different codes were grouped into more conceptual classes and categories were made (Spiggle, 1994). Differences within the codes were identified, compared and used to identify patterns in how the city was ascribed meaning. Three typical ways of spatially constructing place identity were identified and classified as *counter space*, *social media space*, and *absent space*. In the next section, these representational spaces are presented in more detail.

Spaces of identity

Residents' experiences of participating in place branding resulted in different enactments of the city's identity, which manifested representational space in symbolic terms. The organization of space in residents' narratives produces specific social patterns and relationships that affect cultural values, norms, economic opportunities and everyday life. In the following, the three typical spaces of identity in the city are presented. The spaces belong to representational space, that is to say they enact different ideals, history, theories, and imaginaries of the city.

Counter space

One of the primary constructions of place identity evoked by the participants was that of Landskrona as being viewed in a negative way in the media and that people from the outside were not aware of the cultural scene and the natural beauty of the city. Residents conceived of their Instagram posts as counter spaces to the commonly held negative images of Landskrona from where the city could be reclaimed and reimagined. The negative image of the city was used as a reference point against which to construct a new collective identity.

> I mean it takes time to recover the image of the city after a long period of bad associations. Landskrona does not have a local newspaper and there are no established channels to communicate positive things that happen; the national media only reports the bad news. In fact, Landskrona has a very rich cultural scene and I feel that it is unfair that people from the outside view us in such a negative way. I am tired of comments like 'Do you *actually* live in Landskrona?'
>
> (Resident 1)

To counterbalance the negative reputation, the residents wanted to show the positive side of Landskrona. The city's architectural peaks, dramatic nature, and sunny weather are the focus of the photographs uploaded on Instagram. Typical motifs are landmarks and scenic spots, often with sunsets and cloudy skies as backdrops. The residents' production of space here coincides with the space of representation generated by place brand consultants for promotional purposes (cf. Colombino, 2009). The residents were aware of the similarity with promotional images; nevertheless, they reasoned that they added a personal story to these scenic spots, which made them more authentic. Heritage sites and architectural highlights, involving a past temporal orientation, were set against contemporary everyday practices such as shopping and dining, and made relevant in the present.

> Few people are aware of the fine architecture of Landskrona. For me this is an important part of the Landskrona identity – Landskrona's residents should straighten their backs, because we have so much to be proud of … like the architecture. I hope that my image of Landskrona will strengthen the identity of the city.
>
> (Resident 2)

Counter spaces of identity may be further understood in relation to the concept of the tourist gaze and practice (Urry, 2002; see also Jenkins, 2003). Residents explicitly compared their photographs to tourist photography, which was used as a point of reference and ideal. Hence, they relied on the gaze and practice of the tourist to reimagine the city. Tourist gaze may be described as a principle of socially organizing tourist experience and practice (Urry, 2002). It refers to a way of seeing that is in part manufactured by the network of institutions that work to ensure that certain tourist experiences are created, and in part embodied by the practice of the tourist. This way of seeing involves images and myths about what to see and do in a place, what stories to return home with, and what motifs to photograph (Jenkins, 2003). However, in contrast to tourists who are often understood as taking photographs for their private use to remember the journey and to be able to recount it upon returning home, residents published their photographs on the city's Instagram account for a wider anonymous audience. Hence, even though counter space draws on the tourist gaze, it simultaneously follows the logic of social media, which involves a different temporal orientation than tourist practice. While tourist practice is oriented towards experiencing recounting the past, the temporal orientation of social media is perhaps best described as instantaneous. Posts are added to a continuous flow of posts that either confirm or refute one another according to a binary line of reasoning. This means that the complexity of the identity of Landskrona is here condensed to a postcard view of the city that stand in contrast to the negative associations of Landskrona as they are imagined by the residents.

Instantaneous space

Instantaneous space is organized by a discourse of social media, which means that participation was made sense of in relation to the medium of Instagram. 'I can easily upload photographs on my work account during the weekend when I am logged in. I have a smartphone and I enjoy using it. You get such a direct response' (Resident 6). Hence, it is an Instagram view of Landskrona that is presented. This space is governed by ideals concerning instant photography and that the photographic images should not be 'technically perfect' and appear 'spontaneous' (Resident 6, personal conversation). Participating in place branding here converges with residents' everyday use of social media. These spaces of place identity were also produced to counter balance the negative image of Landskrona, but focus on mundane activities and people, rather than on attractions and picturesque images. Spontaneous, natural, relaxed and the real were used to describe what residents wanted to achieve with their posts. Therefore, taking and sharing photos were less planned than in the counter spaces. To be spontaneous and oriented towards the mundane is a way to accomplish authenticity and trustworthiness. Filter was applied in the photographs, but residents often reflected on their use of filters, and even hash-tagged images as 'no filter' to denote more 'real' images of the city.

Common motifs in the posts were smiling people, for instance, friends, role models, entrepreneurs, and local celebrities, captured in the city streets. Posts typically showed residents at work, for instance, in meetings, workshops and seminars, which consequently meant that the content and meaning of the posts were difficult to understand for outsiders.

Instant spaces were also marked by a polarized view on Landskrona and what residents considered worthy and unworthy to show to the imagined audience. People were understood as sources of place identity and key to the representation of the city. The people living and working in the city enact spaces of identity and there are clues in instant spaces to the character of an ideal resident.

> This is Ann who owns the store and her friend. I took a picture of them when I walked past during lunchtime. Ann is a bit of a local profile, runs her own business. She is a very nice, social and engaged entrepreneur in Landskrona. Many people visit her store just for a chat and not primarily for the purpose of buying clothing. I thought it would be nice to include her, since she does a lot of good for the city.
>
> (Resident 3)

Spontaneity and the orientation towards the mundane accomplished authenticity and trustworthiness in the images. The preference for the unprompted and the acceptance of imperfect photographs conveys a glimpse of an unexpected view of the city.

> We are working with creating a new identity for Landskrona ... we use the creative industries and culture as part of the transformation process. The whole city needs to be structurally transformed in order to promote more entrepreneurial businesses and attract entrepreneurs to the city; therefore *creativity* is an important concept in the overriding branding strategy of Landskrona....
>
> (Resident 4)

Residents were careful about promoting themselves at the same time as the city and it was experienced as important to gain gained comments and 'likes' from other Instagram users. In this way, the identities of the city that emerges in these spaces are more closely tied to the self-interest of the residents. Resident 4 works with improving the conditions for local businesses and start-ups in the city. She represents an entrepreneurial discourse that is distinctive for the branding of post-industrial cities. Following on the rise of the entrepreneurial city (Harvey, 1989; Hall and Hubbard, 1996) and the emphasis on the creative class (Florida, 2005), a new type of place brand identity has crystallized, encompassing an ideal resident who is typically defined as an urban professional characterized by being creative, entrepreneurial, and innovative. At the same time residents' preference for the spontaneous and mundane, as well as their acceptance of imperfect photographs, enabled instant glimpses of the city that sometimes contradicted the stereotype image of Landskrona.

Absent space

> My sister and I discussed whether we would include...because there is a Halal meat store, which she suggested that we would enter, have chat, and take some pictures. Perhaps there could be some interesting meat to photograph ... we walked passed it several times, back and forth. But I did not dare to enter. Lots of people were walking in and out from the store, but I was not sure how the staff would react, so I did not go in. Otherwise, it was a good idea, since so many immigrants live here, to portray that in a positive light. But I did not do that.
>
> (Resident 5)

Absent spaces involve themes that are excluded or missing in the official narratives of the city. Immigrant residents living in the city centre were discussed in our interviews, but they were never included or touched upon in the Instagram posts. Hence, they were present in the residents' minds, but not in how they represented the city. While residents could narrate a photo of beautiful eighteenth-century building blocks in the city centre, they would simultaneously add that they would not walk there alone in the evening, because of high rates of criminality in the area. The manager of the place branding project explained that the municipality's communication department had recruited the participants via their personal networks, and that it had not been possible to reach the immigrant population in this way. As previously mentioned, the residents that served as curators for the Instagram account belonged to a homogenous group residing in the outskirts of the city. In the spaces of place identity, therefore, the immigrant population represent the other – the exotic and dangerous. When residents portrayed non-conventional aspects and the dark sides of the city, their posts received less likes and comments, which may explain why most of the posts were fairly homogenous and portrayed 'safe' things like people, buildings, and sceneries.

> My purpose was to be a little subversive and present my picture of Landskrona. I'm quite allergic to doing the same thing as everyone else. But it was not so popular. People thought I was annoying and I did not meet the expectations of the project. My photographs did not generate an awful lot of likes; they were mostly met by silence.
>
> (Resident 8)

Resident 8 sought to give a critical view of the city through a sequence of cartoon episodes. The episodes highlighted economically deprived groups of people, cynicism, lack of faith in politicians, and his own experiences of being bullied every day when walking home from school. The posts received very few likes and comments; consequently Resident 8 experienced that he had imagined the city in the wrong manner.

Absent spaces are about the repressed and that which is not considered worthy to show to others in place identity. These spaces underscore Hayden's (1995, 61) call to identify 'new community-based ways of working with the physical traces of the past beyond its preservation at museums or adaptive use as real estate'. Absent spaces resemble Lefebvre's (1991) differential spaces that interrupt the abstract space and suggest an alternative order. Absent spaces could therefore be useful to include in the place identity to increase the complexity of the place brand and to build community. Absent spaces harbour contradictions, which could generate alternative spaces within it that actually, could produce new images of the city. While the counter spaces are oriented towards a postcard view and the elimination of difference, the absent spaces include many different strands of discourses, which could lead to novel meanings of the city.

Conclusions

This chapter examined the process whereby place identity was spatially constructed in participatory place branding. The aim of engaging residents in imaging the city was to make the place brand more socially inclusive. Informed by a geographical approach to place branding, three typical ways of spatially constructing place identity was identified. These practices were argued to produce three types of representational spaces that were organized by different imaginaries that we connected to the tourist gaze, the Instagram platform, and otherness. The spaces were similar in that they represented spaces that harboured several contradictions that could potentially produce novel meanings of the city. These contradictions were related to producing images that would generate likes on social media, while simultaneously representing the nuances of the city in a novel manner. The images that received most likes and comments were those that portrayed close-ups of people or landmarks in sunsets. Thus, it is the positive, well known and impersonal image of the city that can be expected to generate likes. Another contradiction involved the fostering of a place identity on the basis of contesting the negative images of the city related to unemployment, criminality, and segregation. Instead of addressing these problems, residents produced counter and instantaneous spaces from where the city was cast in a favourable light, for example, by referring to its scenic views, and many entrepreneurs. Due to the selective recruitment of residents and vague purpose, in its effect, the inclusiveness of the project became excluding.

In the beginning of the chapter we posed the question of whether participatory place branding could potentially constitute a more sustainable marketing of cities that could lead to social inclusion. We may now be approaching an answer. There may be a certain naiveté in regard to what participatory place branding can accomplish in terms of social inclusion. Territorial histories are tied to relations of power that shapes and constrain what can be told about a place. These relations are difficult to change, in particular through social media practices, which merely circulate content that add to an already existing flow of messages (Dean, 2005). Social media therefore may be understood as a self-referential system defined by circulation rather than innovation. In addition, as indicated by the instantaneous spaces, social media logic is characterized by a binary logic of 'either or' making the conversation overly simplistic. In the case of Landskrona, there seems to be a need to articulate alternative histories and stories, based on other relations of power that must first be put to place, before becoming subjected to branding. To be able to identify such stories, inviting folklore researchers, feminist, social and architectural historians into the project of reimagining the city may be useful (cf. Hayden. 1995). In addition, contradictions within spaces could be useful in order to accomplish a more inclusive place brand identity. Contradictions highlight asymmetries in power relations between groups and interests in the city and are difficult to resolve, thus they create ambiguous spaces in which the place identity is continuously reworked and negotiated.

Preserving these contradictions in place branding on a strategic level could increase the awareness of marginalized groups and interests and include under-represented and unheard voices in the identity of the city.

References

Bachelard, G. (1994, orig. 1958) *The Poetics of Space*. Boston: Beacon Press.

Bell, D. (1973) *The Coming of Post-industrial Society*. New York: Basic Books.

Braun, E., Kavaratzis, M. and Zenker, S. (2013) 'My city – my brand: the different roles of residents in place branding'. *Journal of Place Management and Development*, 6(1), pp. 18–28.

Christensen, C. (2013) '@ Sweden: Curating a nation on Twitter'. *Popular Communication*, 11(1), pp. 30–46.

Colomb, C. and Kalandides, A. (2010) 'The "Be Berlin" campaign: Old wine in new bottles or innovative form of participatory place branding?' In Ashworth, G. J. and Kavaratzis, M. (eds.) *Towards Effective Place Brand Management: Branding European Cities and Regions*. Cheltenham: Edward Elgar, pp. 173–190.

Colombino, A-L. (2009) 'Multiculturalism and time in Trieste: place-marketing images and residents' perceptions of a multicultural city'. *Social and Cultural Geography*, 10(3), pp. 279–297.

Dean, J. (2005) 'Communicative capitalism: circulation and the foreclosure of politics'. *Cultural Politics*, 1(1), pp. 51–74.

Florida, R. (2005) *Cities and the Creative Class*. New York: Routledge.

Freire, J. R. (2009) '"Local People" A critical dimension for place brands'. *Journal of Brand Management*, 16(7), pp. 420–438.

Hall, T. and Hubbard, P. (1996) 'The entrepreneurial city: new urban politics, new urban geographies?'. *Progress in Human Geography*, 20(2), pp. 153–174.

Harvey, D. (1989) 'From managerialism to entrepreneurialism: the transformation in urban governance in late capitalism'. *Geografiska Annaler. Series B. Human Geography*, pp. 3–17.

Harper, D. (2002) 'Talking about pictures: A case for photo elicitation'. *Visual Studies*, 17(1), pp. 13–26.

Hayden, D. (1995) *The Power of Place: Urban Landscapes as Public History*. Cambridge: The MIT Press.

Jenkins, O. (2003) 'Photography and travel brochures: The circle of representation'. *Tourism Geographies*, 5(3), pp. 305–328.

Kalandides, A. (2011) 'The problem with spatial identity: revisiting the "sense of place"'. *Journal of Place Management and Development*, 4(1), pp. 28–39.

Kavaratzis, M. and Hatch, M. J. (2013) 'The dynamics of place brands an identity-based approach to place branding theory'. *Marketing Theory*, 13(1), pp. 69–86.

Kavaratzis, M. and Kalandides, A. (2015) 'Rethinking the place brand: the interactive formation of place brands and the role of participatory place branding'. *Environment and Planning A*, 47, pp. 1368–1382.

Knez, I. (2005) 'Attachment and identity as related to a place and its perceived climate'. *Journal of Environmental Psychology*, 25, pp. 207–218.

Landskrona City (2013) 'Landskrona is home: Branding strategy for Landskrona'. Available at: www.landskrona.se/documents/landskrona/documents/media/bilaga%20till%20pressmeddelande/bilagor2013/varumarkesstrategi.pdf (Accessed: 8 April 2016).

Lash, S. (2002) *Critique of Information*. London: SAGE Publications.
Lefebvre, H. (1991, orig. 1974) *The Production of Space*. Cambridge, MA: Blackwell.
Massey, D. (2001) *For Space*. London: Sage.
Massey, D. (1994) 'A global sense of place', in Massey, D. (ed.) *Space, Place and Gender*. Cambridge: Polity Press, pp. 146–156.
Proshansky, H. M., Fabian, A. K., and Kaminoff, R. (1983) 'Place-identity: physical world socialization of the self'. *Journal of Environmental Psychology*, 3(1), pp. 57–83.
Relph, E. (1976) *Place and Placelessness*. London: Pion.
Spiggle, S. (1994) 'Analysis and interpretation of qualitative data in consumer research'. *The Journal of Consumer Research*, 21(3), pp. 491–503.
Tuan, Y.-F. (2001) *Space and Place: The Perspective of Experience*. Minneapolis: University of Minnesota Press.
Urry, J. (2002) *The Tourist Gaze*. London: Sage.
Zenker, S., and Erfgen, C. (2014) 'Let them do the work: a participatory place branding approach'. *Journal of Place Management and Development*, 7(3), pp. 225–234.
Zenker, S., and Petersen, S. (2014) 'An integrative theoretical model for improving resident-city identification'. *Environment and Planning A*, 46(3), pp. 715–729.

7 Revitalizing the damaged brand

Place (re)branding in post-Katrina New Orleans

Kevin Fox Gotham and Cate Irvin

Introduction

This chapter investigates several rebranding campaigns launched during the last decade in New Orleans to counter perceptions of urban disaster and misfortune and propagate images of recovery, rebuilding, and resilience. Since 2005, New Orleans has been subject to several unrelenting and overlapping crises – Hurricane Katrina (2005), Hurricane Gustav (2008), the Great Recession (2007–2009), the Deepwater Horizon oil catastrophe (2010), and Hurricane Isaac (2012) – that have projected images of urban chaos, instability, and disaster. The massive displacement of approximately half a million people by Hurricane Katrina put on global display New Orleans's deep and longstanding class and racial disparities and urban problems (Jackson, 2011). The disaster brought international media attention to vulnerable and marginalized communities, such as in the Tremé and the Lower Ninth Ward, and presaged a new insecurity about the future of coastal cities in the context of rising sea levels and increased frequency and destructiveness of storms (Gotham and Lewis, 2015). The unfolding of the Great Recession two years later depressed recovery efforts in New Orleans by slowing physical reconstruction and stifling the delivery of aid to needy communities. In April 2010, the largest marine oil spill in history occurred in the Gulf of Mexico, when the Deepwater Horizon oil rig exploded and approximately 4.9 billion barrels of oil poured into the Gulf of Mexico over the three months that followed. Today, residents and researchers debate the negative impacts and socio-spatial consequences of these traumatic events and public discussions rage over the long-term sustainability of the city and region (Gotham, 2016a, 2016b; Gotham and Campanella, 2013).

We have three goals in this chapter. First, we identify the key actors and organized interests underlying post-disaster rebranding efforts. Second, we describe the major reimaging strategies linked to processes of inclusion and marginalization. Third, we address the challenges of participatory place branding in a post-disaster context. We draw on many years of data collection including ethnographic field observations, dozens of interviews with neighbourhood residents and tourism leaders, and analysis of government reports and planning documents. Tourism destinations are particularly vulnerable to the negative impacts of disasters and economic downturns. Disasters can have serious and long lasting reputational impacts. Disasters turn destinations into locations. Public perception strongly influences people's decisions whether to visit and spend time in a particular community. The challenge for tourism organizations and institutions is to thwart and nullify negative images and perceptions of disaster and destruction through concerted and strategic rebranding campaigns aimed at changing people's opinions, views, and stereotypes of a city (Gotham, 2007a).

We examine place branding as a set of conflictual practices that express and display highly contradictory urban representations linked to struggles over resident participation in decision-making. We use empirical examples from New Orleans to highlight the role of place branding as a post-disaster recovery tool and theorize place branding as a process of both spatial differentiation and spatial dedifferentiation. On the one hand, branding strategies attempt to create new venues for tourist consumption via the production and differentiation of space into spaces of consumption and spectacle. Insofar as possible, advertisers and tourism organizations attempt to represent and portray otherwise mundane neighbourhoods as extraordinary spaces to visit. On the other hand, branding is a process of dedifferentiation in which various place making and reimaging strategies seek to obliterate distinctions between tourist and non-tourist spaces and experiences. In this process, branding campaigns and organizers aim to socialize and coach residents to view their hometown as a tourist attraction and thereby adopt the knowledge and visual orientation characteristic of tourists. Here we focus our analytical attention on how branding activities express local struggles over inclusion, exclusion, and marginalization. New Orleans stands as a valuable laboratory for the study of place branding practices under the conditions of post-disaster recovery and rebuilding, providing a lens to understand the connections among branding and disasters while illustrating the paradoxical impacts of branding for local institutions and residents. By elucidating the localized dynamics of branding in a context of multiple and intersecting crises, our chapter offers a novel processual account of the drivers and impacts of branding processes in a disaster-impacted city.

The Forever New Orleans rebranding campaign

One of the major problems facing political and economic elites in disaster-torn cities is the circulation of images of damage, destruction, pain and suffering. The problem with these negative images is that they signify a damaged brand that invests space with stigma. For tourism professionals and city leaders, Hurricane Katrina caused major damage to the city's long cultivated image – or brand – as a tourist destination. 'We need to restore the brand that is New Orleans', pronounced Alfred Groos, general manager of the Royal Sonesta Hotel, 'that is the biggest challenge that we all have' ('A year after', 2006, para. 8). According to Stephen Perry, President and CEO of the New Orleans Metropolitan Convention and Visitors Bureau (NOMCVB), '[w]e need to dissolve myths that continue to persist about the city's state of recovery and deliver credible messages that illustrate the vibrancy of the New Orleans experience today' (New Orleans Metropolitan Convention and Visitors Bureau (NOMCVB), 2007, para. 15). As one tourism official told the first author:

> brand damage was significant. The world had been inundated with images, television specials, news stories, etc ... promoting the devastation of the city. So our branding campaigns had to be very carefully crafted in order to be accepted as valid.
>
> (Interview with D.S., 2012)

Such concerns were paramount on January 25, 2007 when the NOMCVB announced the launch of a new 'aggressive rebranding campaign to focus on the authentic and dynamic culture of New Orleans' (NOMCVB, 2007, para. 1). Titled *Forever New Orleans*, the international rebranding campaign marked a major shift in New Orleans hospitality marketing toward the development of new cross-scale networks and synergistic relationships linking local and state tourism organizations with global marketing and consulting firms. The various components of this rebranding network included the branding firm, Trumpet, to 'redefine the new Orleans brand vs. the images of despair and failure in the mainstream media following Katrina' (Trumpet, 2012); global public relations firm Weber Shandwick to promote the city as place of rich history and culture; GlobalCastmedia, Inc. to develop a series of advertisements for outdoor and print media; Peter A. Mayer Advertising and CBS Outdoor to create a 12-month advertising campaign in eighteen domestic markets; Pet Bird Entertainment, LLC to produce a 30-minute travel television show, 'A Whole New Orleans'; and the State of Louisiana Office of the Lieutenant Governor and the Louisiana Department of Culture, Recreation and Tourism (CRT) (NOMCVB, 2008, p. 11).

In addition to forging new networked interactions with global advertising firms and state tourism organizations, a novel feature of this rebranding effort was the NOMCVB's utilization of the Cision Corporation to provide media monitoring software to 'analyse key message delivery, frequency and tone of media coverage about the New Orleans brand' (NOMCVB, 2008, p. 20). The NOMCVB, the New Orleans Tourism Marketing Corporation (NOTMC), and Harrah's New Orleans Hotel and Casino established a new alliance whereby each organization adopted each other's advertisements, merged their visitor guidebooks, and settled on *Forever New Orleans* as a shared slogan for their integrated rebranding campaigns.

We can view *Forever New Orleans* as part of a larger attempt by city's tourism organizations to include new cultural imagery in the repertoire of place marketing as an expedient to revitalizing the city. Central to this place promotion effort was the attempt to foster a more inclusive view of the city that would incorporate new voices, new stakeholders, and new collective identities as expressions of New Orleans culture. In the news release announcing the launch of the rebranding campaign, the NOMCVB proclaimed that *Forever New Orleans* marks 'a major shift in New Orleans hospitality marketing' toward promoting 'more aspects of New Orleans culture, including the visual arts' and thereby 'develops a deeper, richer understanding of our culture as unique and authentic, celebrating the very life of New Orleans' (NOMCVB, 2007, para. 1). Emphasizing their 'aggressive' and 'strategic' rebranding effort, NOMCVB officials designed the *Forever New Orleans* campaign 'to celebrate [the city's] authentic culture, lure domestic and international visitors back, preserve the city's leading industry (hospitality) and overcome misperceptions about New Orleans among consumers' (NOMCVB, 2007, para. 1). A major goal of the NOMCVB rebranding campaign was to promote a 'positive' vision of urban 'recovery'. Emphasizing the need to preserve 'the city's largest industry', the CVB recognizes the challenge of 'enticing visitors back despite daily international headlines about slow hurricane recovery, rising crime rates, political scandal and questions about future flood protection', according to the NOMCVB (NOMCVB, 2008, p. 12).

Rebranding campaigns launched in the immediate years after Hurricane Katrina sought to counter negative images of storm and flood damage and to emphasize positive themes of resilience, vibrancy, and phoenix-like recovery (Gotham, 2007b; Gotham and Greenberg, 2014). Tourism officials did not select these themes spontaneously or at random. Rather, rebranding campaigns attempted to connect these themes with inclusive forms of place promotion that could resonate with new stakeholders and more thoroughly represent the city's uniqueness. The downturn in the national economy in 2008 and the BP oil spill in April 2010 added a sense of urgency to their efforts. 'I think what we're seeing now is the national economy has impacted our industry and it has created a sense of nervousness', remarked Doug Thornton, senior vice president of SMG, the company that operates the Superdome and the New Orleans arena for the state of Louisiana, in April 2009 (White, 2009, para. 9). '[A]ll the brand damage that we are suffering in Louisiana this summer with the [BP] spill is devastating' remarked NOMCVB president, Stephen Perry in June 2010. 'It [is] urgent for us to move forward' (White, 2010, para. 10). By August 2010, marketing campaigns sought to move away from brand mitigation campaigns that reacted to and addressed crises like Hurricane Katrina and the BP oil spill to proactive rebranding campaigns stressing that the 'visitor experience today is better than it was prior to Katrina' (NOMCVB, 2010, p. 1). As one advertisement stated,

> Despite post-Katrina infrastructure and reputation damage, a national recession, restrictions in corporate business travel, and the BP oil spill, New Orleans is once again welcoming millions of visitors per year, hosting prominent corporate and association meetings, and earning awards as one of the hottest leisure destinations in America.
>
> (NOMCVB, 2010, p. 1)

A fundamental theme in post-Katrina rebranding efforts was the cultivation of salvation motifs and messianic rhetoric that positioned the tourism sector as a major leader in the recovery and rebuilding of the city (Gotham and Greenberg, 2014). 'The future of New Orleans has never been brighter thanks to the renaissance of the tourism industry', according to one promotional brochure (NOMCVB, 2010, p. 4). In an August 2010 list of 'story ideas' for media and publicity, CVB officials note that one idea, 'Overcoming Crisis' implores officials to alert stakeholders and other interests on 'how the CVB convinced visitors that it was safe to visit post-Katrina New Orleans and managed the destination's reputation during the oil spill in a perception and image-driven tourism business'. (NOMCVB, 2010, p. 2). A related story idea on 'The Business of Tourism' suggests that spokespeople get word out that 'tourism drives the New Orleans economy and has led the recovery of the city since Katrina' (NOMCVB, 2010, p. 3). In short, tourism officials and their staff carefully plotted and disseminated themes of salvation and messianic recovery to not only mollify negative imagery associated with the Katrina disaster and the BP oil spill but, more importantly, position and legitimize themselves as design experts and master planners of a putative post-disaster urban renaissance.

Aestheticizing New Orleans: live the brand, brand the space

In our conversations with tourism professionals in New Orleans, the perspective of 'internalizing the brand' is mentioned as major ingredient in the successful rebranding of the city as a major entertainment destination. This idea is based on the assumption that rebuilding New Orleans is incumbent upon local people coming to accept the branded image as their own and learning to 'live' the brand. Internalizing the brand follows the World Tourism Organization's (WTO) (2006) guidelines that local leaders implement strategies to 'communicate and advocate the brand internally', develop 'practical ways of instilling the brand values within the community', and 'capacitate and enable leadership figures to live the brand and infuse the population ... For the brand to be authentic and deliver on its promise', according to the WTO, 'local community and stakeholders should believe in it and live it' (WTO, 2006, slide 16). Post-disaster rebranding is not just a question of attracting tourists or engineering tourism growth. In addition to imagining an urban future that conforms to a semiotic script, urban rebranding seeks to socialize residents to view the city as a brand. In doing so, place marketers and tourism organizations define and promote the urban brand as a mode of collective identity that connects individuals with a sense of socio-cultural inclusion and 'belonging', whether to a city or neighbourhood.

Broadly, in New Orleans, the rebranding process reflects organized attempts to insinuate tourism practices and discourses into the repertoire of urban culture and inspire residents to embrace the visual orientation and consumption practices of tourists. In May 2007 and again in July 2011, NOMCVB officials launched the 'Be a Tourist in your Own Hometown' campaign 'to encourage New Orleanians to enjoy all of the hospitality offerings that make our city one of the most popular travel destinations in the world', according to the 2011 press release (NOMCVB, 2011, para. 1). Emphasizing themes of uniqueness and authenticity, the campaign invites locals to visit 'art galleries, museums, shops, boutiques, hotels, restaurants, special events and attractions ... that rely on tourism for their survival' (NOMCVB, 2011, para. 1). The NOMCVB partners with WWL-TV and Channel 4 television stations to develop commercials featuring celebrities such as Lenny Kravitz, Irma Thomas, Emeril Lagasse, Drew Brees, among others, who promote specials at restaurants, hotels, shops and attractions. Celebrities are key to post-crisis rebranding efforts because they deliver the 'wow factor' to enchant everyday life and transform otherwise mundane activities into extraordinary and spectacular experiences. As vehicles of spectacle, celebrities provide an entertainment-based incentive to spend money and thereby invite and encourage 'residents' to view their community as consumable entertainment.

While tourism-advertising campaigns directed at residents span many decades, what is new in post-Katrina New Orleans is the intensity and sophistication of the marketing strategies to encourage residents to be tourists in their own hometown. A key feature of these campaigns is the methodical and strategic effort to blur distinctions between residents and tourists using the mechanisms of entertainment, spectacle, and commodified media culture. Unlike tourists who are in a place for a short time for consumption-related purposes, residents are locked into local life and all of its long-time conflicts, struggles, triumphs, and tragedies. A sense of temporariness and looseness of ties with the place – social, physical, and geographic – are built into tourist experiences and are the antitheses of the home experiences of residents. 'Be a tourist in your own hometown' rebranding campaigns attempt to disassociate residents from the mundane and ordinary aspects of home life and encourage them to view their hometown as a cocktail of spectacular sites for consuming pleasurable sensations. In this respect, the marketing of 'be a tourist in your own hometown' becomes an overt and intentional avenue of capitalist accumulation with tie-ins with the buying and selling of a variety of products, activities, and experiences.

Branding activities that coach urban residents to adopt the visual orientation and consumer practices of tourists are both inclusive and exclusive. On the one hand, branding activities seek to include and incorporate a variety of disparate voices, urban stakeholders, and otherwise dissimilar cultural representations in the repertoire of urban place promotion in order to contribute to the production and consumption of space. On the other hand, branding activities tend to marginalize and exclude those individuals and groups that lack the financial means to particulate as consumers in the constitution of urban life and community. Urban branding goes hand-in-glove with urban consumption. That is, branding activities offer an invitation to people to spend money on goods and services as an expression of social status and urban identity. The various actors and organized interests in these rebranding campaigns give people a choice of goods and services to consume. Yet what they seek to limit, if not eliminate, are non-consumption activities and the participation of non-consumers in the constitution of community.

Not everyone accepts the invitation to participate as a consumer, however, and many urban residents actively oppose and resist attempts by place marketers to connect membership in an urban community with consumerism. An important example here is the development of new themed festivals – cuisine, music, art, multicultural, film and literary, theatre, and LGBT, among others – that are organized by grassroots organizations and located in particular neighbourhoods. The St. Patrick's Day festival in the Irish Channel, the Greta Festival, Old Algiers Riverfest, and Bayou St. John Bayou Boogaloo in Mid-City, among many others, seek to attract people to delimited areas of the city to participate in the affirmation of neighbourhood identity, another example of living the brand. For place marketers and rebranding firms, neighbourhood festivals generate awareness of a place's good qualities and result in a positive place brand that can generate increased sales of merchandize, raise home values, and contribute to a shorter home sales cycle because consumers are more informed, thus creating greater profits for the stakeholders. For residents, festivals bring people together, integrate them in the life of the community, and thereby constitute a form of collective participation in reproducing neighbourhood culture. Moreover, festivals are akin to ceremonies and collective rituals that express and affirm neighbourhood identity and solidarity. At the same time, the grassroots and indigenous character of festivals creates opportunities for branding and commodification. That is, urban festivals raise the prestige of neighbourhoods and give real estate agents a new selling tool to convince people that they are buying a 'lifestyle' as well as a neighbourhood.

'Follow Your NOLA' and the selling of New Orleans' neighbourhoods

Expanding on the branding campaigns that emerged to combat the negative imagery of New Orleans after Hurricane Katrina, by 2013 the branding campaigns were increasingly emphasizing selling the lifestyle of the various neighbourhoods of New Orleans directly to the visitor and consumer. The *Follow Your NOLA* campaign, launched in May of 2013, targets visitors of a new demographic of travellers aged 35 to 65 who are interested in expanding their experiences of the city, moving beyond the French Quarter, and instead taking in the city's 'music, food, art, shopping, architecture and history, at their own pace and by following their own path' (Thompson, 2013, para. 3). This campaign intends to sell the less explored corners of New Orleans to the omnivorous consumer, moving beyond the stereotypical French Quarter experience. Coupled with the themed festivals, this campaign targets consumers who seek unique, authentic, and exotic experiences. Even the name, *Follow Your NOLA*, hints at an insider's view of New Orleans, using the abbreviation NOLA – New Orleans, Louisiana.

This branding campaign primarily uses television and social media to target 'the more sophisticated traveller in all age groups' (Thomson, 2013, para. 1). The website provides the visitor with specifics on all of the areas of New Orleans, broadly grouped into nine regions of the city, and encourages visitors to tailor their trips to their interests. Per Mark Romig, the president and CEO of the New Orleans Tourism Marketing Corporation states:

> We're transforming the way we market the city…inviting our visitors to explore and discover the entire city, in addition to our iconic and wonderful French Quarter. We want to raise awareness of every corner of New Orleans to the visitor, to the culture-minded consumer, and we refer to these tourists, our visitors, as the experiential discoverer.
>
> (Thomson, 2013, para. 4)

The experiential discoverer is the type of person who wants to see more than the typical tourist attractions, instead desiring to get off the beaten path and explore the authentic experiences of the city; 'They want an anchor point that lets them follow a trail of breadcrumbs in whichever direction interests them most' (Dyakovskaya, 2015, para. 7).

While the new campaign still incorporates some of the New Orleans stereotypical experiences – second-line parades, eating Cajun and Creole cuisine, jazz music (Dyakovskaya, 2015, para. 6) – it also introduces the visitor to other authentic and more unusual New Orleans experiences, such as bar hopping in the Bywater neighbourhood or exploring the Vietnamese vendors in New Orleans East. Follow Your NOLA was created by the New York advertising firm Dentsu America and 360i, and includes television and digital ads that centre on the fleur-de-lis as a compass for navigating the city's cultural offerings, in order to guide tourists through a journey of discovering New Orleans (Thompson, 2013, para. 5). Unlike previous campaigns, *Follow Your NOLA* campaign advertises all of New Orleans the visitor to consume, demonstrating that New Orleans is safe and recovered from the multiple disasters that catapulted it into national attention.

The website features three curated itineraries that each correspond to three video advertisements created to be played on both television and social media. These advertisements demonstrate three potential visitor experiences: Nightlife New Orleans, The Highlife NOLA, and Family Fun, New Orleans Style. The first video shows the viewer a night out in New Orleans featuring drinking at dive bars in the Marigny and Bywater, listening to music in a traditional jazz club, and dancing in the street of the French Quarter, while the second video highlights the high-brow experiences available in New Orleans, including fine dining, ballet and modern dance performances and craft cocktails. Finally, the third video displays New Orleans' family friendly side, with the video featuring a young family riding the streetcar, visiting the aquarium, and dancing in the street with the Mardi Gras Indians. Each video uses the exact same narration but shows the variety of experiences New Orleans has to offer, selling the viewers on the friendly locals the fun public street culture, and the arts, food, and music options. These advertisements aim to showcase the city as a unique, one-of-a-kind authentic experience.

The NOTMC also uses social influencers, including BuzzFeed, and bloggers, to create their own ideal New Orleans trips and share them on Instagram,

YouTube as well as their own blogs. Furthermore, as with previous branding campaigns, *Follow Your NOLA*, features celebrities to increase the 'wow factor', with travel itineraries created by Anthony Bourdain, Emeril Lagasse and John Besh. Furthermore, using the interactive website and embedded online maps, visitors can craft their own itineraries based around their specific interests throughout New Orleans.

The interactive map divides New Orleans into ten areas to explore, each area encompassing a subset of smaller neighbourhoods: Uptown, Lakeview, Esplanade Ridge, Tremé, Mid-City, CBD/Downtown, French Quarter, Gentilly, Marigny, and Algiers. This campaign directly advertises the particularities of the New Orleans' neighbourhoods to the visitor, emphasizing and selling the traditional aspects of African American culture, while glossing over the on-going tensions in the neighbourhoods. The descriptions of these neighbourhoods offer a conflict-free view of New Orleans that erases the deep and consequential inequalities that characterize neighbourhoods. Instead, these descriptions highlight the stereotypical aspects of the public culture that appeal to visitors of the city, yet still being sure to appeal to the omnivorous consumer seeking authentic experiences. For example, the description of Gentilly and New Orleans East highlights this out-of-the-way authentic New Orleans experience:

> New Orleans East is the New Orleans few know, but many should… Sample Vietnamese restaurants and food markets or visit the House of Dance and Feathers, a Seventh Ward Museum celebrating the Mardi Gras Indians and social aid and pleasure clubs, both centuries-old African-American traditions. Both history and home, New Orleans East is a place to explore.
>
> (Follow Your NOLA, 2015)

Capitalizing on the consumer desire for unique and authentic experiences, and using the local African American and Vietnamese cultures, this campaign targets these areas of the city to the urban pioneer seeking an authentic and exotic experience. Here visitors can '… [d]iscover the Lower Ninth Ward, where new architecture and a new hope rise from Katrina', (Follow Your Nola, 2015) all the while obfuscating the processes of exclusionary displacement and rapid gentrification that have spread throughout the city since Katrina. The emphasis of the language employed by this campaign constructs the visitor not as a tourist, but rather an explorer, a discoverer of new worlds and experiences in New Orleans, to which not everyone is privy. This is the visitors' NOLA, simply awaiting their discovery, breaking substantially from the *Be a Tourist in Your Own Hometown* campaign.

Follow Your NOLA demonstrates how this convergence and co-branding between corporations, celebrities, and neighbourhoods can go even further than the neighbourhood festivals, in this case selling each individual area of the city to the traveller to explore. Furthermore, the launch of the *Follow Your NOLA* video and social media campaign occurred at a time when short-term rental options became available en masse in New Orleans, changing how tourists visit cities by allowing visitors to rent rooms in owner-occupied houses as well as entire homes throughout various neighbourhoods of the city. While short-term home rentals were technically illegal in New Orleans, they were allowed to flourish without enforcement (Adelson, 2016, para. 9), and in recent years, as many as 5,000 short-term rentals have proliferated across the city, bringing in an estimated $316 million in revenue from Airbnb alone (Litten, 2016b, para. 2). These rentals provide visitors with numerous alternatives to the traditional hotel experience and are primarily located outside of the French Quarter, where the laws are more strictly enforced.

The addition of short-term rentals with the emphasis on experiencing the 'real' New Orleans has helped to push tourism into many regions of the city, though the distribution of rentals has not been even throughout the city, with many rentals concentrated in the Marigny, Bywater, St. Roch, and Mid-City neighbourhoods of the city. These neighbourhoods offer tourists close proximity to the French Quarter and downtown areas while also allowing them the opportunity to experience different types of residential neighbourhoods of New Orleans. While Airbnb and other short-term rental organizations were not directly tied to the NOMCVB's tourism campaigns, they did replicate similar language to the *Follow Your NOLA* discourse; for example, one of Airbnb's slogans, 'Live there. Book unique homes and experience a city like a local' (Airbnb, 2016), emphasizes that no longer are you only a tourist, you can experience the city as a local now, staying in their homes, exploring their neighbourhoods, and discovering your own New Orleans.

While this proliferation of short-term home rentals, corresponding to the *Follow Your NOLA* campaign, introduced tourism to multiple neighbourhoods across New Orleans, this has not been without local critique. Multiple signs have appeared all over New Orleans neighbourhoods, though most concentrated in the Marigny, Bywater, and Mid-City neighbourhoods, criticizing short-term rentals and Airbnb specifically, calling for 'neighbours not tourists' (Dall, 2016). In September of 2016, ahead of the City Council vote on short-term rental restrictions, community activists and residents from the St. Roch, Marigny, and Bywater neighbourhoods held a protest on the steps of City Hall, featuring floats, props, local actors and artists (Jing, 2016, para. 1). The main critique of short-term rentals is that they have been responsible for the rapid rate of gentrification and the loss of residential neighbours in the areas with the highest concentration of these whole-house short-term rentals aimed at bringing tourists to the regions of the city outside of the traditional tourist areas. As one resident stated in an interview:

> No offense to the French Quarter, but I think the French Quarter lost much of its residential character in the 70s, 80s and 90s…I wouldn't want that to happen in my neighbourhood. I wouldn't want my neighbourhood to be all that tourism, because real people live there and that's how it should be.
>
> (Litten, 2016a, para. 11)

Another resident explained, 'When you remove the people in the neighbourhood that's filled with culture, love and history, you remove what makes New Orleans great' (Litten, 2016a, para. 5).

While short-term rentals encountered protests from local residents, claiming that whole house short-term rentals will rapidly increase the processes of gentrification already on-going in the city, on October 20th, 2016 the New Orleans City Council passed legislation legalizing short-term rentals, though placing some restrictions on whole-house short-term rentals (Litten, 2016b, para. 1). As has become a common trend with regulating short-term housing, enforcement is a consistent issue as the specific addresses of the rentals are unknown and the online short-term rental platforms, such as Airbnb, VBRO, and Homeway, refused to aid the city in enforcing specific restrictions (Litten, 2016b, para. 12).

While these home rentals are not a specific component of the city branding campaign, they do, in conjunction with the *Follow Your NOLA* campaign, encourage visitors to explore the lesser-known corners of New Orleans. They reinforce each other's marketing platform, appealing to a new demographic of visitor, who wishes to explore outside the confines of the traditional New Orleans experience. *Follow Your NOLA* emphasizes that New Orleans has recovered from the disasters but still maintains its uniqueness, and now this uniqueness is available for exploration and participation, while short-term rentals allow the tourist to play at being a local, if only for a weekend.

Concluding points

This chapter has identified the key actors and organized interests underlying post-disaster rebranding efforts and described the major reimaging strategies in New Orleans since 2005. As this chapter reveals, place branding is both visual and material, combining sophisticated marketing with the creation of new synergistic relationships and social structural transformations to reimage and reinvigorate the damaged place brand. From a marketer's perspective, damaged and tarnished brands reduce sales, erode market share, and eviscerate a consumer base. The solution is to develop new networked connections among diverse brand stakeholders and implement new reimaging strategies to neutralize negative brand perceptions and create new brand values. Yet what distinguishes place branding from branding in general is that the former has to deal with a variety of stakeholder interests, conflicting community concerns and place identities, and struggles over who speaks for the community.

One of our major contributions has been to examine place branding as a set of practices that reflect local conflicts and urban realities that can be highly contradictory. Critics have conceived of branding as a global process of standardization and homogenization that hallows out the rich texture and cultural depth of everyday life (Ritzer, 2007). In contrast, we have depicted place branding as a hybrid global-local process that reflects macrostructural trends but also expresses the particularities of the local in the making of urban space. That is, we have developed our investigation to shed light on the internal orientation of place branding practices, an orientation that emphasizes the key dimensions of places, such as the cultural fabric of place and the experiences of people living in the place. Such an approach recognizes the positive and progressive aspects of place branding as a vehicle of urban revitalization while acknowledging that place branding practices can have uneven outcomes and unforeseen consequences. As we have argued and demonstrated, branding can reinforce relations and patterns of exclusion and marginalization while creating new opportunities for more socially inclusive and participatory forms of urban decision-making.

Another contribution has been to introduce novel and critical ways of thinking about branding with a particular focus on theorizing place branding as a dual process of spatial differentiation and spatial dedifferentiation. Our empirical examples draw attention to the ways in which branding practices can discursively reconstruct neighbourhood culture and identity to create symbolic value for consumers and valorize real estate markets. As we have shown, the commercial areas of New Orleans flooded neighbourhoods now function increasingly to market each neighbourhood's residential real estate market. This process of branding-to-gentrify is no longer confined to specific commercial spaces in neighbourhoods but is a widespread practice, goal, and outcome. On the one hand, branding-to-gentrify seeks to marginalize and exclude those people who cannot afford rising rents and housing prices. On the other hand, branding-to-gentrify creates new opportunities for people to include previously marginalized cultures in the place marketing repertoire of the city and to cultivate new place-based identities. Processes of spatial differentiation and dedifferentiation exist together and each one complements that other. Branding a neighbourhood means constructing and deploying a set of images, motifs, and symbols that clearly differentiate the specific neighbourhood from other neighbourhoods. The intent and goal is to explicitly highlight the neighbourhood's unique and distinctive characteristics, to turn a neighbourhood from a location into a destination.

Branding a neighbourhood also implies a process of obscuring distinctions between tourist and non-tourist spaces and experiences (Gotham, 2007b). In this process, branding campaigns and organizers seek to educate and inculcate residents to view their neighbourhood and other hometown spaces as tourist destinations. An indicator of success of any place branding effort will be that residents will freely adopt the visual orientation characteristic of tourists and therefore learn to view the city as a tourist, a consumer, a person that does not have ties to the place. This process is not new, however. For decades, tourism organizations have launched promotional campaigns to elide the distinction between residents and tourists, to urge residents to acquire the consumption practices and visual orientation characteristic of tourists, to be tourists in their own hometown (Gotham, 2007b). As we have shown, tourist modes of staging, visualization, and experience increasingly penetrate into everyday life as branding campaigns and practices play a major role in post-disaster recovery and rebuilding efforts.

We have highlighted the tensions of this process of dedifferentiating tourists and residents for meanings and processes of inclusion, exclusion, and marginalization. Like tourists, residents consume the cuisine, history, entertainment, music, and culture of the city. Unlike tourists, however, residents are embedded into local struggles and indigenous conflicts, shared experiences of tragedies, and collective practices that reflect the mundane and commonplace. Also, as members of a community, residents create and reproduce rituals and ceremonies that express local cultural beliefs and convictions. Such actions and experiences are the antithesis of touristic experiences, which are explicitly designed to be worry-free, spectacular, extraordinary, and short-term. Thus, whether residents can or should become destination-brand users is an open question. The larger implications of blurring the lines between tourists and residents to foster more inclusive and participatory branding practices and activities remain to be seen.

References

'A year after the storm, business remains unusual' (2006) *New York Times*, 25 August. Available at: www.nytimes.com/2006/08/25/us/a-year-after-the-storm-business-remains-unusual.html.

Adelson, J. (2016) 'Temporary' whole-home rentals get long life in mayor's latest proposal'. *The Advocate*, 18 October. Available at: www.theadvocate.com/new_orleans/collection_4ab76522-965c-11e6-a312-2391b73ecd5d.html (Accessed: 5 November 2016).

Airbnb (2016) *Airbnb*. Available at: www.airbnb.com (Accessed: 5 November 2016).

Dall, T. (2016) 'Short-term rentals during Jazz Fest sparks new public fight' WWLTV, 26 April. Available at: www.wwltv.com/news/local/short-term-rentals-during-jazz-fest-sparks-new-public-fight/154961500 (Accessed: 8 November 2016).

Dyakovskaya, A. (2015) 'How #FollowYourNOLA used content marketing to put New Orleans back on the map'. *Business 2 Community*, 17 February. Available at: www.business2community.com/brandviews/newscred/followyournola-used-content-marketing-put-new-orleans-back-map-01159640#S3sYWeArdJzCFKEM.97 (Accessed: 20 October 2016).

Gotham, K. F. (2007a) *Authentic New Orleans: Race, Culture, and Tourism in the Big Easy*. New York: New York University (NYU) Press.

Gotham, K. F. (2007b) '(Re)branding the Big Easy: tourism rebuilding in post-Katrina New Orleans'. *Urban Affairs Review*, 42(6), pp. 823–850.

Gotham, K. F. (2016a) 'Coastal Restoration as Contested Terrain: Climate Change and the Political Economy of Risk Reduction in Louisiana'. *Sociological Forum*. 31(S1), pp. 787–806. September 2016. doi:10.1111/socf.12273.

Gotham, K. F. (2016b) 'Antinomies of risk reduction: climate change and the contradictions of coastal restoration'. *Environmental Sociology*, 2(2), pp. 208–219.

Gotham, K. F. and Campanella, R. (2013) 'Constructions of resilience: Ethnoracial diversity, inequality, and post-Katrina recovery, the case of New Orleans'. *Social Sciences*, 2(4), pp. 298–317.

Gotham, K. F. and Greenberg, M. (2014) *Crisis Cities: Disaster and Redevelopment in New York and New Orleans*. New York: Oxford University Press.

Gotham, K. F., and Lewis, J. (2015) 'Green tourism and the ambiguities of sustainability discourse: the case of New Orleans's Lower Ninth Ward'. *International Journal of Social Ecology and Sustainable Development* (IJSESD), 6(2), pp. 60–77.

Follow Your NOLA (2015) Available at: https://followyournola.com (Accessed: 18 October 2016).

Jackson, A. T. (2011) 'Diversifying the dialogue post-Katrina – race, place, and displacement in New Orleans, USA'. *Transforming Anthropology* 19(1), pp. 3–16.

Jing, J. (2016) 'Anti-Airbnb rally ahead of City Council's short-term rental regulations vote'. *WGNO*, 27 September. Available at: http://wgno.com/2016/09/27/anti-airbnb-rally-ahead-of-city-councils-short-term-rental-regulations-vote/ (Accessed: 6 November 2016).

Litten, K. (2016a) 'New Orleans City Council legalizes short-term rentals, limits whole-home listings'. *Time Picayune*, 20 October. Available at: www.nola.com/politics/index.ssf/2016/10/short_term_rentals_council.html (Accessed: 25 October 2016).

Litten, K. (2016b) 'Short-term rental showdown slated for City Council meeting'. 19 October 2016. Available at: www.nola.com/politics/index.ssf/2016/10/short_term_rentals_marigny.html (Accessed: 13 September 2017).

New Orleans Metropolitan Convention and Visitors Bureau (NOMCVB) (2007) 'New Orleans CVB announces aggressive rebranding campaign'. *Hotel Online Special Report*, 25 January. Available at: www.hotel-online.com/News/PR2007_1st/Jan07_NewOrleansCVB.html (Accessed: 19 June 2012).

New Orleans Metropolitan Convention and Visitors Bureau (NOMCVB) (2008) *Annual Report*. New Orleans, LA: New Orleans Metropolitan Convention and Visitors Bureau.

New Orleans Metropolitan Convention and Visitors Bureau (NOMCVB) (2010) *Tourism, Hospitality and Cultural Economy Fact Sheet: Five-year Anniversary of Hurricane Katrina*. New Orleans, LA: New Orleans Metropolitan Convention and Visitors Bureau. Available at: www.neworleansonline.com/pr/releases/releases/Tourism,%20Hospitality,%20and%20Cultural%20Economy%20Fact%20Sheet_1.pdf (Accessed: 20 June 2012).

New Orleans Metropolitan Convention and Visitors Bureau (NOMCVB). (2011) *New Orleans CVB Launches Summer Campaign 'Be a Tourist in Your Own Hometown'*. News release. 29 July 2011. Available at: http://www.neworleanscvb.com/articles/index.cfm?action=view&articleID=6281&menuID=1604 (Accessed: 13 September 2017).

Ritzer, G. (2007) *The Globalization of Nothing 2*. Thousand Oaks, CA: SAGE Publications.

Thompson, R. (2013) 'New Orleans tourism officials make their pitch: "Follow Your NOLA"'. *Times Picayune*, 14 May. Available at: www.nola.com/business/index.ssf/2013/05/new_orleans_tourism_officials_1.html (Accessed: 20 October 2016).

Trumpet (2012) 'New Orleans CVB'. Available at: www.trumpetgroup.com/work/cvb/ (Accessed: 27 June 2012).

White, J. (2009) 'Task force tackles tourism study; 17-member group has 10 year vision'. *Times-Picayune*, 2 April. Available at: www.gnohla.com/news/latest-news/Task-force-tackles-tourism-study (Accessed: 10 April 2017).

White, J. (2010) 'Louisiana will launch media campaign to mitigate oil spill's damage to tourism industry'. *Times-Picayune*, 2 June. Available at: www.nola.com/news/gulf-oil-spill/index.ssf/2010/06/louisiana_will_launch_media_ca.html (Accessed: 10 April 2017).

World Tourism Organization (WTO) (2006) *Destination Positioning, Branding and Image Management*. Addis Ababa, 27–29 March, PowerPoint Presentation. Available at: www.visitmyphilippines.com/ (Accessed: 10 April 2017).

8 Maps and tours as metaphors for conceptualizing urban place representation for marketing/branding purposes

Gary Warnaby, Richard Koeck and Dominic Medway

Introduction

An important theme in place marketing/branding theory and practice is the development of a strong, consistent and attractive image to actual and potential target audiences (Kavaratzis and Ashworth, 2008; Ward and Gold, 1994). To date, this has been accomplished primarily through *visual* representation (Kotler *et al.*, 1999; Warnaby and Medway, 2010), consistent with the fact that the majority of human perception of the environment is through our eyes (Porteous, 1990). It has been suggested that in this specific marketing context, places are 'constituted through a plethora of images and representations' (Hubbard and Hall, 1998, p. 7), a fact highlighted by Hospers (2009, p. 232) who describes city marketing in terms of 'the public selection of photogenic images of [the] city and their reproduction'. Such reproduction has primarily occurred through traditional media, and more recently online.

However, recent trends in marketing theory and practice arguably require a more critical re-examination of these stereotypical aspects of place representation/promotion. These trends include a more overt focus on the *experiential* (see Tynan and McKechnie, 2009), linked to which are principles of the Service-Dominant logic of marketing (see Vargo and Lusch, 2004, 2008), emphasizing experiences and value co-creation between marketer and customer/consumer. This has been – at least partially – enabled and facilitated by technology, which allows a wider variety of stakeholders to potentially participate in place marketing activity. This resonates with Cova and Dalli's notion of 'working consumers', whom they describe as 'more active and constructive' in their relationships with market entities (2009, p. 315), with significant implications for value creation and communication. More specifically, in relation to place marketing/branding there are various stakeholders who could potentially contribute to such activities, foremost among whom are the residents of the place in question (see Stubbs and Warnaby, 2015). However, notwithstanding the important roles residents may play in relation to place marketing/branding (see Braun *et al.*, 2013), their viewpoint(s) and perspective(s) are often neglected by those responsible for developing and implementing such activities (Braun and Zenker, 2012).

In this chapter, we problematize the role of civic participation and engagement in place marketing/branding arising from these recent trends drawing on the work of Michel de Certeau. De Certeau's well-known cultural theories, as described in *The Practice of Everyday Life* (1984), *Heterologies* (1986) and *Culture in the Plural* (1997), have contributed to a rethinking of the relationship between consumption, people and place in everyday life. In the specific context outlined in this chapter, the act of walking, as a space-inscribing act, is for us of particular importance and Duff (2010, p. 881) argues for the need of 'an analytics of place that refines de Certeau's narrative of practice and tactics to include the affective measure of place, identity, and belonging'. Such a 'felt' and 'affective' dimension of the city, which arguably de Certeau neglected in his writing (Duff, 2010, p. 881), becomes particularly pertinent if we recognize cities not only as fixed material/architectural constructs, but also as media landscapes that connect 'digital cultural objects' and 'mediated commodities' within the everyday (Poster, 2004, p. 409). In terms of the design of urban/architectural spaces, Poster notes that:

> the consumer for de Certeau is one who brings a repertoire of practices into a space that was designed for someone else. The consumer brings otherness into society and inscribes a pattern into space that was not accounted for in its design.
>
> (Poster, 1992, p. 102)

This sets the context in which we believe it is time to revisit one particular aspect of de Certeau's work, namely his concepts of *maps* and *tours*, outlined in *The Practice of Everyday Life* (1984) – in the context of urban place representation and marketing/branding, where we use maps and tours as metaphors for urban place representation. We begin by outlining – and distinguishing between – these two concepts, before moving to consider the implications for place representation for marketing purposes via three key questions (following Warnaby and Medway, 2013): namely, (1) *what* is being represented; (2) *how* does this representation occur; and (3) *who* is implementing representation activities?

Telling the 'spatial story' of a city: maps and tours

De Certeau, in *The Practice of Everyday Life*, proposes the concepts of maps and tours as a means of conveying spatial 'stories', which 'traverse and organize places … select and link them together … make sentences and itineraries out of them' (1984, p. 115). He describes maps in terms of 'a totalizing stage on which elements of diverse origin are brought together' (1984, p. 121) to create a tableau comprising, in this specific context, an assemblage of place elements. This could include maps in their traditional cartographic understanding, but might equally incorporate pictures, photographs or other graphics – or indeed anything that visually captures the elements making up a place's essence. In so doing, maps describe these different elements in relation to one another in an essentially static way. Thus, they constitute visual representations of the place as a whole, at least from the perspective of their creator and for the moment in time in which they were created. By contrast, de Certeau describes tours as descriptions of places 'that are made for the most part in terms of operations' (1984, p. 119): in other words, emphasising movement in, and experience of, place.

Tours and maps are therefore 'two poles of experience', in respect of 'the relation between the itinerary (a discursive series of operations) and the map (a place projection totalizing observations)'. De Certeau has noted that description of place:

> ... oscillates between the terms of an alternative: either **seeing** (the knowledge of an order of places) or **going** (spatializing actions). Either it presents a **tableau** ('there are...'), or it organizes **movements** ('you enter, you go across, you turn...').
>
> (1984, p. 119. Original emphasis)

We suggest that marketing/branding activities could be thought of essentially as a means of telling the 'spatial story' of a particular place, in order to attempt to create distinctiveness/identity – a key motivation for place marketing/branding (Kavaratzis and Ashworth, 2008). However, at the same time, we argue that through processes of co-creation, increasingly facilitated by the use of information technology (especially Web 2.0 applications), spatial stories do not emerge solely from 'top-down', marketing considerations alone, but also from the landscape and its people, incorporating more participatory, 'bottom-up', tendencies, and thereby emphasizing civic participation in place marketing/branding activities. Indeed, Colomb and Kalandides (2010, p. 175) note that place branding has a dual aim: 'to form a 'unique selling proposition' that will secure visibility to the outside and reinforce 'local identity' to the inside'. We suggest that the representations emanating from such grass-roots, participatory sources can, potentially, be as – if not more – effective in communicating the experiential dimensions of a place and its *genius loci*. The following three sections of the chapter consider these issues in more detail.

What is being represented?

As noted above, de Certeau (1984) describes maps in terms of a tableau. This has some resonance with an earlier chapter in *The Practice of Everyday Life* on 'Walking in the City', where, using the analogy of the story of Icarus and Daedalus from Greek mythology, he contrasts what he terms the 'panorama city' as viewed from above, with how it may be experienced by 'the ordinary practitioners of the city' who 'live 'down below', below the levels at which visibility begins'. To view the city from above, he argues 'is to be lifted out of the city's grasp', transforming 'the bewitching world [i.e. of the city's streets] by which one was "possessed" into a text that lies before one's eyes' (De Certeau, 1984, p. 92).

Consequently, from a place marketing perspective, the panorama city could be thought of as constituting the 'map', whereby all the individual contributory and visual elements of a place 'product' are arrayed in order to appeal to the prospective target audience. Such an approach arguably resonates with the stereotypically visual aspects of marketing communications activity and related representations and conceptualizations of the place product, made up of an assemblage of different attributes (e.g. Ashworth and Voogd, 1990; Warnaby *et al.*, 2010; and also, Getz, 1993; Jansen-Verbeke, 1986, in a tourism context), or a place brand (e.g. Balakrishnan, 2009; Hankinson, 2004; Hanna and Rowley, 2010; Parkerson and Saunders, 2005). While some conceptualizations incorporate both tangible and intangible elements, the emphasis is on place *materiality*, which is more susceptible to effective communication by visual means.

However, it must be emphasized that the choice of the particular place aspects on which to focus in this way is not a neutral activity. The highlighting of those attributes to be paraded upon what Degen (2008) has termed the global catwalk for investment and tourism will reflect to some extent the perspectives and priorities of the hegemonic 'strategic network' (van den Berg and Braun, 1999) responsible for urban place marketing activity. Using a metaphor of light and shadow in describing urban representation, Short (1999, pp. 40–41) identifies 'two distinct discourses', comprising an accentuation of the positive aspects of the city, and in contrast, a 'dark side that has to be contained, controlled or ignored'. Griffiths (1998, p. 53) notes that '[p]lace marketing works by creating a selective relationship between (projected) image and (real) identity'. The inherent selectivity – and subjectivity – of place representation for marketing purposes, which can reflect existing urban hegemonies (Eisenschitz, 2010; Sadler, 1993), has parallels in the representational cartography literature relating to maps (see Black, 1997; Monmonier, 1996; Robinson and Petchenik, 1976). Thus, Harley notes the concept of 'cartographic silence', which can arise from 'deliberate policies of secrecy and censorship' as well as 'the more indeterminate silences rooted in often hidden procedures or rules' (2001, p. 84). We will return to issues of hegemony and power in this context in terms of the 'who' question.

Moving to consider 'tours' (and in contrast with the essentially static 'panorama city' implied by the map), de Certeau argues that the real urban *experience* occurs 'down below', especially by those that walk, which he describes as 'an elementary form of this experience of the city' (Harley, 2001, p. 93). This is echoed by writers such as Iain Sinclair and Rebecca Solnit, who describe walking through urban space as 'the best way to explore and exploit the city' (Sinclair, 1997, p. 4) and as 'what links up reading the map with living one's life' (Solnit, 2001, p. 176). Indeed, such exploration and exploitation (to use Sinclair's terms) might mean entering into the 'dark' parts of the city mentioned above. Here, one may (to paraphrase the title of Lou Reed's famous 1972 song) 'take a walk on the wild side', with a consequent frisson which may add to the experience enjoyed by the individual. However, the possible risk and danger inherent in this might be something that place marketers may not wish to highlight!

Such experiential aspects are highlighted by De Certeau, who regards 'lived space' as a place of 'tactile apprehension and kinesthetic appropriation' – a territory in which seemingly unremarkable pedestrian movement begins to, in turn, actively shape spaces in the city (1984, p. 97). This creative act is linked to the enunciating power of the body in space. He makes a noteworthy analogy between the movement of pedestrians and the act of speech: 'The act of walking is to the urban system what the speech act is to language or to the statements uttered' (De Certeau, 1984 p. 97), and alludes to a triple 'enunciative function' that is connected to the act of walking: the appropriation of space and spatial elements; the acting-out of place; and the implying of relations. Hence, the pedestrian engages in a process of appropriating the topographical system which consists of almost endless choices. The walker is, therefore, selective; one chooses a path and brings certain urban elements to the forefront while at the same time omitting others. This means that the walker 'transforms each spatial signifier into something else' (De Certeau, 1984, p. 98) or, in other words, the walker creates space. In this sense, our movement in urban landscapes can be regarded as a dialectic process with which we relate to – and moreover, create our own – spatial narratives.

This has implications for notions of the place 'product' and how it is constructed. Thus, rather than an assemblage of urban facilities and attributes compiled (and subsequently promoted, typically visually) by urban place marketers (as implied by the map concept), the place product becomes a co-created phenomenon, where the main creative act is carried out by the place user – an issue highlighted by Ashworth (1993) in his assertion of the primacy of the consumer as creator of a place product. This resonates with some of the axiomatic principles underpinning the service-dominant (S-D) logic of marketing, promulgated by Vargo and Lusch (2004, 2008), who acknowledge its relevance to spatial entities. Indeed, the application of the S-D logic in the context of places has been considered by Warnaby (2009) and Warnaby and Medway (2013, 2015). Some 'foundational premises' of the S-D logic state that the customer (rather than the organization/marketer) is always a co-creator of value, and such co-creation occurs through the integration of consumer and organizational (or in this case, place) resources, to create value, which 'is always uniquely and phenomenologically determined by the beneficiary' (Vargo and Lusch, 2008, p. 7). In the context of places, we suggest that this value be articulated in terms of *experience*, resulting from active engagement with place, given that human perception of urban environments is inevitably multi-sensorial. Moreover, whilst the visual sense is dominant, the non-seeing senses can provide an immersive and experiential impression of the environment (Drobnick, 2002), which has the potential to be capitalized upon by urban place marketers. We turn to this now, by considering the 'how' question outlined above.

How does this representation occur?

As noted above, the importance of visual images and representations for place marketing is acknowledged, and particularly the importance of collage as a means of efficiently highlighting multiple place attributes (Gold, 1994), especially those with 'iconic' visual appeal. This is linked to the notion of the 'map', but arguably more from a *chorographic* (as opposed to *cartographic*) perspective. Chorography is usually described in terms of the portrayal of a local area (Gregory, 2009), and stylistically is more subjective and aesthetically oriented than contemporary mapping/cartographic practice (which according to Cosgrove, 2008, is much more analytically oriented and stylistically practical), to the extent that Casey (2002) presents chorography as a commingling of cartography and landscape painting. This is most evident in town portraits, common in the Renaissance period (see Frangenberg, 1994; Nuti, 1999). These Cosgrove (2008, p. 175) argued, formed a distinct cartographic genre which was 'overwhelming celebratory' in its motivation, and was 'intended to frame in a comprehensive image the city's complex social and spatial totality', and moreover, could equally be regarded as attempts to convey the symbolic significance of the city (Cosgrove, 1982 – see also Koeck and Warnaby, 2015). Such representations were, according to Whitfield, 'pictures, bird's-eye views or panoramas', their purpose being, 'to present to us, directly and vividly, a picture of living in the city', and whose spirit was 'aesthetic rather than cartographic' (2005, p. 17). The parallels with much contemporary visual representation of urban places for the purposes of marketing are obvious (and explored in more detail by Warnaby, 2015), and link quite explicitly with de Certeau's use of the term 'seeing' to describe how such place representations are discerned (1984, p. 119).

However, as noted above, recent technological advances have enabled and facilitated the use of different approaches to place representation that have much resonance with 'tours' in that they aim to replicate the kinaesthetic experience of *movement* in – and through – a place. Such applications can be commercially oriented: for example, Google Street View, and also Google Earth, which now has the facility to represent 3D cityscapes whereby the user can move easily between aerial and ground-based perspectives (Dredge, 2012), thereby combining both the 'panorama city' and 'down below' (de Certeau, 1984). Additionally, these applications could also act as mobile portals to access further information about the place in question, which may be explicitly linked to the specific location of the user at that point in time.

An example of this is the mobile application *GhostCinema* – produced as part of the *Cinematic Geographies of Battersea* research project, led by the universities of Cambridge, Liverpool and Edinburgh. This application makes a distinct contribution to place-making in the context of the London Borough of Battersea. It is based on the assumption that film and moving images more generally have not only shaped our everyday experiences and environments, but have also transformed our society into one in which *reel* realities are readily incorporated into our contemporary sense of self and space. This project built a database of over

600 films that were (partially or entirely) shot in Battersea, or were in some way emblematic of the area. The mobile app was then developed to convey the convergence of geographic and historical material in accessible narrative and visual terms, in which users can engage in and share (through, for example, a social media link) the discovery of lost local cinemas, and movies shot in Battersea. By placing some of the database content literally in the hands of citizens, the physical city becomes not just a source of filmic and architectural heritage or a cultural space in which the filmic and urban heritage is inscribed, but is, in a sense, an interface through which one could investigate ways of engaging the public (see Koeck and Flintham, 2017). In doing so, the *GhostCinema* mobile app not only promotes a database that would otherwise be primarily academic in its orientation, it engages in the narration of 'spatial stories' and it takes part in the transformation of Battersea as a perceived space through a co-creative act of walking and the sharing of local memories and histories.

Linking back to the attributes emphasised (or ignored) in the representation of urban places (both cartographic, and more generally for marketing purposes), the ability of these applications to 'serve up whatever information and/or content is useful to that particular person [using the app] at that particular time' is, according to Dredge (2012, p. 2), an important issue. Dredge quotes a representative of Google, as follows:

> For cartography, it's never been what you include on the map, but what you take off that's important ... We're now taking that beyond traditional cartography: if you're looking through your augmented reality glasses, what information would be relevant to you at that particular time? ... We're perhaps getting to the point where every map is unique for every individual for their particular task ... A map I would see might be different to a map you'd see.
>
> (2012, p. 2)

With such commercial tour-oriented place representation methods, the full potential for the co-creation of how a place is represented is arguably still constrained by the 'menu' of available place information decided upon by the organizations/groups creating the applications (although users can select which aspects of this information are useful to them, albeit from possibly a limited range of options). However, in relation to Cova and Dalli's (2009) notion of working consumers mentioned above, the fact that the threshold for the effective use of technology is now much lower, thereby enables the possibility of a far greater diversity of – potentially alternative – place representations, created by a much more diverse range of place stakeholders. This echoes more overt participatory, 'bottom-up' approaches to the representation of places, some of which might be relevant in marketing terms, but which might potentially threaten the hegemony of the more traditional 'strategic networks' (Van den Berg and Braun, 1999) responsible for place marketing.

Such trends are evident, for example, with participatory cartography, defined as, 'local mapping, produced collaboratively, by local people and often incorporating alternative local knowledge' (Perkins, 2007, p. 127). This development is part of a series of significant changes impacting on mapping practices from the widespread deployment of Web 2.0 technology (see Gartner, 2009), which has democratized cartography (Dorling and Fairbairn, 1997; Krygier and Wood, 2005) by allowing people to make their own maps. This depends in part on the open-source movement, which has enabled competition with proprietary monopolistic products (Perkins, 2014), offering through co-creative processes 'new possibilities for articulating social, economic, political or aesthetic claims. Formerly marginalised groups can gain a voice' (Perkins, 2007, p. 127). Thus, the production of maps can emphasise practice and performance (Crampton and Krygier, 2005) to create perhaps more aesthetically oriented representations of places, which (resonating with the aims and characteristics of chorography) could be thought of in artistic terms, as opposed to the practical, navigational aspects of contemporary cartographic practice. Cosgrove (2005) provides various examples of this more artistically-oriented approach, including for example, Guy Debord's widely reproduced *Situationist Map of Paris Using G Peltier's 1956 Vue de Paris à vol d'oiseau*. Indeed, members of the Situationist International – especially Debord, along with Asger Jorn and Michèle Bernstein in particular – were interested in alternative forms of mapping that investigated the relationship between language, narrative, and cognition in urban landscapes (Sadler, 1999). Resonating with de Certeau's notion of the tour, Debord developed the idea of drifting (*dérive*), or the playful strolling through urban spaces which was seen as a form of surveying of the psychogeographic conditions of the modern city in order to reveal its hidden delights (Knabb, 2006). Whilst Debord's psychogeographical map dates from the late 1950s, current technology facilitates the creation and much wider dissemination of such alternative place representations, which brings us to the last question.

Who is implementing representational activities?

As noted above, more stereotypical place marketing has arguably been characterized by a 'top down' approach, exemplified by, for example, notions of the 'strategic network' (van den Berg and Braun, 1999) which creates a vision for the place and enabling 'organizing capacity', defined as, 'the ability to enlist all actors involved and, with their help, to generate new ideas and to develop and implement a policy designed to respond to fundamental developments and create conditions for sustainable development' (van den Berg and Braun, 1999, p. 995). However, such notions with their focus on institutional frameworks and administrative structures, arguably neglect a broader range of stakeholders who can influence the nature of the place, and whose perspectives should be incorporated into the development of place marketing/branding initiatives, according to Stubbs and Warnaby (2015). Particularly important here is the role of place residents who, as noted above, have been identified as crucial stakeholders in urban place marketing (Braun *et al.*, 2013; Braun and Zenker, 2012; Kavaratzis, 2012; Stubbs and Warnaby, 2015). Warnaby and Medway (2013) note that place residents can have a dual role: they can be both targets of place marketing activity, and (co-)creators of place brands, playing what Braun *et al.* (2013) term an ambassadorial role, and moreover, as citizens and voters, who are instrumental in the political legitimization of place branding.

Drawing on social constructionist and phenomenological approaches towards the definition of place, Cresswell and Hoskins (2008, p. 394) describe place as a lived concept' in that place inherently involves practice and performance, arising from the fact that it is inhabited. Thus, Cresswell (2004) argues, place becomes an 'event', and drawing on the work of Pred (1994), he argues that a sense of place is developed through the interaction of structure and agency: 'Places are constructed by people doing things and in this sense are never "finished" but constantly being performed' (Cresswell, 2004, p. 37). The resonance with de Certeau's notion of the urban walker creating space through the act of walking is readily apparent, as is the co-created communication of a place 'product' in the specific context of urban place representation for the purposes of marketing, through the agency of working consumers (Cova and Dalli, 2009), be they residents, or a range of other place stakeholders remaining outside the 'strategic network' responsible for place marketing activities. Thus, Warnaby and Medway (2013) argue that if the place as 'product' is regarded as a dynamic and fluid entity composed as much from the changing (and potentially competing) narratives in and over time that are (co-)created by a range of stakeholders, then this in turn requires urban place marketers to cede some control over how the place is represented. Thus, if these more overtly experiential aspects of the place 'product' can be considered in terms of 'tours', then there could be numerous alternative 'tours' being promoted which are informed by the perspectives of a range of different stakeholders. Indeed, if as mentioned above, the individual place user creates his or her own place product by choosing from an array of specific place attributes and facilities (see Ashworth, 1993), then the place becomes a smorgasbord, which place marketers, at best, merely curate rather than control. The implication, Warnaby and Medway state, is that this 'may take many place marketers out of their 'comfort zone', but the potential benefits arising from such a course of action may richly repay the effort' (2013, p. 358).

Discussion and conclusions

This chapter presents a theoretical framework for rethinking the way in which places are represented in place marketing/branding effort. We have argued that in this context the predominant focus of representing places can be described using the metaphor of de Certeau's 'map' concept. To reiterate, this is not just about maps in their usual cartographic sense, although it does not exclude the marketing communication and promotion of place through sponsored maps of a locale which are free to visitors/residents, and which detail selected attractions (e.g. the town and city maps that are made available in hotels, and other outlets, for tourists). Instead, our acknowledgement of the importance and relevance of maps for place representation widens out to an amalgam of visual forms (photographs, pictures, graphic design, symbols) and characteristics (colour, lighting, shading), which translate easily to the ocular vehicles of printed (leaflets, brochures, billboards) and screen-based media channels (TV, cinema, mobile, tablet and PC).

A criticism of this approach concerns the viewpoint from which maps are constructed. Thus, de Certeau's contention that to view the city from above 'is to be lifted out of the city's grasp' highlights an inherent problem with maps as a means of representing place, at least for marketing/branding purposes. Critically, such a perspective shakes off the grounding details that make a place unique. Thus, as the gaze angles out to the panorama view, and the scale of representation gradually diminishes, the viewer is left with a representation of place that highlights the most striking visual features (e.g. the oldest/tallest buildings; an iconic bridge or vista). Echoing the work of a caricaturist, these features can easily become over-emphasized. A problem with caricatures is that they can make every*one* look quite similar. Equally, we suggest that place marketing and branding campaigns that utilise maps as an approach to place representation can make every*where* look quite similar – and this has been an important part of the critique of place marketing activities.

A related criticism is that the representation of place through maps for marketing/branding purposes assumes directional control of the place consumer's gaze, and his/her subsequent potential perceptions of the place in question. We argue that such campaigns are understandably promoting their own 'map' of a place to the tourist, visitor or resident. Consequently, recipients of place marketing/branding effort become metaphorically reduced to the position of aeroplane passengers looking from the window. Assuming such a perspective, many urban places again look very similar, typically to the extent where they are often unidentifiable and indistinguishable from one another. Furthermore, this viewpoint cannot be changed or influenced unless you are able to change the pilot's height and trajectory. Extending the analogy, a better approach to place marketing/branding might be one which liberates the place user, allowing them to develop their own map rather than have one imposed on them, and to move from the position of passenger to pilot. But how might this be achieved?

Here, it is useful to (re)engage with de Certeau's notion of tours. By promoting a place via the concept of tours, specifically through helping/facilitating individuals to easily (and sometimes not so easily, thereby engendering a sense of exclusivity) discover a place through walking, living and experiencing it 'down below', the targets of place marketing/branding activities could be provided with an ability to become the 'pilot' and develop their own view (from whatever perspective), unique and special to them. Because this approach instils the place consumer with a sense of responsibility and personal investment in their own interpretation and understanding of place, we contend it has the potential to form the basis of genuine place attachment. In turn, such attachment is more likely to deliver associated economic benefits such as repeat visits amongst tourists (e.g. Yuksel *et al.*, 2010) and civic pride among residents (e.g. Warnaby and Medway, 2013). Additionally, place-marketing activity can facilitate this process by considering the content of augmented reality platforms that might accompany tours. The *GhostCinema* mobile app described above is a good example. In the context of Battersea, it performs a dual role of enhancing an individual's appreciation (and understanding) of, and engagement with, the place, whilst also promoting the sharing of co-created content (stories, memories, histories) about the place from individuals or 'ordinary practitioners'. This arguably engenders the construction of a collective perspective for a place, whereby the whole is greater than the sum of the parts, and which may provide the basis for development of place identities and related branding from the bottom-up.

Thus, it could be argued that the notion of a tour emphasizes the experiential aspects of places, but if, as Warnaby and Medway (2013) suggest, places are kaleidoscopic entities with multiple different facets, then decisions about which facts to explore become important. For many place users (and especially tourist visitors) some curation of the assemblage of place product elements becomes essential if they are to get the maximum benefit from their time in the place. Here, the role of the tour guide comes to the fore in order to 'edit' the place experience, and offer a degree of 'directional control' as mentioned above in a 'map' context. Is *curation*, therefore, the future role of the place marketer in an environment where *experience* assumes greater importance? If so, then do we run into the same dangers of more stereotypical place marketing activities, where only certain elements of the place are offered as parts of the 'tour', and consequently the place becomes reduced to a set of stereotypes and caricatures of the kind mentioned above? Of course, there is a danger of this. However, we would argue that the user of the place has more scope to choose from a range of different 'tour guides' depending on preference. Moreover, place users now have much greater ability (via information technology and web 2.0 applications) to develop – and importantly, communicate – their own 'bespoke' tours in order to reflect the facets of the place kaleidoscope that best reflect the perspective and interests of the individual in question.

Thus, in encouraging and facilitating an understanding of place through tours, place marketing holds the ability to make flâneurs or flâneuses of us all. In turn, we posit that such heightened individual engagement with place at the level is likely to lead to a greater desire to contribute to a collective narrative of that place, reminiscent of Therkelsen *et al.*'s (2010) 'city of words', through mechanisms such as social media, arguably leading to a more authentic and collective 'map', incorporating a variety of different (and possibly competing) perspectives. From this emerges the raw material for a more meaningful and wider inculcation of place branding, bought about not by the passive subjugation of individuals, who are 'being lifted' (in de Certeau's terms) from the grounding grasp of places, but one of active and collective elevation. Put another way, this is place marketing as an act of 'doing together' rather than 'being done to'. In this instance, those who hold the role of place marketers need to move from a position of making the message about a place to nurturing and curating one from all place users and consumers.

References

Ashworth, G. (1993) 'Marketing of places: What are we doing?', in Ave, G. and Corsico, F. (eds.) *Urban Marketing in Europe*. Turin: Torino Incontra, pp. 643–649.

Ashworth, G. J. and Voogd, H. (1990) *Selling the City: Marketing Approaches in Public Sector Urban Planning*. London: Belhaven.

Balakrishnan, M. S. (2009) 'Strategic branding of destinations: a framework'. *European Journal of Marketing*, 43(5–6), pp. 611–629.

Black, J. (1997) *Maps and Politics*. London: Reaktion Books.

Braun, E. and Zenker, S. (2012) *I am the city – Thus I Own the Brand! The Problem of Ownership in Place Branding*. Paper presented at Special Session on Rethinking Place Marketing: The Necessity of Marketing to Citizens, European Marketing Academy Conference, Lisbon, May.

Braun, E., Kavaratzis, M. and Zenker, S. (2013) 'My City – My brand: the role of residents in place branding'. *Journal of Place Management and Development*, 6(1), pp. 18–28.

Casey, E. S. (2002) *Representing place: Landscape, painting and maps*. Minneapolis and London: University of Minnesota Press.

Colomb, C. and Kalandides, A. (2010) 'The "be Berlin" campaign: Old wine in new bottles or innovative form of participatory place branding?', in Ashworth, G. and Kavaratzis, M. (eds.), *Towards Effective Place Brand Management: Branding European Cities and Regions*. Cheltenham and Northampton MA: Edward Elgar, pp. 173–190.

Cosgrove, D. (1982) 'The myth and stones of Venice: An historical geography of a symbolic landscape'. *Journal of Historical Geography*, 8(2), pp. 145–169.

Cosgrove, D. (2005) 'Maps, mapping, modernity: Art and cartography in the Twentieth Century'. *Imago Mundi*, 57(1), pp. 35–54.

Cosgrove, D. (2008) *Geography and vision: seeing, imagining and representing the World*. London and New York: I B Tauris.

Cova, B. and Dalli, D. (2009) 'Working consumers: the next step in marketing theory?'. *Marketing Theory*, 9(3), pp. 315–339.

Crampton, J. W. and Krygier, J. (2005) 'An introduction to critical cartography'. *ACME: An International E-Journal for Critical Geographies*, 4(1), pp. 11–33.

Cresswell, T. (2004) *Place: A Short Introduction*. Oxford: Blackwell Publishing.

Cresswell, T. and Hoskins, G. (2008) 'Place, persistence, and practice: evaluating historical significance at Angel Island, San Francisco, and Maxwell Street, Chicago'. *Annals of the Association of American Geographers*, 98(2), pp. 392–413.

De Certeau, M. (1984) *The Practice of Everyday Life* (trans. S. Rendall). Berkeley/Los Angeles/London: University of California Press.

De Certeau, M. (1986) *Heterologies: Discourse on the Other* (trans. B. Massumi). Minneapolis: University of Minnesota Press.

De Certeau, M. (1997) *Culture in the Plural* (trans. T. Conley). Minneapolis: University of Minnesota Press.

Degen, M. (2008) *Sensing Cities: Regenerating Public Life in Barcelona and Manchester*. London and New York: Routledge.

Dorling, D. and Fairbairn, D. (1997) *Mapping: Ways of Representing the World*. Harlow: Longman.

Dredge, S. (2012) 'Google unveils 3D cities in Google Earth and offline Google Maps for Android', *Guardian*, 6 June. Available at: www.theguardian.com/technology/appsblog/2012/jun/06/google-maps-3d-street-view1 (Accessed: 1 April 2015).

Drobnick, J. (2002) 'Toposmia: art, scent and interrogations of spatiality'. *Angelaki – Journal of the Theoretical Humanities*, 7(1), pp. 31–46.

Duff, C. (2010) 'On the role of affect and practice in the production of place'. *Environment and Planning D: Society and Space*, 28(5), pp. 881–895.

Eisenschitz, A. (2010) 'Place marketing as politics: the limits of neoliberalism', in Go, F. M. and Govers, R. (eds.) *International Place Branding Yearbook 2001: Place Branding in the New Age of Innovation*. Houndmills: Palgrave Macmillan, pp. 21–30.

Frangenberg, T. (1994) 'Chorographies of Florence: the use of city views and city plans in the Sixteenth Century'. *Imago Mundi*, 46, pp. 41–64.

Gartner, G. (2009) 'Web mapping 2.0', in Dodge, M., Kitchin, R. and Perkins, C. (eds.) *Rethinking Maps; New Frontiers in Cartographic Theory*. Abingdon: Routledge, pp. 68–82.

Getz, D. (1993) 'Planning for tourism business districts', *Annals of Tourism Research*, 20, pp, 583–600.

Gold, J. R. (1994) 'Locating the message: place promotion as image communication', in Gold, J. R. and Ward, S. V. (eds.) *Place Promotion: The Use of Publicity and Marketing to Sell Towns and Regions*. Chichester: John Wiley & Sons Ltd, pp. 19–37.

Gregory, D. (2009) 'Chorology/chorography', in Gregory, D. Johnston, R. Pratt, G., Watts, M. J. and Whatmore, S. (eds.), *The Dictionary of Human Geography*. 5th edn. Chichester: Wiley-Blackwell, pp. 82–83.

Griffiths, R. (1998) 'Making sameness: place marketing and the new urban entrepreneurialism', in Oatley, N. (ed.) *Cities, Economic Competition and Urban Policy*. London: Paul Chapman Publishing, pp. 41–57.

Hankinson, G. (2004) 'Relational network brands: towards a conceptual model of place brands'. *Journal of Vacation Marketing*, 10(2), pp. 109–121.

Hanna, S. and Rowley, J. (2010) 'Towards a strategic place brand-management model'. *Journal of Marketing Management*, 27(5–6), pp. 458–476.

Harley, J. B. (2001) 'Silences and secrecy: The hidden agenda of cartography in early modern Europe', in Harley, J. B., *The New Nature of Maps: Essays in the History of Cartography*. Baltimore and London: The Johns Hopkins University Press, pp. 83–107.

Hospers, G.-J. (2009) 'Lynch, Urry and City marketing: taking advantage of the city as a built and graphic image'. *Place Branding and Public Diplomacy*, 5(3), pp. 226–233.

Hubbard, P. and Hall, T. (1998) 'The entrepreneurial city and the "new urban politics"', in Hall, T. and Hubbard, P. (eds.), *The Entrepreneurial City: Geographies of Politics, Regimes and Representations*. Chichester: John Wiley & Sons, pp. 1–13.

Jansen-Verbeke, M. (1986) 'Inner-city tourism: Resources, tourists and promoters'. *Annals of Tourism Research*, 13, pp. 79–100.

Kavaratzis, M. (2012) *Participatory Place Brands: Stakeholders in the Foreground*. Paper presented at Special Session on Rethinking Place Marketing: The Necessity of Marketing to Citizens, European Marketing Academy Conference, Lisbon, May.

Kavaratzis, M. and Ashworth, G. (2008) 'Place marketing: how did we get here and where are we going?'. *Journal of Place Management and Development*, 1(2), pp. 150–165.

Knabb, K. (2006) *Situationist International Anthology*. Berkeley CA: Bureau of Public Secrets.

Koeck, R. and Warnaby, G. (2015) 'Digital chorographies: Conceptualising experiential representation and marketing of urban/architectural geographies'. *Architectural Research Quarterly*, 19(2), pp. 183–191.

Koeck, R. and Flintham, M. (2017, forthcoming) 'Geographies of the moving image: Transforming cinematic representation into geographic information', in Penz, F. and Koeck, R. (eds.). *Cinematic Urban Geographies*. London: Palgrave Macmillan.

Kotler, P., Asplund, C., Rein, I. and Haider, D. (1999) *Marketing Places Europe: Attracting Investments, Industries, and Visitors to European Cities, Communities, Regions and Nations*. Harlow: Financial Times Prentice Hall.

Krygier, J. and Wood, D. (2005) *Making Maps: A Visual Guide to Map Design for GIS*. New York and London: The Guilford Press.

Monmonier, M. (1996) *How to Lie with Maps*. Chicago and London: The University of Chicago Press.

Nuti, L. (1999) 'Mapping places: Chorography and vision in the Renaissance', in Cosgrove, D. (Ed.) *Mappings*. London: Reaktion Books, pp. 90–108.

Parkerson, B. and Saunders, J. (2005) 'City branding: Can goods and services branding models be used to brand cities?'. *Place Branding*, 1(3), pp. 242–264.

Perkins, C. (2007) 'Community mapping'. *The Cartographic Journal*, 44(2), pp. 127–137.

Perkins, C. (2014) 'Plotting practices and politics: (Im)mutable narratives in OpenStreetMap'. *Transactions of the Institute of British Geographers*, 39(2), pp. 304–317.

Porteous, J. D. (1990) *Landscapes of the Mind: Worlds of Sense and Metaphor*. Toronto: University of Toronto Press.

Poster, M. (1992) 'The Question of Agency: De Certeau and the History of Consumption'. *Diacritics*, 22, pp. 94–107.

Poster, M (2004) 'Consumption and digital commodities in the everyday'. *Cultural Studies*, 18 (2–3), pp. 409–423.

Pred, A. R. (1984) 'Place as historically contingent process: Structuration and the time-geography of becoming places'. *Annals of the Association of American Geographers*, 74(2), pp. 279–297.

Robinson, A. H. and Petchenik, B. B. (1976) *The Nature of Naps: Essays Towards Understanding Maps and Mapping*. Chicago and London: The University of Chicago Press.

Sadler, D. (1993) 'Place marketing, competitive places and the construction of hegemony in Britain in the 1980s', in Kearns, G. and Philo, C. (eds.) *Selling Places: The City as Cultural Capital Past and Present*. Oxford: Pergamon Press, pp. 175–192.

Sadler, S. (1999) *The Situationist City*. Cambridge MA: MIT Press.

Short, J. R. (1999) 'Urban imagineers: boosterism and the representation of cities', in Jonas, A. E. J. and Wilson, D. (eds.) *The Urban Growth Machine: Critical Perspectives Two Decades Later*. New York: State University of New York Press, pp. 37–54.

Sinclair, I. (1997) *Lights out for the Territory*. London: Granta Books.

Solnit, R. (2001) *Wanderlust: A History of Walking*. London and New York: Verso.

Stubbs, J. and Warnaby, G. (2015) 'Working with stakeholders: Rethinking place branding from a practice perspective', in Kavaratzis, M. Warnaby, G. and Ashworth, G. (eds.) *Rethinking Place Branding: Comprehensive Brand Development for Cities and Regions*. Heidelberg: Springer Verlag, pp. 101–118.

Therkelsen, A. Halkier, H. and Jensen, O. B. (2010) 'Branding Aalborg: building community or selling place?', in Ashworth, G. and Kavaratzis, M. (eds.), *Towards Effective Place Brand Management: Branding European Cities and Regions*. Cheltenham/Northampton MA: Edward Elgar, pp. 136–155.

Tynan, C. and McKechnie, S. (2009) 'Experience marketing: A review and reassessment'. *Journal of Marketing Management*, 25(5–6), pp. 501–517.

Van den Berg, L. and Braun, E. (1999) 'Urban competitiveness, marketing and the need for organising capacity'. *Urban Studies*, 36(5–6), pp. 987–999.

Vargo, S. L. and Lusch, R. F. (2004) 'Evolving to a new dominant logic for marketing'. *Journal of Marketing*, 68(1), pp. 1–17.

Vargo, S. L. and Lusch, R. F. (2008) 'Service-dominant logic: Continuing the evolution'. *Journal of the Academy of Marketing Science*, 36(1), pp. 1–10.

Ward, S. V. and Gold, J. R. (1994) 'Introduction', in Gold, J. R. and Ward, S. V. (eds.), *Place Promotion: The Use of Publicity and Marketing to Sell Towns and Regions*. Chichester: John Wiley & Sons, pp. 1–17.

Warnaby, G. (2009) 'Towards a service-dominant place marketing logic'. *Marketing Theory*, 9(4), pp. 403–423.

Warnaby, G. (2015) 'Rethinking the Visual Communication of the Place Brand: A Contemporary Role for Chorography?', in Kavaratzis, M., Warnaby, G. and Ashworth, G. (eds.), *Rethinking Place Branding: Comprehensive Brand Development for Cities and Regions*. Heldelberg: Springer Verlag, pp. 175–190.

Warnaby, G. and Medway, D. (2010) 'Semiotics and Place Branding: The Influence of the Built and Natural Environment in City Logos', in Ashworth, G. J. and Kavaratzis, M. (eds.) *Towards Effective Place Brand Management: Branding European Cities and Regions*. Cheltenham and Northampton MA: Edward Elgar, pp. 205–221.

Warnaby, G. and Medway, D. (2013) 'What about the "Place" in Place Marketing?'. *Marketing Theory*, 13 (3), pp. 345–363.

Warnaby, G. and Medway, D. (2015) 'Rethinking the Place Product from the Perspective of the Service-Dominant Logic of Marketing', in Kavaratzis, M., Warnaby, G. and Ashworth, G. (eds.) *Rethinking Place Branding: Comprehensive Brand Development for Cities and Regions*. Heidelberg: Springer Verlag, pp. 22–50.

Warnaby, G., Bennison, D. and Medway, D. (2010) 'Notions of Materiality and Linearity: The Challenges of Marketing the Hadrian's Wall Place Product'. *Environment and Planning A*, 42(6), pp. 1365–1382.

Whitfield, P. (2005) *Cities of the World: A History in Maps*. London: The British Library.

Yuksel, A., Yuksel, F. and Bilim, Y. (2010) 'Destination attachment: Effects on customer satisfaction and cognitive, affective, and conative loyalty'. *Tourism Management*, 31(2), pp. 274–284.

9 Brand conformity in a food place context

Anette Therkelsen

Introduction

This chapter takes its empirical point of departure in a critical analysis of the recent local food wave sweeping over the branding efforts of Danish rural tourism destinations. Fraught by a declining economy and challenged by few significant differentiators, these places are increasingly bringing local food and gastronomy into play. In order to position themselves on the global market and to tap into consumer trends of local food and authentic experiences, destinations across Denmark are eager to bring locally sourced food and meals into their place narratives.

It is interesting to study the food narratives employed by Danish coastal destinations in their attempts to brand themselves as attractive places for at least two reasons. First, at a general conceptual level, the case study constitutes an empirical lens through which the issues of culturally situated vs. generic place branding may be viewed and further developed. These discussions have implications within as well as beyond a food place branding context. 'Sameness' of communication efforts (Kavaratzis, 2012) and generic place brands (Therkelsen *et al.*, 2010) have been debated among scholars within recent years and reflect a recurring problem in place branding practices that hamper the development of differentiated and culturally situated place brands. To shed light on these challenges the concept of 'the conformity trap' (Antorini and Schultz, 2005) also lends itself useful, but it is equally important to identify ways out of this trap based on a participatory approach to place branding. Local stakeholders are central in defining a place and their voices in formulating the promotional stories of the place are key to a culturally situated place brand. Moreover, building relationships with relevant consumer groups may also be a way out of conformity (Louro and Cunha, 2001), though this does not necessarily ensure place specific characteristics. Second, the case of food place profiling is particularly interesting to study as local food is closely intertwined with the cultural traditions and natural conditions of a place, i.e. its terroir (Barham, 2003), and therefore offers ample opportunity for place-specific place branding efforts. However, what is particularly interesting by the case of Danish coastal places is that they are characterized by a modest culinary heritage which may make them an easy target for a copycat approach. Hence through discussions of local food and terroir (Barham, 2003; Hughes, 1995; Sims, 2010) and the related term of authenticity (Cohen, 1988; MacCannell, 1976; Wang, 1999), the discussion of place specific vs. generic place brands is nuanced even further.

On this basis, the present chapter seeks to understand contemporary place branding narrative strategies, and not least the challenges involved in communicating place-specific stories that resonate with the identity of the place. Empirical point of departure is taken in a comparative mapping of concurrent food narratives in four Danish destinations characterized by modest culinary heritage and contemporary food traditions. The study is based on both extensive and in-depth analyses of the online communication undertaken by local stakeholders along the food tourism value chain (i.e. local destination management organizations, food producers and outlets and restaurants) to find out whether place-specific food place brands are established across numerous stakeholder interests. The contribution of this chapter is hence to inform a discussion about the implications of imitative place branding and subsequently identify areas of improvement for places in general and food places in particular.

Generic vs. culturally situated place branding: the case of food places

In the fairly limited literature on food place promotion (Bessiére, 2013), one of the issues that has received attention is the usage of identical food themes across regions, which are characterized by a predominance of non-processed produce at the expense of dishes and meals as well as the cultural and social aspects of consuming food (Frochot, 2003). As similar food themes clearly point towards conformity and an undifferentiated approach to place branding narratives, it seems expedient to discuss the challenges of generic place branding in this context. Prior to that, it is, however, necessary to delve into the concept of local food, including its territorial and temporal construction, to display its culturally situated nature but also its interplay with food traditions from other locations which challenges 'the localness' of local food.

Defining local food through territory and temporality

The concepts of terroir and authenticity are deemed useful when trying to get to grips with the place-based nature of local food. Terroir denotes, on the one hand, the soil and climate's influence on food produce, and, on the other hand, customs related to the cultivation, manufacturing, preparation and cooking of food (Barham, 2003; Hughes, 1995). Hence terroir is basically to be understood as an interplay between the nature-based conditions and cultural traditions of a place that together imparts distinctive qualities on foods and meals.

In the face of the globalization of food products and health threats associated with industrialized food, many producers and consumers have become increasingly interested in food and eating experiences that encapsulate more traditional characteristics, in contrast to the more standardized offerings that have emerged during the last several decades (Miele and Murdoch, 2002; Nickelsen and Scheuer, 2009). This desire for the traditional points towards a search for some kind of authenticity, though without consumers realizing the contested nature of the 'authentic' (Barham, 2003). There is a long, and some would say never-ending, discussion on authenticity in tourism literature. What is interesting to highlight here is the distinction between the object-oriented (Cohen, 1988; MacCannell, 1976) and subject-oriented (Brown, 1996; Wang, 1999) approaches to authenticity. The nature-based conditions and cultural traditions inherent in the terroir concept point to an object-oriented understanding of authenticity in that focus is on locally sourced products, craftmanship of chefs and the culinary heritage of the place – all characteristics of the food resources of a given locale. Interestingly, the subject-oriented approach to authenticity, what Brown (1996) terms the search for the authentic Self, is quite neglected in scholarly literature, both in terms of the personal stimulations and insight which culture-specific or personally challenging food experiences may provide, and in terms of social relations to travelling companions, other tourists, tourism providers or locals that food experiences may result in (Smithers *et al*., 2008; Therkelsen and Blichfeldt, 2012). Whether, and if so how, food place profiling efforts manage to combine object- and subject-oriented authenticities will be an integral part of the analysis. Such analyses will help identify both the place-specific character of place branding narratives and the level of consumer engagement aimed for.

This discussion, furthermore, points towards territorial food practices originating from the natural and cultural characteristics of a given locale. However, as James (1996) and Warde (2009) argue food discourses also exist that cross spaces and build on a mix of local, regional and national cuisines. Cuisines such as Modern British Cooking (Warde, 2009) and New Nordic Cuisine (Bjyrkeflot *et al*., 2013) are based on locally sourced products, but inspired by cooking traditions and methods from across the world. On a spatial scale ranging from territorialized to cosmopolitan such cuisines may be placed quite centrally as the food products are local but the cooking methods are global. Globally available, familiar foods and meals that possess no territorial signifiers can, on the other hand, more clearly be defined as cosmopolitan food.

Considering food places in view of a time dimension, a predilection for past food practices is widespread in that focus is directed at the history of food products and culinary offers. However, food practices are not static but evolve over time, which brings innovation into the picture and so the time aspect arguably ranges from 'historical' to 'innovative' food. Some innovations will become socially constructed as typical of a given place, and with time they may even become mainstream and part of the food history of the place. Differentiation between food products and cooking methods may also have its merits when discussing the time aspect of local food, in that these may be classified according to their traditional or innovative characteristics respectively (Boyne and Gyimóthy, 2014).

Based on this discussion and with inspiration from Boyne and Gyimóthy (2014), a classification which differentiates between two categories of typicality arguments and two categories of temporality arguments is suggested (Figure 9.1). As such, product typicality exists characterized by narrative strategies built around food products and commodities, as opposed to culinary typicality which emphasizes meals, recipes, culinary habits and serving styles. Narrative strategies can, furthermore, be described along arguments focusing on historical vs. innovative characteristics and qualities.

This conceptual framework will be useful in the empirical analysis for characterizing the narrative strategies of the individual stakeholders and determining whether distinctive food place brands set in specific cultural contexts are established.

The conformity paradox of food place brands

References to terroir-specific and authentic place and its foods do not, however, guarantee distinctiveness if similar staging arguments are used across places. As argued by Antorini and Schultz (2005) in relation to corporate branding, similar brands are frequently the outcome of commercial drives towards differentiation. Organizations easily end up in a 'conformity trap' due to, not least, leadership monopolizing brand definition and in that process following the paths of yesteryear or, just as detrimental, copycatting so-called 'best practices'. Hence an organization may find itself trapped in conformity, reproducing own or other's previous strategies, instead of continually developing a differentiated, culturally situated brand. This is supported in a place branding context by Kavaratzis (2012) and Therkelsen *et al.* (2010), who argue that similar sets of values, catch

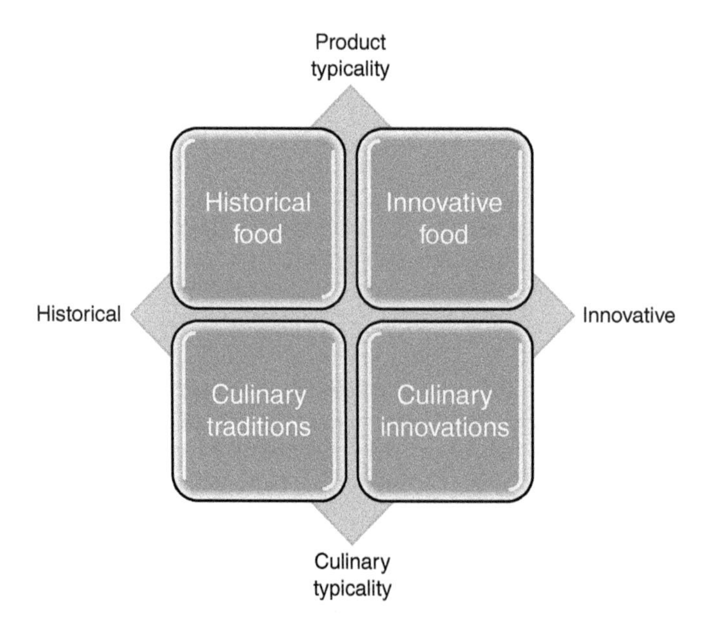

Figure 9.1 The typicality-temporality framework of food place promotion.

phrases and slogans are formulated across places that leave place brands vague and indistinct and thereby reduce place branding to a communication-promotional tool. In relation to food place branding, staging arguments often centre on: high quality, freshness, seasonality, and some degree of typicality insofar as the product (or preparation, i.e. a dish) is closely connected with its place of origin (i.e. the tourism destination). However, if these staging arguments are not imbued with substance exemplifying practices of high food quality and typicality, the differentiation potential remains low. Hence a close interrelation between symbolic representation and physical place-making (Therkelsen *et al.*, 2010) needs to exist to ensure the place brand is culturally situated, i.e. in tune with place practices.

Antorini and Schultz (2005) assert that one way out of the conformity trap is to adopt a relationship-based approach to corporate branding, in which stakeholders of the organization, including markets, together create the brand. This is also coined participatory branding (e.g. Jernsand and Kraff, 2015; Kavaratzis, 2012) and co-creation of brands (Hatch and Schultz, 2010) and rests with the idea that product as well as place brands lie outside the control of marketers but are instead co-created by the various people who relate to them. And as people typically relate to, even identify with, the places they inhabit both as private and commercial actors, an inclusive approach is a necessity for making brands place-specific. In their work on brand communication, Louro and Cunha (2001) and Dahlen *et al.* (2010) likewise argue for relationship-building, however, in their case towards potential and established market. They hold that a product-oriented company monologue is gradually being replaced by a consumer-oriented relationship-building dialogue. Customers increasingly become co-authors of brand meaning i.e. through social media dialogues and posting of consumer experiences on commercial websites. Hence engaging consumers in co-creating food experiences could be a possible way out of conformity. This may in particular be pertinent to places with limited culinary heritage to boast, as the strength inherent in the object may be restricted whereas the food relationships to be built with consumers may be plenty.

In a food place branding context, a relationship-based, participatory approach directed at the supply side is supported by Askegaard and Kjelgaard (2007), who argue for 'leveraging on and developing/constructing local cultural capital' (p. 145) when branding places on food. Leveraging on local cultural capital takes place, on the one hand, when external influences are barred off and attention is directed at cultivating for instance old crops and livestock as well as historically correct version of a given dish – what James (1996) terms a nostalgic food discourse; or on the other hand, cultural capital also comes into play when local food and dishes are combined with ingredients and preparation methods from other locales – what James (1996) terms a creolization food discourse. In both types of discourses, local culture is seen as resource that can enrich both food place narratives and development, and so local does not necessarily have to be regarded as something traditional or pure to be authentic (Askegaard and Kjelgaard, 2007). These reflections fit well into the typicality-temporality framework developed above and underscore the potential inherent in both the historical and innovative cultural capital existing in given places. But they also call for close interaction between the numerous stakeholders that are to transform the cultural capital into concrete food and meal offers if a distinct and integrated food place brand is to be established. Furthermore, Askegaard and Kjelgaard are critical towards a destination management organization that monopolizes brand definition, which has been the path that many tourism places have followed for years on end.

All in all, the theoretical discussion has proposed a conceptual model useful for understanding food place narratives based on a combination of typicality (food products and meals) and temporality (historical and innovative). Critical consideration has, furthermore, been given to the conformity characterizing place branding efforts, and arguments are put forward for a participatory, relationship-based approach that may unlock this conformity trap both in terms of forming close ties with consumers and producers of local food and meals.

Methodology and empirical data

Before offering details on the specific empirical studies undertaken, a profile of Danish culinary heritage is sketched out. This should help contextualize the empirical analyses and thereby explain the characteristics identified.

Opposed to most Mediterranean destinations, the Nordic region, and not least Denmark, features significantly fewer authenticity markers through the EU geographical indications (PDO, PGI) and traditional specialities designations (European Commission, 2012). Whereas part of the explanation for these North–South differences may be found in different practices and attitudes towards such international standards, it may also reflect different concerns with culinary heritage. Hence it has been argued that due to a long-standing international food export success, Danish cuisine has, to a large degree, been characterized by left-overs from export products (Hjalager and Corigliano, 2000). Being tuned into global market demands, rather than cultivating a unique food culture attractive to the local population and visitors to the country, seems to have been the guiding principles during most of the twentieth century. These principles have, however, been challenged by a rising opposition towards industrialized and globalized food (Miele and Murdoch, 2002; Nickelsen and Scheuer, 2009), and with inspiration from the slow food movement in Italy, the New Nordic Cuisine movement has recently left a mark on Danish cuisine (Bjyrkeflot *et al.*, 2013). Hence local food with an innovative twist has become fashionable, primarily in the capital and other major cities. The question is whether rural Denmark has also realized the market potential of this and is capable of creating culturally situated as opposed to generic place brands on this basis.

Four Danish coastal destinations were chosen as the objects of analysis: Fyn, Odsherred, Vadehavet and Djursland. These destinations are characterized by a number of common traits: like other Danish coastal destinations their main attraction is the sea, sandy beaches and the surrounding nature; they mainly attract self-catering tourists from the domestic and neighbouring markets; and their business structure is characterized by a number of small tourism actors for which reason the public destination management organization (DMO) plays a central role in the tourism development, including branding of the destinations.

Textual as well as visual data was collected from forty websites, ten from each destination, in the summer/ early autumn of 2014 covering in broad terms the food tourism value chains of these places (local DMOs, food producers and outlets, and restaurants). In their capacity as umbrella organization for the local tourism trade, DMOs play a particular role in profiling Danish coastal destinations and they are therefore in a unique position to establish food and culinary offers as a central part of the destination's brand. For this reason, the data collection took its point of departure in the website-based promotion of the DMOs, and the additional websites analysed are all linked up with these DMO websites. Only the parts of the DMO websites that deal with local food and culinary offers and only individual stakeholders promoting themselves on local food and dishes were analysed.

Due to the central position of the DMOs, both a content analysis and a narrative analysis were carried out of their websites. The former was carried out to identify the salience of local food, in terms of allocated space and the main themes used, the latter to go into details with the promotional arguments employed. The websites from individual stakeholders were analysed solely through qualitative analysis. It is the Danish language versions of the websites that have been analysed. Most websites also have foreign language versions, however, as these are typically reduced versions of the Danish one, the most detailed food narratives are available via the Danish version. In the analysis, all quotes from the websites are translated into English by the author.

Analysis: food narrative strategies at Danish coastal destinations

An initial quantitative content analysis indicates that each of the selected coastal DMOs emphasizes food products that are typical to these respective areas by means of terroir-specific narratives. The 'Taste of …' section of the DMO websites introduces readers to local specialities, although as Figure 9.2 illustrates one destination (Djursland) lists significantly less culinary experiences and local delicacies than the three other destinations (eighteen as opposed to fifty-plus items).

Taking a closer look of the 189 listed items, words referring to generic foods (asparagus, honey, vegetables, apples, meat, etc.) dominate and a limited number of processed products and dishes are mentioned. Figure 9.2 also shows that only one destination (Vadehavet) seems to position itself along its culinary traditions as well as its food products. In other words, only one out of four DMOs broadly supports the business portfolios of the individual tourism and food actors in whose interest they work. This is also critical in view of the fact that coastal tourists demand both availability of food items for self-catering and restaurant meals (Therkelsen, 2015).

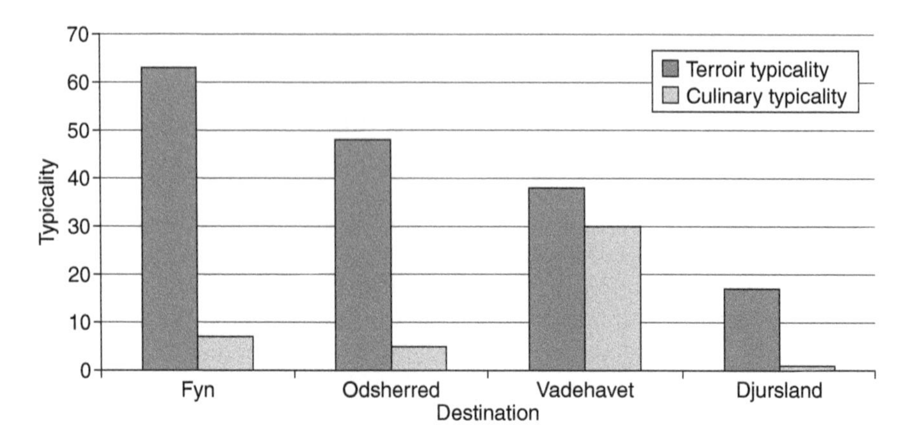

Figure 9.2 Product and culinary typicality across the four destinations.

Typicality and temporality across promotional efforts

Using Boyne and Gyimóthy's (2014) model as a structuring framework, the subsequent analysis will take its point of departure in Figure 9.3 and delve into the typicalities and temporalities present at the analysed websites. The individual stakeholders are placed within the matrix square that predominantly characterizes the promotional narratives that they employ, however, arrows indicate a slide towards other narratives where relevant.

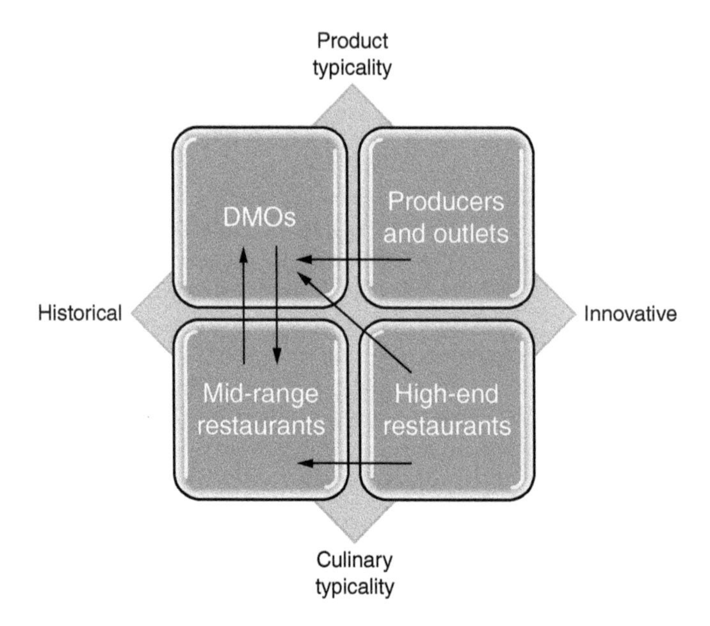

Figure 9.3 Food place promotion along the destination value chain.

In line with the content analysis, *the DMO stakeholder category* is placed predominantly in the product typicality part of the matrix as generic produce and food products are the promotional focus of three out of four DMOs. This confirms Frochot's (2003) point that tourist destinations give scant attention to gastronomy. Irrespective of whether one or both types of typicalities are used, the main temporality employed by DMOs is historical. This appears for instance in these two extracts:

> Temptations from Denmark's pantry. Enjoy a broad culinary selection of high quality and produced in an area with a unique history. Containment of the fjords in the last part of the 1800s made possible present-day cultivation of vegetables at a previous seabed.
>
> (www.visitodsherred.dk)

> The eel roll is one of the area's really old dishes. When eels are skinned and boned, they are filled with chopped onion, salt and pepper. Next, rolled from the tail and upwards, they are cooked. The roll is served chilled, sliced and garnished with potatoes in white sauce. The eels served in Venø Inn can make the angels sing.
>
> (www.sydvestjylland.com)

References to, in these cases, the geological and culinary history of the places are supplemented by widespread references to dedicated local producers, which bring forward associations of bygone times characterized by a slower pace and smaller scale. This is clearly underscored by the words of one of the DMOs: 'You can taste that it is people, not machines, who stand behind the production' (www.visitsvendborg.dk).

The discourses of *the food producers* are mainly directed towards product typicality as well, which is not surprising as these actors are specialized in certain types of produce or manufactured products. In contrast to the DMOs, the individual producers are more oriented towards innovative aspects of food products, in that several of them use untraditional ingredients in their products and their production methods are inspired from abroad. An example of this is an ice cream producer that portrays innovative production methods and ingredient combinations: 'Our ice cream differs from other ice creams by being made from birch juice which has reduced the sugar content by 50% … we use sugar tongs as a spice to give the ice cream a taste of umami' (www.isfraskaroe.dk/Omos/Video). However, this producer, along with others, also brings up associations of a pre-modern society when they describe their personal involvement in and closeness to their products. A fruit aquavit producer for instance uses this phrase: 'it is craftmanship from when we receive the fruit – and cut away possible bad parts with a pocket knife – until it is fermented into wine, burnt, stored, bottled and ready to drink' (www.aquavitaesydfyn.dk). The terms 'aquavit' and 'craftmanship' as well as the image conjured up of the producer with his pocket knife sorting the fruit anchor the narrative in a historical temporality which is parallel to the discourse utilized on the DMO websites. Several producers also stress their belonging to the place where they are situated, including the importance of contributing to the local economy, which underscores the pre-modern image conjured up, just as descriptions of food production as a family project adds to this impression, as illustrated below:

> Vaeverslund is a family business where Peter takes care of the daily operation and management. Pia works away from the nursery at the moment but takes care of most of the paper work. In addition we have 4-year-old Viktor and 11-year-old Anna. The family also consists of three dogs, Lunde, Luna and Lilli and four ponies, Laban, Paddington, Birk and Mattis.
>
> (www.vaeverslund.dk)

Being in the business of preparing meals, *restaurants* naturally stress culinary typicality. A difference is, however, detectable between mid-range and high-end restaurants in that the former lean mainly towards a historical temporality whereas the latter stress innovative aspects of their offers. For instance, one mid-range restaurant describes its offers as: 'food as it used to be' and 'food you can relate to and plenty of it' (www.restaurantsvendborgsund.dk) – statements that are supported by a menu dominated by classical Danish dishes. In other words, an explicit attempt to differentiate itself from gastronomic influence from abroad, including the dish sizes of nouvelle cuisine. High-end restaurants, on the other hand, have a tendency of using local produce in innovative ways much along the lines of the New Nordic Cooking (Bjyrkeflot *et al.*, 2013). One such restaurant describes itself as 'a unique place of world class standards, but in the true fashion of West Jutland'[1] (hennekirkebykro.dk). Combinations of local food with imported foods underscores its innovative approach which is reflected in the menu, for instance: 'Spicy Henne sausage, pimento and oregano'[2] and 'Wadden Sea oysters, horseradish, oyster leaves, green chili and coriander' (hennekirkebykro.dk). Moreover, place branded food products (Henne sausage and Wadden Sea oysters) and not only generic produce are here brought to the fore, which further situates the localness of the restaurant. This is not an often-used strategy by other stakeholders than the individual food producers in relation to their own products.

As Figure 9.3 and the discussion above shows, the discourses of the actors of the food value chain are to a significant degree overlapping in that all of the actors refer to product typicality and the historical roots of their food offers. There are, however, also salient differences, some of which rest with the different businesses the actors represent (food producers naturally focus on produce and food products; restaurants on culinary offers). The most critical difference in discourses relates to the DMOs, in that they, as umbrella organizations, are to represent the interests of all food actors in the value chain and are those that are the drivers of a common food place branding effort. They are, however, focused on the terroir typicality of food products with only one DMO giving attention to culinary traditions. This means that the interests of restaurants are poorly supported. Moreover, the food discourses of the DMOs are mainly centred on historical references, which neglect the innovative characteristics of many of the actors that they represent. Along the lines of Askegaard and Kjelgaard (2007) it is possible to argue that the stakeholders represent the various facets of the cultural capital of the place (i.e. historical, innovative, culinary and product typicalities), which are only partly considered by the umbrella organization and so the food place branding efforts appear uncoordinated and thereby indistinct. Thus, stakeholder inclusion in formulating the overall brand narrative is minimal.

Struggling with conformity and ways out

Having a closer look at how product and culinary typicality is portrayed in the food narratives, it appears that the various stakeholders struggle to imbue these with substance. In line with Sims' (2010) research, an ambiguous use of geographical ear-markers characterizes the promotional efforts, in that the country, region, town or village is referred to quite interchangeably as 'the local place' from where food and meals originate. Those food producers and restaurants that name their company, restaurant, product series or dishes after the local town or island, where they are situated, stand out as more consistent in their reference to a given locale than other actors. Hence in terms of geographical scale, local food is difficult to define and as no consensus exists across stakeholder groups on what place is to be promoted on food, the place brand becomes ambiguous.

Apart from geographical signifiers, the rhetoric is built on a number of similar phrases at all four destinations, such as: 'locally grown', 'high quality', 'seasonal produce', 'fresh fish', 'tasty vegetables', 'delicious apples', 'personal engagement and skills of producers'. On the one hand, this creates a common line in the promotional discourse across the destination's food value chain, which was lamented by Boyne and Hall (2004) to be non-existent in their UK-based study. On the other hand, these phrases hold very little differentiation potential as they both refer to generic produce and are widely used words within food-oriented place promotion (Frochot, 2003; Warde, 2009). By using such staging arguments, the promotional effort becomes locked in a conformity trap (Antorini and Schultz, 2005) which offers very little substance to local food and does not leverage on the diverse cultural capital of the given place (Askegaard and Kjelgaard, 2007). Narrative exceptions exist that manage to attach more specific terroir markers to food products across the food actors involved. In the case of Odsherred, the contained fjord and the mild nature is referred to by several stakeholders to have a special influence on the taste of local food, for instance: 'The old fjord bed contains a mixture of sand and mineral-based clay that provides taste for carrots, onions, potatoes and much else' (www.visitodsherred.dk). And in the case of Vadehavet several actors refer to the Wadden Sea and the rough nature as crucial for the taste experience, as in this example:

> The lambs at the dikes grow at a different speed because they have to fight both for their food and to keep warm. Their rough lives result in good taste when they are served as a delicacy at the destination's restaurants.
>
> (sydvestjylland.com)

The terroir concept is mainly interpreted as nature-based conditions by the DMOs, to which are added some cultural traditions and innovations by the food producers and restaurants in their description of the cultivation, manufacturing and cooking of food products. Hence the public destination management seeks to leverage on the existing nature-based conditions of the place whereas the private stakeholders display both a broader understanding of terroir and an approach to cultural capital as something that can be constructed through innovative processes. This tallies with the point made by Sundbo (2013) that innovation mainly happens among chefs and food producers, and this clearly spills over into their communicative efforts as well. Hence a complexity of food discourses (James, 1996) is occasionally acknowledged by private stakeholders. This may prove to be one possible way out of the conformity trap as it constitutes a more nuanced reflection of the cultural capital of a place and may appeal to a broader range of consumer groups. Commitment across stakeholder groups to such a communicative strategy is, however, necessary for this to become a distinctive feature of the place brand.

It is also, however, possible to look beyond the cultural capital of places in search of distinctive place branding features. As argued in the theoretical section, the object-oriented approach to place-based authenticity (Cohen, 1988; MacCannell, 1976) does not provide the only basis for place differentiation and distinctiveness, and particularly for localities that are in a process of (re)inventing their culinary identity, the potential inherent in a more subject-oriented approach to authenticity (Brown, 1996; Wang, 1999), i.e. placing the consumer experience at the centre, may be worth considering. The promotional efforts across the four destinations, however, have a clear product focus and an absence of people buying, selling and sharing foods and meals. Hence the places are staged as quite 'empty meeting grounds', overlooking the central social aspects of tourism in general and food tourism in particular (Smithers *et al*., 2008; Therkelsen and Blichfeldt, 2012). Only a few examples of storytelling that establish a sense of place are detectable which would likewise have supported consumer involvement. One example being a West Coast restaurant that manages to convey the destination's rough nature, the robustness of its crops and local people through this engaging food narrative:

> Let me start by making one thing clear: There are many things that can't grow out here. Easy solutions are just one of them. Because here you face the sea, go against the wind and shield the crops. When you finally gain a foothold, and that goes for people as well as crops, then you stick to it. Everything also grows a little slower. In exchange the return is less but the taste is more.
>
> (www.cafestranden.dk)

A connection between the characteristics of nature, the taste of local produce and the mentality of the people is here created through an informal tone and accompanied by a picture of a weather-beaten person, who comes across as the storyteller. Such examples are, however, few and far between. Finally, there are barely any possibilities for co-producing the food experience via social media feedback options or food-related activities (apart from eating) at the destinations. All in all, company monologue rather than a relationship-building dialogue (Dahlen *et al.*, 2010; Louro and Cunha, 2001) mainly characterizes the food discourses of the coastal destinations and hence a management-driven rather than a participatory approach to place branding appears to be the strategy in use. This clearly neglects a current trend of consumer-involvement and co-production that sweeps marketing efforts these years, and these food places may be missing out on an important opportunity to generate satisfied and possibly loyal customers.

Conclusion

The conceptual model combining food product and culinary typicality with historical and innovative temporality has demonstrated its usefulness in deciphering food place branding narratives. By means of a specific case study, it has identified overlapping food narratives characterized by product typicality and historical references employed by various stakeholders along the food value chain. Equally interesting, the model has helped identify significant differences in that public actors restrict themselves to historical, product-oriented food narratives, whereas private actors employ a broader range of food narratives including culinary typicalities and innovative solutions. Being responsible for the overall tourism destination branding, the public actors seem to approach this task in a non-inclusive manner, in that the business portfolios of some the stakeholders, in whose interest they work, are not supported. Lack of stakeholder inclusion and participation may result in a brand not firmly situated in the local context and may make the external food-place profiling generic and thereby indistinct. Moreover, food narratives that stage the interplay between food and place as something continually constructed and not only anchored in history may be a viable strategy for food places in general, and perhaps specifically for places with a limited culinary heritage. Likewise giving priority to the consumer experience may lend itself useful for such places as it invites the potential tourist to become a co-producer of the food-place experience. For instance, culturally situated storytelling efforts may both engage the consumer and shun the comformity trap of place branding.

All in all, this chapter has aimed at contributing to the place branding literature by critically discussing generic place branding efforts and has highlighted the qualities inherent in culturally situated efforts, characterized by participation and relationship-building with both producers and guests. These points are not restricted to a food-place branding context but apply for place branding in general. Moreover, the conceptual model differentiating between different kinds of territorial materialities and temporalities may be translated into other place branding contexts and help decipher the various place narratives employed here as well as their possible interconnectedness. This is one way of determining whether place branding efforts are built on inclusiveness and co-participation among stakeholders.

Acknowledgements

The study builds on data from the project 'Food as experience strategy for Danish coastal destinations' sponsored by Knowledge Center for Coastal Tourism, Denmark. Thanks are also extended to Szilvia Gyimóthy for valuable input for this chapter.

Notes

1 West Jutland is the name of the region where the restaurant is based.
2 Henne is the name of the village where the restaurant is based.

References

Antorini, Y. M. and Schultz, M. (2005) 'Corporate branding and the "Conformity Trap" ', in Schultz, M., Antorini, Y. M. and Csaba, F. F. (eds.) *Corporate Branding*. Copenhagen: Copenhagen Business School Press, pp. 57–76.

Askegaard, S. and Kjeldgaard, D. (2007) 'Here, there and everywhere: Place branding and gastronomical globalization in a macromarketing perspective'. *Journal of Macromarketing*, 27(2), pp. 138–147.

Barham, E. (2003) 'Translating terroir: The global challenge of French AOC labeling'. *Journal of Rural Studies*, 19, pp. 127–138.

Bessière, J. (2013) ' "Heritagisation", a challenge for tourism promotion and regional development: an example of food heritage'. *Journal of Heritage Tourism*, 8, pp. 275–291.

Bjyrkeflot, H., Pedersen, J. S., and Svejenova, S. (2013) 'From label to practice: The process of creating New Nordic Cuisine'. *Journal of Culinary Science and Technology*, 11, pp. 36–55.

Boyne, S., and Hall, D. (2004) 'Place promotion through food and tourism: Rural branding and the role of websites'. *Place Branding and Public Diplomacy*, 1(1), pp. 80–92.

Boyne, S. and Gyimóthy, S. (2014) 'Tradition, innovation and authenticity: Narrative hybridity in Danish regional food promotion'. Working paper presented at the ATLAS Expert Meeting on Regional Gastronomy: Between tradition and innovation, Ponte de Lima, Portugal, 29–31 May 2014.

Brown, D. (1996) 'Genuine fakes', in Selwyn T. (ed.), *The Tourist Image. Myths and Myth Making in Tourism*. Chichester: John Wiley & Sons.

Cohen, E. (1988) 'Authenticity and commoditization in tourism', *Annals of Tourism Research*, 15(3), pp. 371–386.

Dahlen, M., Lange, F. and Smith, T. (2010) *Marketing Communication. A Brand Narrative Approach*. Chichester: John Wiley.

European Commission (2012) Regulation (EU) No 1151/2012 of the European Parliament and of the Council of on quality schemes for agricultural products and foodstuffs. *Official Journal of the European Union*, L 343/1.

Frochot, I. (2003) 'An analysis of regional positioning and its associated food images in French tourism regional brochures'. *Journal of Travel and Tourism Marketing*, 14(3–4), pp. 77–96.

Hatch, M. J. and Schultz, M. (2010) 'Toward a theory of brand co-creation with implications for brand governance'. *Journal of Brand Management*, 17(8), pp. 590–604.

Hjalager, A. M. and Corigliano, M. A. (2000) 'Food for tourists – determinants of an image'. *International Journal of Tourism Research*, 2, pp. 281–293.

Hughes, G. (1995) 'Authenticity in tourism'. *Annals of Tourism Research*, 22(4), pp. 781–803.

James, A. (1996) 'Cooking the books: Global or local identities in contemporary British food cultures', in Howes, D. (ed.). *Cross-cultural Consumption: Global Markets, Local Realities*. London: Routledge, pp. 77–92.

Jernsand, E. M. and Kraff, H. (2015) 'Participatory place branding through design. The case of Dunga beach in Kinsumu, Kenya'. *Place Branding and Public Diplomacy*, 11(3), pp. 226–242.

Kavaratzis, M. (2012) 'From "necessary evil" to necessity: Stakeholders involvement in place branding'. *Journal of Place Management and Development*, 5(1), pp. 7–19.

Louro, M. J., and Cunha, P. V. (2001) 'Brand management paradigms'. *Journal of Marketing Management*, 17, pp. 849–875.

MacCannell, D. (1976) *The Tourist. A New Theory of the Leisure Class*. Schocken Books.

Miele, M. and Murdoch, J. (2002) 'The Practical Aesthetics of Traditional Cuisines: Slow Food in Tuscany'. *Sociologia Ruralis*, 42(4), pp. 312–328.

Nickelsen, N. C. and Scheuer, J. D. (2009) 'Tilblivelsen af det nye nordiske køkken – Claus Meyer som institutionel entreprenør'. *Psyke and Logos*, 30, pp. 695–713.

Sims, R. (2010) 'Putting place on the menu: The negotiation of locality in UK food tourism, from production to consumption'. *Journal of Rural Studies*, 26(2), pp. 105–115.

Smithers, J., Lamarche, J. and Joseph, A. E. (2008) 'Unpacking the terms of engagement with local food at the Farmers' Market: Insights from Ontario'. *Journal of Rural Studies*, 24, pp. 337–350.

Sundbo, D. I. C. (2013) 'Local food: The social construction of a concept'. *Acta Agriculturae Scandinavica*, Section B, 63, supplement 1, pp. 66–77.

Therkelsen, A. (2015) 'Catering for yourself. Food experiences of self-catering tourists'. *Tourist Studies*, 15(3), pp. 316–333.

Therkelsen, A. and Blichfeldt, B. S. (2012) 'Understanding Tourists' Complex Food Relations', in Mair, M. and Wagner, D. (eds). *Culinary Tourism: Products, Regions, Tourists, Philosophy*. Wien: Springer, pp. 119–128.

Therkelsen, A., Halkier, H. and Jensen, O. B. (2010) 'Branding Aalborg. Building Community or Selling Place?', in Ashworth, G. J. and Kavaratzis, M. (eds.), *Towards Effective Place Brand Management: Branding European Cities and Regions*. Cheltenham, UK and Northampton, MA, US: Edward Elgar.

Wang, N. (1999) 'Rethinking Authenticity in Tourism Experience'. *Annals of Tourism Research*, 26(2), pp. 349–370.

Warde, A. (2009) 'Imagining British cuisine. Representations of culinary identity in the *Good Food Guide*, 1951–2007'. *Food, Culture and Society*, 12(2), pp. 151–171.

10 Stockholm

The narcissistic capital of Sweden

Johan Gromark

Introduction

Since 2005, Stockholm, the capital of Sweden, has tried to convince the world that Stockholm is the capital of Scandinavia by launching the brand represented by a logotype containing the text 'Stockholm – The Capital of Scandinavia' and a symbol in the form of a crown which is placed above the text. For people living in Scandinavia, the problem is quite obvious – there is no capital of Scandinavia. Therefore, it may come as no surprise that representatives of the other two Scandinavian countries, Norway and Denmark, have protested against this new soft form of trademarked imperialism exhibited by the Swedish capital in its branding efforts (Ågren, 2013). Despite massive and loud criticism from both outside and inside of Stockholm, the representatives of the place branding network (PBN) do not listen to the criticism or simply, based on questionable premises, reject it. This case study is an attempt to understand the antagonistic and aggressive form of brand orientation displayed by the PBN. The case presented here illustrates a brand orientation that may stimulate arrogance, inhibit learning and impair relationships. This brand orientation may effectively decouple external perspectives and input, and instead turn into some form of organizational narcissism. The hallmark of a narcissistic organization is an ego-fixation and, consequently, a lack of interest in others. This may in the pathological form result in a lack of empathy and a strong belief in the entitlement of exploiting and using others for the organization's own gains (Brown, 1997). This is not desirable in any organization, but even more problematic in place branding organizations. The public and political nature of place branding require an inclusive approach in order to engage, communicate and build relationships with a wide range of stakeholders (Kavaratzis, 2012). The monological approach to communication displayed by narcissistic organizations represents the opposite of the capability of engaging in dialogues or 'multilogues' suggested by Aitken and Campelo (2011) as an essential management skill in place branding processes. The ambition in this case study is therefore to contribute to a more balanced form of brand orientation theory, which should be of special interest in a place branding context. There are of course other contexts where this approach may also prove useful.

Brand orientation

The early 1990s saw the beginning of a massive interest in brands and brand management. The brand was no longer perceived as a peripheral and tactical sales tool. This era also marked a shift in interest from brand image to brand identity. The central role of brand identity is evident in Urde's (1999, p. 188) frequently quoted the definition of brand orientation: 'an approach in which the processes of the organization revolve around the creation, development and protection of brand identity in an ongoing interaction with target customers with the aim of achieving lasting competitive advantages in the form of brands'. This definition highlights the fact that brand identity is the key principle and resource upon which the organization builds all of its activities.

Brand orientation as an alternative to market orientation

Throughout the years, a great deal of effort has been spent on trying to position brand orientation against market orientation, which is the dominating paradigm and strategic orientation; not only in marketing, but in business administration as a whole. According to Urde (1999), the crucial difference between the two concepts is that market orientation represents an approach to brands as an unconditional response to customer needs. With regard to brand orientation, on the other hand, the long-term vision, the core values and the strategic intent of the brand create an integrity of the brand lacking in market orientation. In Urde's (1999) conceptualization, the choice between brand orientation and market orientation is ultimately an inevitable choice between letting either identity *or* image be the guiding principle for the organization. Another way of approaching brand orientation is to look at it as an evolution from market orientation (Baumgarth *et al.*, 2010). Within the evolutionary approach, the brand is seen as the interface between the internal and the external (Kornberger, 2010; Gromark and Melin, 2013).

Two different forms of brand orientation

Louro and Cunha (2001) delineate two different forms of brand orientation: a *projective* and a *relational* brand orientation. The fundamental dimension separating the two orientations is customer centrality. In the projective version of brand orientation, customer centrality is low and based on a unilateral approach with regard to customers. This means that the relationship is based on a transmission of value from the company to passive customers. In the relational form of brand orientation, on the other hand, the approach is multi-lateral, where the customer plays a central role as a co-creator of value. The difference between a projective and relational approach to branding is a central issue in recent place branding literature (see Kavaratzis, 2012; Aitken and Campelo, 2011), as well as in general brand management literature (see Antorini and Schultz, 2005). However, the benefits of the relational approach and the risks of the projective approach have largely gone unnoticed in the brand orientation literature. Hatch and Schultz (2002) do not discuss brand orientation per se, but create a framework for corporate branding that captures organizational dysfunctionalities regarding extensive focus on customers or on the organization. In the framework of Hatch and Schultz, there is no need to choose between image and identity, as they inform each other. Both concepts become meaningless if one of them is missing. In fact, there is a risk that organizational dysfunctionalities develop when there is not sufficient interaction between image, identity and culture. Kavaratzis and Hatch (2013, p. 82), who further develop this framework in a place branding setting, stress that 'place branding is best understood as dialogue, debate, and contestation'. When the organization is not attentive to, or able to engage in, such activities, there is fertile ground for organizational narcissism (Hatch and Schultz, 2002). By adopting a corporate brand perspective on the projective and relational brand orientation developed by Louro and Cunha (2001), and by including the organizational dysfunctionalities presented by Hatch and Schultz (2002), it is possible to discuss three different strategic orientations. Two of these represent a risk of imbalances in the form of either narcissism (projective brand orientation) or hyper-adaptation (market orientation). In the third orientation, there is a balance between internal and external perspectives (relational brand orientation). Table 10.1 below is a framework for further discussions on the concept of brand orientation.

The dialogical nature of relational brand orientation highlights the importance of having an inclusive approach with regard to the branding process. The brand is co-created by both internal and external stakeholders. In fact, the brand is seen as an interface for interaction. This represents obvious democratic and ethical benefits in a place branding setting, but also a strategic value for the place, as the inclusive approach may facilitate learning and change (Hatch and Schultz, 2002). The organizational narcissism that may develop within the projective brand orientation is discussed further below.

Organizational narcissism

Narcissism is one of the most important concepts in psychoanalysis. The concept was originally used for diagnosing individuals, but has also been utilized in organizational studies in order to analyse and discuss organizational needs for regulating self-esteem (Brown, 1997). Duchon and Burns (2008) argue that every organization is narcissistic to some extent, but that extreme narcissism may be devastating, as the pre-occupation with the organization itself will ultimately lead to stakeholders abandoning it in search of more appealing alternatives. Brown and Starkey (2000) suggest that a psychodynamic explanation of why previously successful organizations fail to adapt to changing environments may be found in narcissism. Brown and Starkey highlight that if the organization's identity is too narrow, rigid and based on past performances, there is a risk of developing an omnipotent and grandiose identity, which will effectively impede organizational learning. However, apart from inhibiting learning, Duchon and Drake (2009) argue that organizational narcissism also leads to

Table 10.1 Strategic orientations

	Market orientation	*Projective brand orientation*	*Relational brand orientation*
Metaphor (Louro and Cunha, 2001)	Listening – What do *they* need?	Monologue – This is *me*!	Dialogue – How about *you* and *me*?
The role of the brand (Urde, 1999; Gromark and Melin, 2011; Kornberger, 2010)	The brand as an unconditional response to customer needs	The brand as a strategic resource and an expression of a strategic intent	The brand as an interface for interaction
Managerial focus (Urde, 1999; Gromark and Melin, 2011; 2013)	Customer needs and wants (image)	Identity (image)	Identity, image and relationships
Identity formation (Urde, 1999; Antorini and Schultz, 2005)	Tactical and short-term. Based on customer needs and wants	Visionary, long-term and constructed by management	Evolving, fluid and negotiable by stakeholders
Corporate brand 'ownership' (Urde, 1999; Antorini and Schultz, 2005)	The corporate brand is owned by the customer	The corporate brand is owned by the organization and management	Joint ownership. The corporate brand is seen as an interactive co-creation process
Risk of organizational dysfunctionality (Hatch and Schultz, 2002; Kavaratzis and Hatch, 2013)	Imbalance: Hyper-adaptation	Imbalance: narcissism	Balance: neither internal nor external perspectives dominate

unethical behaviour, since the motive to protect and enhance the organization's identity is stronger than the motive to behave virtuously. These behaviours will become institutionalized in the organization and become a part of its identity. This is emphasized by Brown (1997), who argues that organizational members actively deny, conceal and omit information in order to maintain the organization's reputation when this is threatened by a controversy. These kinds of organizational behaviours are therefore similar to how individuals act in order to preserve their own identity. Morgan (2006) presents a similar notion when it comes to egocentric organizations, which he argues:

> have a rather fixed notion of who they are or what they can be and are determined to impose or sustain that identity at all cost. This leads them to overemphasize the importance of themselves while underplaying the significance of the wider system of relations in which they exist.
>
> (p. 248)

The diagnosis of organizational narcissism

Based on the seminal article by Brown (1997), Duchon and Burns (2008) have developed a diagnostic framework, which is utilized in this study. These traits are *self-aggrandizement*, which captures the 'tendency to overestimate merits and accomplishments: overestimate one's importance, power, reputation' (p. 356), followed by *entitlement*, which describes a 'sense of having the right to use/exploit situations/people' (p. 357). *Denial*, finally, describes the 'inability or refusal to acknowledge problems' (p. 357). In addition to these three traits, a fourth trait from the literature on organizational narcissism is also added to the framework. This is *rationalization* (Brown and Starkey, 2000, p. 106), which represents 'an attempt of development of self-deceiving explanations to justify unacceptable behaviours and feelings'.

Methodological considerations

The primary aim of this study is to illuminate the risk of organizational narcissism that comes with a projective form of brand orientation in a place branding setting. The research strategy that has been chosen is the case study, as it is well-suited for advancing theory by utilizing context dependent knowledge (Flyvbjerg, 2006). Studies on organizational narcissism, just like psychoanalytical work, are normally based on single cases.

The empirical material collected for this case ranges over the whole ten-year period during which the place brand Stockholm – The Capital of Scandinavia (SCS) has been in active use. First, a close, in-depth qualitative content analysis was carried out on a motion by an opposition politician in the city of Stockholm, where he asks the city council to remove the SCS brand and replace it with a brand that corresponds better to reality. The document also contains the appurtenant replies from the mayor of Stockholm and different organizations in the PBN. Using this data enables us to get a unique understanding of how organizational narcissism is evident even in the official documents and rhetoric produced by agencies in this PBN. In the motion, the very existence of the brand is questioned and the rhetoric justifying the use of the brand will therefore be clarified. Second, official statements from websites and social media platforms of the numerous actors in the place brand network were also analysed. Third, articles in Scandinavian newspapers as well as social media platforms and blogs were also a rich source for non-official voices and interpretations of the SCS brand and provided additional perspectives in the analysis. Fourth, at this stage a couple of relevant academic articles, dissertations and books discussing the SCS brand have been published, and these sources have also been useful for the interpretation of this case. The iterative analysis has been characterized by using different data sources, where the researcher alters between a close and more distant stance examining different voices and texts, including the researcher's own, where there is interplay between data and theory. This approach provides opportunities for methodical and data triangulation, where multiple perspectives facilitate validation of the research (Denzin, 1978).

The brand orientation of the capital of Sweden

The Scandinavian nations have been characterized by peaceful relations for the last 200 years. However, during much of the modern era between the 1500s and the 1800s, war, rather than peace, was the norm between the Scandinavian nations. The period of war ended in 1814 when Sweden forced Norway into a union. This union lasted until 1905, and the centennial anniversary of the dissolution of the union was celebrated on a grand scale in Norway in 2005. The fact that this celebration coincided with the launch of the SCS brand makes it somewhat tragicomic (Ohlin, 2007). The former days of militaristic imperialism are now replaced by a trademarked imperialism, where the competition over physical space has changed into a communication-led battle for 'mind space'. However, prior to SCS, the place marketing tradition of the Scandinavian countries has been characterized by cooperation rather than competition. For many years, the Scandinavian countries carried out joint marketing efforts, for instance in the United States, via the Scandinavian Tourist Board. The launch of the SCS brand has severely damaged this cooperation and created tension between the Scandinavian countries (Ågren, 2013; Lucarelli and Hallin, 2015).

The genesis of the SCS brand

The idea behind the brand came from an ad campaign for Stockholm Arlanda Airport that used the text 'Stockholm, the capital of Scandinavia' (Lucarelli and Hallin, 2015). In 2003, this campaign attracted interest in the Stockholm City Hall, which at the time felt that the city needed a strong brand to be internationally competitive. They hired the same marketing consultant who developed the ad campaign, and after a two-year-long strategy project, the brand was launched (Stockholm Business Region, 2016). The logotype is owned by the Stockholm Business Region (SBR), which is a company owned entirely by the municipality of Stockholm. The logotype was registered as a trademark in 2006. All the way from the start, the intention was that the brand could be used by different actors for targeting tourists or investors. For this purpose, the Stockholm Business Alliance (SBA) was formed in 2006. Already a year after it was launched, forty-three municipalities had joined the alliance. Every municipality belonging to the SBA must pay 4 SEK[1] per inhabitant annually (Lucarelli and Hallin, 2015). This gives the municipality the right to use the SCS brand in its own marketing and participate in the network.

SCS and identity work on the regional level

SBA must be discussed in relation to the organization called Mälardalsrådet; something that highlights the role of the SCS brand in a classic tug of war between centre and periphery, but also between two political levels, the local and the regional. Mälardalsrådet is a membership-based organization founded in 1992, for five county councils and fifty-seven municipalities in the Stockholm

Metropolitan Area, focusing on regional development. An important factor when it comes to understanding the success of the SCS brand is that the Swedish government system is characterized by a strong central and local government, with a weak regional level, often described as the 'hourglass-model'. Since the late 1980s, EU policy has clearly favoured the development of strong regions. All Swedish regions have been affected by this policy and have more or less been pushed into developing a competitive and attractive regional identity. In some of the newly formed and informal regions, such as the Stockholm-Mälarregion, there are no cultural or historical roots to use as a starting point. Westholm (2008) who has interviewed officials in the region, concludes that there is a strong belief among these individuals that the success of the region relies heavily on *the ability to describe it as a region.* As pointed out in the literature on organizational narcissism, these types of processes can induce anxiety, which in connection to the organizational members' collective strive for self-esteem and legitimacy may lead to pathological narcissism (Brown, 1997). An illustration of how the SCS brand may be seen in relation to existential anxiety comes from a text on Mälardalsrådet's website: 'We still lack a comprehensive story about how we have become the Capital of Scandinavia. Until now. We are absolutely convinced that we have now found the common history of our region' (Mälardalsrådet, 2008 cited in Westholm, 2008, p. 123, own translation). SCS has led to all ambitions to market the Mälarregionen or Stockholm-Mälarregionen as the brand of the region having vanished. In fact, Mälardalsrådet today describes itself as a part of Stockholm – The Capital of Scandinavia.

The expansion of the SCS-brand

The SBA network has experienced a steady growth during its ten years of operations. In 2016, there are fifty-three municipalities belonging to the network. The SCS brand fills an important gap not only in the regional but also in the local identity work. It is easy to see how the smaller municipalities around Stockholm prefer to co-brand themselves with the metropolitan city of Stockholm rather than with the unknown and vague brand of Stockholm-Mälarregionen or Mälarregionen. As noted by Lucarelli and Hallin (2015), the municipalities participating in the PBN are in some cases quite large cities and municipalities, some located as far away as 250 kilometres from Stockholm. The geographical boundaries defined by Stockholm-Mälarregionen are also challenged by the SBA since they do not overlap.

The brand as a vehicle for regional change

In the complex PBN consisting of different public and private actors, which frequently have competing agendas, it is obvious that the SCS brand is the glue that binds these actors together (Lucarelli and Hallin, 2015). The PBN has undoubtedly adopted a very brand-oriented approach with regard to its operations. In fact, the brand is the *hub of the networks processes*, which is pointed out in the brand orientation literature as being a decisive trait of this strategic orientation (Urde, 1999). A communication executive interviewed by Lucarelli and Hallin (2015, p. 9) describes this: 'Stockholm Business Alliance is an alliance that has different functions. It helps us learn from each other; however it's the brand that is at the centre of it'. One of the expectations of the counties outside of Stockholm when Mälardalsrådet was launched in 1992 was that the dominance of the capital would decrease in the new region (Mälardalsrådet, 2015). The effect of the SCS initiative is undoubtedly the opposite, and the participating municipalities in the PBN also use their inhabitants' tax money to further reinforce this dominance. The SCS brand should be understood as a key vehicle in the shift in focus from region to city region and from decentralization to centralization (Falkerby and Westholm, 2008) and embracing of trickle-down economics.

SCS as internal branding in Stockholm

Apart from the impressive horizontal expansion of the brand into a new space, the SCS brand also expanded vertically. The SCS brand was initially legitimized by means of a rhetoric arguing for the relevance of the Capital of Scandinavia positioning due to the need to create attention in the international market for tourism and investments. However, six years after the launch of SCS-brand, the city of Stockholm acknowledged the need for internal branding towards its residents as well. Since 2012, it is mandatory to use the slogan Stockholm – The Capital of Scandinavia in all corporate communications produced by the municipality (Stockholm stad, 2011). In practice, this means that the slogan is included in material such as recruitment ads for kindergarten teachers. Since the City of Stockholm is an organization with many and diverse communication channels, and also an actor buying a lot of advertising, this has substantially increased the visibility of the SCS brand in the city. Stockholm is therefore a prime example of the idea of *one brand – one voice* in a place branding context (for a critique, see Skinner, 2005).

Resistance towards the SCS brand

Apart from various protests concerning the brand originating from various sources in Oslo and Copenhagen, there have been a couple of formal objections towards the SCS brand. The first complaint arrived at Marknadsetiska rådet (a self-regulating organization responsible for handling complaints regarding unethical advertising) in 2008. The second objection came in 2009 and focused on language issues (Swedish law stipulates that the Swedish language should be used in the communication produced by governmental agencies). None of these objections had any effect. The third objection, which we analyse in detail, came in 2012, seven years after the launch of the brand Stockholm – The Capital of Scandinavia, when a representative of the Green Party in the Stockholm city council proposed the following motion to the governing body (Stockholm stad, 2013, p. 6, own translation):

> 2012:13 Motion regarding replacing the slogan 'The Capital of Scandinavia'
>
> Stockholm's slogan 'The Capital of Scandinavia' has caused irritation in Sweden and abroad. First, the claim is not true. Second, it may be perceived as boastful.
>
> People who live in Scandinavia obviously realize that the slogan is not true. But many people in other parts of the world have limited knowledge concerning both Stockholm and Scandinavia, and may therefore believe that the statement is correct. A classic example is that people confuse Switzerland and Sweden. This lack of correct knowledge concerning Scandinavia is reinforced by this misinformation from the city of Stockholm.
>
> PROPOSAL
>
> In light of the above, the city council may decide to replace 'Stockholm – the Capital of Scandinavia' with 'Stockholm – the Capital of Sweden'. Or anything else that reflects reality and may be produced, for example, through a competition among locals.
>
> (Stockholm, 22 March 2012)

In the preparatory work concerning the motion, the City Executive Office and the Stockholm Business Region voiced their opinion regarding the motion, which the mayor (a Liberal-Conservative Party representative) then summarized as (p. 1):

> The City Executive Office believes that the motion should be denied. The message of Stockholm – The Capital of Scandinavia has been used for seven years. This marketing effort needs to attract attention and be long-term in nature. The message fills these requirements and should therefore continue to be used in the city's international marketing efforts.
>
> The Stockholm Business Region believes that Stockholm – The Capital of Scandinavia should not be confused with a physical name, as it is a positioning and as such cannot be false. A thorough strategy process lasted a few years before the launch in 2005. Changing Stockholm – The Capital of Scandinavia would be a breach of contract towards the 49 other municipalities included in the municipality cooperation body of the Stockholm Business Alliance. The contract has the clear ambition of jointly marketing Stockholm internationally by using this message.

The recommendation made by the mayor before the city council's decision to reject the motion (p. 2):

> Stockholm is a successful and attractive region with major financial and cultural offerings. Stockholm – The Capital of Scandinavia has been a part of the city's marketing efforts for seven years and is mediated through cooperation with 49 other municipalities in the Stockholm region. The now well-known message, together with a long-term effort, provides results – the number of investments and visitors to the region has increased.

> The marketing campaign has created, and still creates, attention, which is also the purpose of the message itself. I therefore rejected the motion and refer to the City Executive Office's official statement.

From this text, we can see that the main arguments given by administrators and politicians in defence of the brand originate from an economic and marketing perspective. The problem of impaired relations with Sweden's Scandinavian neighbours is met with silence. The brand is also contracted out of the democratic control of the citizens of Stockholm, since it would be a breach of contract to abandon the slogan with regards to the forty-nine other municipalities engaged in the branding of Stockholm as the Capital of Scandinavia. In the text, we see that the brand is given almost magical properties, as it is believed that the brand is behind the increase in visitors and investments in the city. Attention thus seems to be valued above fairness and truth. For the Stockholm Business Region, the 'truth' does not seem to have anything to do with the brand, since it is only a 'positioning' and thus cannot be false. This statement is quite contradictory to what the Stockholm Business Region (2013) claims on its website – The Capital of Scandinavia – where it provides 'logical' arguments for why Stockholm is the natural capital of Scandinavia:

> There are many reasons why Stockholm is the natural Capital of Scandinavia. Stockholm is the largest city in the largest country and is located in the heart of Scandinavia, with world-class communications. Stockholm is also Scandinavia's economic centre with the largest gross regional product and most multinational companies. It also has one of the world's leading ICT clusters, one of the largest biotech clusters and is the financial centre of northern Europe. Moreover, Stockholm is Scandinavia's leading cultural city with a unique range of galleries and museums, international cuisine and a centre for music production.

Here, it is thus proposed that Stockholm is the *natural* capital of Scandinavia due to its size, the size of Sweden, the central position in Scandinavia (most geographers would here object and rather describe Stockholm as having a peripheral position in Scandinavia) and its economic and cultural capital. The claim of being the natural capital must be seen in an antagonistic light, since the function of this claim is to signal that all other claims would be futile and that it is Stockholm's given right to be the Capital of Scandinavia.

The diagnosis of PBN narcissism

With the assistance of the diagnostic framework developed by Duchon and Burns (2008), we now summarize the PBN in relation to the three narcissistic traits of *self-aggrandizement*, *entitlement* and *denial*. We also discuss *rationalization* as a fourth trait (Brown, 1997).

Self-aggrandizement

The use of the slogan and symbolic crown can be interpreted as an exaggerated form of grandiose fantasy. SCS is believed to have almost magical powers, as the PBN representatives argue that the brand is *the* reason for increased tourism and investments in Stockholm. In spite of claims from actors associated with the PBN that the brand is behind the increase in tourism and investments, it is very hard to find any solid evidence of the SCS brand having external effects outside of Sweden, except for the angry responses from Sweden's Scandinavian neighbours (Ågren, 2013). Another example of self-aggrandizement is making grandiose claims, such as portraying Stockholm-Mälarregionen as a more important economic centre than Berlin, Rome and Madrid (Westholm, 2008).

Entitlement

The PBN believes that Stockholm has the natural right to be the Capital of Scandinavia. By using the argument of Stockholm's central location in Scandinavia, the actors belonging to the PBN show that they believe that they are entitled to alter official geographic definitions by including Finland in their definition on Scandinavia, acknowledged and used by all Scandinavian and Nordic countries, to fit their purpose. The willingness to exploit and the lack of concern for others is another central aspect of the SCS case. In an interview (Axelsson, 2005) on the negative reactions towards the brand, the newly appointed communication director/brand manager for the SCS brand comments: 'The fact that people react means that there is an inherent power in "The Capital of Scandinavia." We then must reckon with both positive and negative reactions. What someone does not like, someone else will like very much' (p. 46, own translation).

Denial

The critical voices are not heard or taken seriously by the PBN. The mayor claims that relations with Oslo and Copenhagen are good despite overwhelming evidence to the contrary (Tottmar, 2012). PBN representatives also intentionally use various techniques for concealing and distorting information to support their own gains. For instance, the use of the contradictory argument that the word 'capital' is not to be interpreted as 'capital city', but rather as 'main' and 'important'. Or claiming that 'a positioning can never be false' (Stockholm stad, 2013, p. 4, own translation).

Rationalization

A rationalization technique used by several of the PBN representatives is when they argue that Oslo and Copenhagen are just jealous: 'If they had come up with the slogan first, they would have used it'. (Ågren, 2013, p. 199, own translation). Or when a PBN representative interprets a single comment from a Danish fair visitor as a universal perception: 'at first they were angry, but now they say we are sorry that we did not come up with the slogan ourselves' (Ohlin, 2007, own translation). The PBN actors see themselves as smart, not malevolent.

Discussion and conclusions

The SCS case is an illustration of how organizational narcissism may thrive in a loosely connected network. Previous studies on organizational narcissism are not discussed in relation to networks or explicitly in connection to brand orientation. This case also gives special attention to the brand itself as a narcissistic device. The brand itself may thus be seen as both the cause and the effect of organizational narcissism, as it is a symbolic device with inherent narcissistic qualities. The continued use of this device feeds and strengthens the narcissism of the PBN. A participant in the PBN might have to use various defence mechanisms in order to align him- or herself with the brand identity (Brown and Starkey, 2000). The PBN will also reward members who demonstrate support of the brand identity (Duchon and Burns, 2008). In the place branding literature, it is sometimes suggested that the field must move beyond discussions of logos and catchy slogans (Ashworth and Kavaratzis, 2009). However, at a closer look, SCS is a very potent logotype and slogan with performative qualities that have been instrumental in changing power relations on many levels.

Brand orientation was once founded on the premise of being a strategy for survival (Urde, 1994). The key for survival in this strategy was increased knowledge, appreciation and loyalty towards the organization's own brand identity. However, as the story of Narcissus tells us, an extreme focus on the organization's own identity may be a path to failure and, in the worst case, the end of the organization, like in the case of Enron as reported by Duchon and Burns (2008). A closed and narrow projective brand orientation, as displayed in the case of SCS, carries the risk of impaired relationships and decoupling of external input, which may impede learning and change. A more open and dynamic relational brand orientation could be an approach for handling these problems. A key for developing this latter orientation is to adopt the holistic approach towards identity and image, where these concepts are truly seen as interdependent, as proposed by Hatch and Schultz (2002) and Kavaratzis and Hatch (2013). In this orientation, the brand is conceptualized as an interface, co-created by both internal and external stakeholders. This has been proposed by Hankinson (2004) as being a way forward for place branding, which he argues has been limited by the focus on brands as perceptual entities.

Towards a relational brand orientation

The decisive difference between the projective and relational brand orientation is to shift the focus on brand identity towards relations and adopt a genuine interest in others, not only from an instrumental perspective (i.e. as an audience to the play performed by the brand). This requires a deep understanding that value creation is a cooperative enterprise performed jointly by the organization's stakeholders. This is important for every organization, but perhaps even more so for organizations that are responsible for place branding, due to its dependence on an interconnected network of stakeholders (Hankinson, 2004). A distinctive feature of narcissism in organizations is that they fail to understand their role in a larger context. Several place branding scholars have argued that the simplistic competitive mindset offered by the product branding tradition is not particularly relevant in a place branding context and may even produce the opposite results (see Kalandides, 2007; Kavaratzis and Ashworth, 2008; Pasquinelli, 2013). This is clearly the case when it comes to SCS, as the former cooperative cross-national marketing efforts of Scandinavia are damaged by the PBN's behaviour (Ågren, 2013). The findings from this case support the suggestion of Kalandides (2007) that a '[p]rerequisite of a different city marketing concept would be a deep understanding of the interrelatedness between places. The consequence would be prioritizing cooperation and networks over competitive strategies' (p. 14). A helpful metaphor for this could be to envision the city as consisting of flows (Doel and Hubbard, 2002) instead of as a fixed place with assets. One must then realize that Stockholm's strengths also reside outside of its geographical borders (e.g. in Oslo and Copenhagen). A truly inclusive place branding concept would not only focus on internal, but also on external, stakeholders (Kavaratzis, 2012). To conclude, let us hope that Stockholm, this beautiful city on water,[2] may soon leave this narcissism behind and instead embrace the cooperative mindset it used to have.

Notes

1 In April 2017, 1 EUR equals about 9.5 SEK.

2 The slogan 'Stockholm – beauty on water' preceded 'Stockholm – the Capital of Scandinavia'. This slogan was most certainly developed without any reference to Narcissus.

References

Ågren, K. (2013) *Att sälja en stad: Stockholms besöksnäring 1936–2011*. Stockholm: Stockholmia.

Aitken, R. and Campelo, A. (2011) 'The four rs of place branding'. *Journal of Marketing Management*, 27(9/10), pp. 913–933. doi:10.1080/0267257X.2011.560718

Antorini, Y. M. and Schultz, M. (2005) 'Corporate branding and the conformity trap', in Schultz, M., Antorini, Y. M., Csaba, F. F. (ed.) *Corporate Branding, Purpose/people/processes: Towards the Second Wave of Corporate Branding*. Frederiksberg: Copenhagen Business School Press, pp. 57–78.

Ashworth, G., and Kavaratzis, M. (2009) 'Beyond the logo: Brand management for cities'. *Journal of Brand Management*, 16(8), pp. 520–531.

Axelsson, C. (2005) 'Hon ska sälja Stockholm Anne Årneby bygger varumärken'. *Svenska Dagbladet*, 4 May, p. 46.

Baumgarth, C., Merrilees, B. and Urde, M. (2010) 'From market orientation to brand orientation–back tracking and mapping routes forward', in Proceedings 6th Thought Leaders International Conference on Brand Management (14 pages).

Brown, A. D. (1997) 'Narcissism, identity, and legitimacy'. *The Academy of Management Review*, 22(3), pp. 643–686.

Brown, A. D. and Starkey, K. (2000) 'Organizational identity and learning: A psychodynamic perspective'. *The Academy of Management Review*, 25(1), pp. 102–120.

Denzin, N. K. (1978) *The Research Act*. 2nd edn. New York: McGraw-Hill.

Doel, M. and Hubbard, P. (2002) 'Taking world cities literally: Marketing the city in a global space of flows'. *City*, 6(3), pp. 351–368.

Duchon, D. and Burns, M. (2008) 'Organizational Narcissism'. *Organizational Dynamics*, 37(4), pp. 354–364.

Duchon, D. and Drake, B. (2009) 'Organizational narcissism and virtuous behavior'. *Journal of Business Ethics*, 85(3), pp. 301–308. doi:10.1007/s10551-008-9771-7.

Falkerby, J. and Westholm, E. (2008) 'Stockholm – The Capital of Scandinavia', in Amcoff, J., Falkerby, J., Stenlås, N., Westholm, E. and Gossas, M. (ed.), *Regionen som vision: det politiska projektet Stockholm-Mälarregionen*. Stockholm: SNS Förlag, pp. 66–74.

Flyvbjerg, B. (2006) 'Five misunderstandings about case-study research'. *Qualitative Inquiry*, 12(2), pp. 219–245. doi:10.1177/1077800405284363.

Gromark, J. and Melin, F. (2011) 'The underlying dimensions of brand orientation and its impact on financial performance'. *Journal of Brand Management*, 18(6), pp. 394–410.

Gromark, J. and Melin, F. (2013) 'From market orientation to brand orientation in the public sector'. *Journal of Marketing Management*, 29(9–10), pp. 1099–1123.

Hankinson, G. (2004) 'Relational network brands: Towards a conceptual model of place brands'. *Journal of Vacation Marketing*, 10(2), pp. 109–121.

Hatch, M. J. and Schultz, M. (2002) 'The dynamics of organizational identity'. *Human Relations*, 55(8), pp. 989–1018.

Kalandides, A. (2007) 'Marketing the Creative Berlin and the Paradox of Place Identity'. *Lo sviluppo territoriale nell'Unione Europea. Obiettivi, strategie, politiche*. Bolen: Associazione Italiana di Scienze Regionali.

Kavaratzis, M. (2012) 'From "necessary evil" to necessity: stakeholders' involvement in place branding'. *Journal of Place Management and Development*, 5(1), pp. 7–19.

Kavaratzis, M. and Ashworth, G. (2008) 'Place marketing: How did we get here and where are we going?'. *Journal of Place Management and Development*, 1(2), p. 150. doi:10.1108/17538330810889989.

Kavaratzis, M. and Hatch, M. J. (2013) 'The dynamics of place brands: An identity-based approach to place branding theory'. *Marketing Theory*, 13(1), pp. 69–86. doi:10.1177/1470593112467268.

Kornberger, M. (2010) *Brand Society: How Brands Transform Management and Lifestyle*. Cambridge: Cambridge University Press.

Louro, M. J. and Cunha, P. V. (2001) 'Brand management paradigms'. *Journal of Marketing Management*, 17(7–8), pp. 849–875.

Lucarelli, A. and Hallin, A. (2015) 'Brand transformation: A performative approach to brand regeneration'. *Journal of Marketing Management*, 31(1), pp. 84–106. doi:10.1080/0267257X.2014.982688.

Morgan, G. (2006) *Images of Organization*. Thousand Oaks, CA: SAGE.

Mälardalsrådet (2015) *Mälardalsrådet 20 år 2012*. Available at: www.malardalsradet.se/20ar/ (Accessed: 10 May 2015).

Ohlin, J. (2007) *Hej stormakt igen! Arbetaren*. Available at: http://arbetaren.se/artiklar/hej-stormakt-igen/ (Accessed: 10 May 2015).

Pasquinelli, C. (2013) 'Competition, cooperation and co-opetition: Unfolding the process of inter-territorial branding'. *Urban Research and Practice*, 6(1), pp. 1–18.

Skinner, H. (2005) 'Wish you were here? Some problems associated with integrating marketing communications when promoting place brands'. *Place Branding*, 1(3), pp. 299–315.

Stockholm Business Region (2013) *The Capital of Scandinavia*. Available at: www.thecapitalofscandinavia.com (Accessed: 10 September 2013).

Stockholm Business Region (2016) *Frequently Asked Questions*. Available at: www.stockholmbusinessregion.se/en/FAQ/ (Accessed: 28 November 2016).

Stockholm stad (2011) *Kommunikationsprogram för Stockholm stad 2012-2015*. Stockholm: Stockholm stad.

Stockholm stad (2013) Utlåtande 2013:8 RI. Ersättande av slogan 'The Capital of Scandinavia'. Available at: https://insynsverige.se/documentHandler.ashx?did=1711085 (Accessed: 29 November 2016).

Tottmar, M. (2012) 'En pr-grej, men det är lite dumt att ljuga'. *Svenska Dagbladet*, 22 March, p. 45.

Urde, M. (1994) 'Brand orientation–a strategy for survival', *Journal of Consumer Marketing*, 11(3), pp. 18–32.

Urde, M. (1999) 'Brand orientation: A mindset for building brands into strategic resources', *Journal of Marketing Management*, 15(1–3), pp. 117–133.

Westholm, E. (2008) 'Den nyregionala paradoxen', in Westholm *et al.* (ed.): *Regionen som vision: det politiska projektet Stockholm-Mälarregionen*. Stockholm: SNS Förlag, pp. 120–127.

11 A branding stranglehold

The case of Florida's orange tie

Staci M. Zavattaro and Daniel L. Fay

Introduction

> 'In 2013? Really?' she said. 'They didn't think half of the people in the state would be offended by this? Really?'
>
> (Penny Hulbert, Links Financial President)

When one thinks of Florida's state brand, some common words and phrases usually come to mind: Disney World, 2000 election debacle, hot and humid, crazy people, alligators everywhere. Florida residents often make the news for seemingly odd acts. In a story that almost perfectly encapsulates Florida stereotypes, a customer threw a three-and-a-half-foot alligator through a fast food restaurant drive-through window as a prank (Payne, 2016). Acts such as these spurred the creation of the popular FloridaMan and FloridaWoman Twitter accounts, harkening to how many headlines for weird stories begin with 'Florida man…' or 'Florida woman…'.

Stories and images such of these are closely intertwined with Florida's brand image. The state is perhaps best known for tourism offering at world famous theme parks, Key West, Miami, the beautiful beaches that line the peninsula, and much more. In 2015, 66.1 million people visited Orlando alone, making the city the U.S.'s most-visited travel destination (Visit Orlando, 2016). The business climate is less well known so in 2013, Gov. Rick Scott directed the state's economic development agency, Enterprise Florida, to develop a branding campaign to promote the state's industry, workforce, diversity, and business climate benefits. There is a tension in Florida between its popular tourism industries and a developing business arena that aims to attract major international corporations and events, making state branding a political process as well (Bellini *et al.*, 2010). In Florida, there was a slight problem: the brand identity Enterprise Florida created centred upon the image of an orange tie as the 'I' in Florida. This chapter's epigraph is from a Florida business leader who was outraged at the highly gendered branding direction given that men often wear ties. The association, then, was that business acumen is the purview of males rather than men and women alike. Needless to say, the brand image did not see much success.

This chapter delves into this case study using Zavattaro's (2012) framework of place branding through Baudrillard's phases of the image. The framework relies on critical theory to understand potential consequences – positive or negative – of branding strategies. As our analysis highlights, the focus on the orange tie image excluded more than half of the state's population from the growth efforts. The implication became that the business climate in Florida was by men, for men. Critical theory as used here shines light on what happens when entities focus too much on image rather than balancing image with substance in place branding campaigns. The first portion of this chapter further details the framework, while the second half expands more on the case study to show what happens when branding ideas lose sight of critical stakeholder groups. The conclusion offers points for future research and comments on the particular case.

The framework

When researching place branding from a public management perspective, much of the relevant literature comes from outside the discipline. Scholars in tourism management, traditional marketing, and hospitality management, for example, have been publishing widely on the topic. Within public administration and management, however, studies into this growing practical trend remain nascent. Recently, scholars from Europe have begun publishing their place branding scholarship in popular public management journals (Braun *et al.*, 2013; Eshuis *et al.*, 2013; Eshuis *et al.*, 2014; Eshuis and Edwards, 2012; Klijn *et al.*, 2014). In our joint work, we have examined branding strategies among U.S. colleges and universities from a public management perspective (Fay and Zavattaro, 2016). This emergence is recent and much needed within public management scholarship given the widespread practical application of place branding strategies in public and non-profit agencies.

Given this, the idea was to create a framework that looks at what might happen *after* entities try to develop branding and marketing strategies. Many articles and books are written about how to brand well, and those tomes are absolutely necessary. The framework presented here (and published previously in Zavattaro (2012) and Zavattaro (2014)) is a critical approach to understanding what might happen between the organization and its stakeholders after branding initiatives take place. From the public management perspective, a main reason branding and marketing are becoming so popular to study is the acceptance of business-based forms of governance, explained later in this chapter as a building block to the framework. Put simply: public entities are seeing the importance of branding and marketing strategies to set themselves apart from other, similar locales. We chose the case of Florida for this chapter because the state exemplifies what can happen when branding efforts aimed at public-sector economic development go awry without proper inclusion of relevant stakeholder groups. By being seemingly blind to the connotative meanings of images, officials in Florida excluded the female population from the image of business success. Critical theory illuminates the move from the status quo – and the status quo narrative is that men excel at business while women do not. As Bellini *et al.* (2010, p. 91) illuminate, 'image is a filter that influences the perception of the area', so with the focus on the orange tie, the image did not match reality in a state where women are key players in the business world.

The framework guiding this chapter, shown in Figure 11.1, is based upon three key items: critical theory, public relations theories that help understand communication styles, and market-based forms of governance. The first building block is Jean Baudrillard's phases of the image (Baudrillard, 1994). People might be familiar with his work and not even know it. We presume readers of this chapter have seen the move *The Matrix*. The film, released in 1999, depicts the story of Neo, a computer hacker who falls deeper into a digital world, realizing that the question of 'What is real?' is simultaneously perplexing and disturbing. That the movie relies on Baudrillard's *Simulacra and Simulation* (Baudrillard, 1994), which is made crystal clear in the beginning of the film in the form of a hollowed-out book where Neo hides some of his computer discs (Constable, 2006) and when Morpheus quotes directly from the book when he says: 'Welcome to the desert of the real' (Constable, 2006).

Baudrillard has been called both a postmodernist and a poststructuralist because of his focus on symbolism and its effects on modern social life (Ashley, 1990). Some might argue his *Simulacra and Simulation* takes a nihilistic view of the world; indeed, his last chapter in the book is titled 'Nihilism'. He spends the majority of his narrative questioning reality and criticizing today's reliance on symbolism and imagery. He argues that all objects will one day lose their connections to reality, writing that

> the era of simulation is inaugurated by a liquidation of all referentials … It is a question of substituting the signs of the real for the real, that is to say of an operation of deterring every real process to its operational double … Never again will the real have a chance to produce itself …
>
> (Baudrillard, 1994, p. 2)

As an example, he cites Disneyland in California. People forget, he argues, that Main Street U.S.A. is an idealized version of main streets and not found anywhere else but Disneyland itself. People tend to lose a sense of reality when they enter the Disney theme parks – though that is exactly what the company wants. It is this blurring of reality and fantasy that concern Baudrillard.

We are not convinced that everything is fake, but we do know that images become powerful symbols that people can use to stand in for reality (see also Bellini *et al.*, 2010), as the case study herein illustrates. Other scholars disagree with all of Baudrillard's assumptions. Huyssen (1989) takes issue with Baudrillard's depiction of Main Street U.S.A, arguing instead that Disney employees drew inspiration from real main streets to create the stylized areas in global theme parks. (Baudrillard likely would call this kind of research a reach for nostalgia.) Huyssen (1989) remains critical, noting that Baudrillard relies too heavily on McLuhan:

> To put the shoe on the proper foot, the ideology critique of Baudrillard's theorizing is urgent precisely because the theory of simulation offers nothing but the solace of instant intellectual gratification to those who are uninterested in understanding media or in analysing them as vehicles for ideology. Simulation, after all, may simply be the latest version of the ideology of the end of all ideology.
>
> (Huyssen, 1989, p. 9)

Huyssen is accusing Baudrillard of taking McLuhan's work, distorting it, and drawing erroneous conclusions that ultimately lead to the end of ideology. For many, it is problematic to think that society can be reduced to only simulations and simulacra. There has to be something out there that is real, right?

Despite the debate about Baudrillard's work, his framework is one building block of this chapter. Baudrillard outlines four phases of the image:

- Phase one: image reflects a profound reality; the image shows truth.
- Phase two: the image masks and denatures a profound reality; the image hides the truth.
- Phase three: the image masks the absence of a profound reality; the image is empty.
- Phase four: the image has no connection to reality; the image is unhinged, a simulacrum.

The phases show how an object can move from a connection to reality to a pure symbol. Political discourse is ripe with such happenings. A couple of examples come to mind to show this progression. Take a rose for example. As it is, a rose is a flower. That is known and a fact. Symbolism comes when we dissect the colour of the rose and its associated meaning (red for love, yellow for friendship), the quantity, and the person to whom the roses are given. A rose becomes so much more than a flower in a quick amount of time.

This progression of reality towards symbolism is the crux of the framework. Two additional portions of the framework should first be explained before proceeding. The framework was originally developed based on research of U.S. cities. In this chapter, we expand its application to a state-wide branding campaign to show how images associated with place branding campaigns can include or exclude certain populations. Bellini *et al.* (2010) showed similar occurrences in Tuscany, Italy when its powerful images – tourism, wine country, outdoors – became diluted with place confusion and competition. There was a movement towards what the authors call 'the other Tuscany' and this mirrors the Florida case detailed below – know the other Florida beyond tourism.

The framework as adapted herein relies on two other pieces of information: Grunig and Grunig's (1995) styles of public relations communication, and the marketization of public administration.

Public relations communication styles

As the second building block of the framework, we briefly detail Grunig and Grunig's (1995) styles of public relations (PR) communication. There is not enough space to delve fully into the applications of these styles, but they do make up a portion of the framework shown herein. Grunig and Grunig (1995) offer four styles of communication: press agentry, public information, two-way asymmetrical, two-way symmetrical. The press agentry model involves the organization pushing out information about itself without caring about relationships or dialogue. The public information model emerged as a way to professionalize public relations but still relies upon organizationally generated content. The two-way asymmetrical style begins to bring in more behavioural science research but as a way to tell people what they want to hear. The goal is pushing information but in a seemingly more scientific way. Finally, they argue that the two-way symmetrical version PR communications is the ideal because it relies on research and dialogue to mutually craft messages and push the discussion. This is, understandably, difficult to achieve in practice given the time, resources, and energy such endeavours take (Waters and Williams, 2011).

The concern in their framework, though, is how two-way symmetrical approaches can become one-way asymmetrical approaches. Put simply: auto-communication can occur when the organization wants people to think it is being responsive and dialogic but still only pushes out its messaging rather than engaging in a meaningful dialog. The organization, for example, might tout its research into the topic at hand as a way to get people to believe the information veracity. Even if stakeholders were included in the research process, we often are left wondering the extent, level, and inclusion of stakeholder information into the information campaigns. Auto-communication happens when the organization essentially is talking to itself – putting out information and having people parrot it back (Christensen, 1995). This can lead to organizational stagnation. To quote Christensen (1995, p. 662):

> through marketing communications such as advertising, sales promotion, PR etc., the organization, on the one hand, enacts, that is, defines, specifies or simulates its own specific environment. On the other hand, this construction, identified as 'the market', constitutes a 'mirror' in which the organization reflects on itself and evaluates its performance *vis-a-vis* the external world.

What we see is the organization dictating ahead of time 'which *kind* of feedback is needed … thus potentially enhancing established preconceptions about consumers and their needs' (Christensen, 1995, p. 662, emphasis in original).

Put differently, people internalize organizational messages as meant for them and attach meaning to that information based on their worldview or thought processes. People give meaning to symbols all the time, so it is not surprising when people attach meaning to organization language or imagery. Broms and

Gahmberg (1983) explain auto-communication as a flip of the normal sender-receiver model of communication. They offer an example of a Congressional research report, which on its surface is quite benign and informational. In the normal model, someone will read it to understand the information. When auto-communication occurs, people then attach emotion to the report and then use the report information to tell their own tales. This is how, for example, we often hear people say that the same set of numerical data is subject to interpretation based on the person's views.

Figure 11.1 shows the progression of phases of the image related to place branding. For a full explanation of the figure, see Zavattaro (2012, 2014) as the figure has been adapted from Zavattaro (2012).

Market-based forms of governance

The final building block for the framework used in this chapter is market-based forms of governance. Within the United States and abroad, movements towards 'running government like a business' took hold in the 1990s in light of New Public Management and Total Quality Management theories and practical implementation. These governance strategies can range from adopting business-like strategies to contracting-out goods or services to organizational privatization (Fay, 2016). Scholars sometimes refer to this as the commodification of public services (Kelly, 2005). According to Pierre (1995, p. 56):

> 'marketization of the state,' namely, to employ market criteria for allocating public resources and also to measure efficiency of public service producers and suppliers according to market criteria. Additionally, the 'marketization of the state' is strongly sustained by – indeed perhaps even part of – what is normally referred to as 'new public management,' which is shorthand for business-style, results-oriented, public sector management ... The perception of recipients of such services as 'customers' have contributed to this change in the relationship between the public and private sectors.

The business ethos shifted how government delivered services, pushing more of a focus onto efficiency rather than effectiveness (Kelly, 2005; Fay, 2016). Citizens *qua* customers are put into a passive relationship with government. Customers are either right or wrong and form relationships based on exchange. This logic does not translate directly to the public sector. For example, someone could decide they are a customer of the Internal Revenue Service and decline to pay taxes even after audit. There are, of course, serious consequences for this action so the customer is not and cannot always be right in governance settings. Market-based models offer 'reduced opportunities for collective citizen decision making through *discourse*' (Box, 1999, p. 20) because citizen ideals are compartmentalized and selected for them within the market framework, lessening the need for dialogue (Ventriss, 2000).

While much more can be written about market-based forms of government, the main point here is that the business-based ethos has increased the use of branding and marketing practices in the public sector (Eshuis *et al.*, 2014; Fay and Zavattaro, 2016; Zavattaro, 2010). A critical approach is needed to look at the effects of this shift on traditional forms of governance such as citizen participation, decision- and policy-making, and transparency. If auto-communication takes place as noted above, then trust in government could wane and stakeholders might not buy into the branding strategies. Figure 11.1 brings all the building blocks together.

The Florida case: an orange tie derails a branding effort

The framework relies on critical theory to understand the after effects of place branding and marketing strategies and is based on research of U.S. cities (see Zavattaro, 2012 and 2014 for further explanation). Cities in phase four, for example, rely heavily on branding and marketing communications and put an express focus on image sometimes forsaking substance. Cities in phase four risk auto-communication, as shown above, because of this express focus on tightly controlling the message. In today's digital age, such message control is becoming increasingly more challenging. Organizations focus on pushing out messaging in so many places (social media, website, TV, magazine, radio, fliers, brochures, etc.) that people might ignore the messaging or become part of the simulation process, whereby citizen input into branding strategies is only seen as lip service (Zavattaro, 2012). As the framework shows, an organization does not have to proceed to phase four. An organization could focus largely on informational communication without hints of branding and remain in phase one or phase two. Organizations find themselves moving into phase three when rebranding initiatives begin – new images try to mask the absence of reality as the

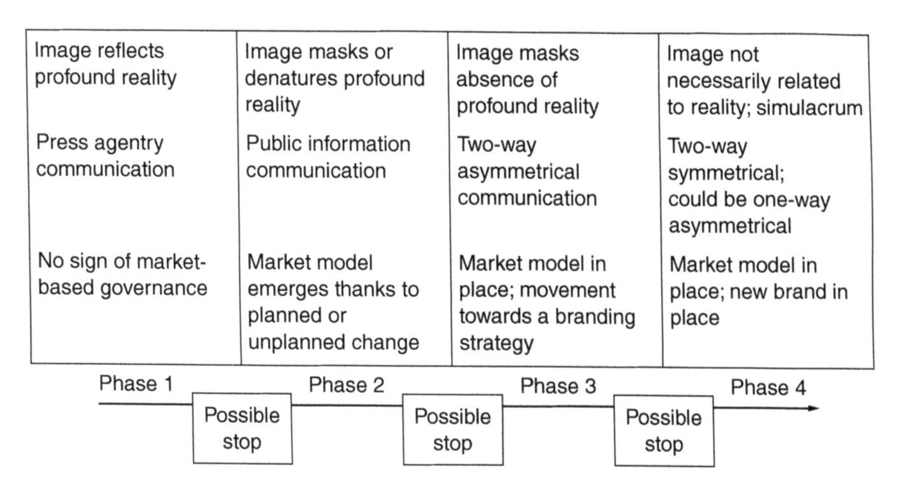

Figure 11.1 Place branding through phases of the image.

branding processes take place. Sometimes there is image mixing that can be confusing for people, for example, when the old logo still appears in places while the new one is rolled out. These efforts result in an impasse (Miller and Fox, 2007) where symbolic ways of ordering the world clash (Bellini *et al.*, 2010).

Such was the case for Florida after officials launched a business-minded branding endeavour that went awry. In 2013, Enterprise Florida, the state's economic development agency, found itself moving from phase two into phase three with a rebranding campaign. Enterprise Florida is a public-private partnership created in 1996 responsible for economic development in the state. Many states have followed this organizational structure, but Florida claims to be the first (Enterprise Florida, 2016a). Given the brand image of Florida detailed above, coupled with a Republican governor who wants to improve the state's business climate, Enterprise Florida launched a new branding campaign: Florida – The Perfect Climate for Business. State officials contracted with North Star Destination Strategies, a popular place branding agency based in Nashville, Tennessee, to develop the campaign. As Kavaratzis and Hatch (2013) note that this kind of contracting often leads to problems when experts are brought in to distil a brand identity rather than actually listening to the local community and stakeholders. This highly privatized effort may also decrease accountability to the general public and thus the effectiveness of the programme (Fay, 2016).

We can look at some of the numbers to figure out the economic development picture in Florida prior to the 2013 branding campaign launch. According to research from the Florida Chamber Foundation, about 22 per cent of survey respondents who relocated a business to the state were not satisfied with the talent pool (Florida Chamber Foundation, 2012). Business owners indicated that they needed skilled labour, which was hard to find in the state. The recession and housing market crash also hit Florida hard. According to Office of Economic and Demographic Research (OEDR), the 2008 recession placed the state forty-eighth in terms of real economic growth, a precipitous slide from second in the nation in 2005 (Office of Economic and Demographic Research, 2009). Personal income in the state dipped, more people migrated out of than into Florida, and credit lending slowed. All of these factors led to little or no economic growth in the state during the recession period.

Regarding the business climate, the OEDR data indicate that since 2009, the state has marginally increased its appropriations to businesses but has increased its reliance on tax-based incentives. In 2009, the state relied upon about $4.9 million in tax incentives, while that number increased to $5.7 million during the 2015–2016 fiscal year (Office of Economic and Demographic Research, 2016). The same report suggests the state can improve its future business climate by focusing on: growing in-state businesses rather than only recruiting relocating businesses, developing a holistic policy approach to spur development that includes education, job training, and graduate retention, and honing pools of local resources and talent (Office of Economic and Demographic Research, 2016).

In other words, the state suffered severe economic blows during the recession periods and tried to dig out through branding and marketing strategies, among other tools. The 2013 Enterprise Florida campaign can be seen as a means through which the state could tout its economic recovery efforts and move away from the negativity associated with the recession and foreclosure rates.

Methodology: qualitative media analysis

To examine the Florida branding campaign, the authors used Qualitative Media Analysis (QMA) (Altheide and Schneider, 2013). QMA is a version of textual analysis that also accounts for the presence of images and includes them as vital texts (see also Fairclough, 1993). In brief, QMA encourages researcher involvement in the analysis process, constantly finding and retooling patterns that emerge from the data. QMA is similar to grounded theory in that patterns are allowed to emerge instead of the authors bringing in preconceived notions about correct answers. In this case, we had a theoretical framework and used documents related to the Florida branding campaign to determine where, if at all, that emerged in the phases of the image.

Document and discourse analysis, interpreted to include images, is a methodology familiar in place branding studies. Many studies rely on case analysis and qualitative methodologies to examine place branding plans (Lucarelli and Berg, 2011). Koller (2008) uses cognitive critical discourse analysis to examine documents related to branding strategies in two cities, finding that few representational differences emerged, meaning the two brands were practically interchangeable. Document analysis and qualitative methods in general remain dominant within place branding studies (Chan and Marafa, 2013).

Figure 11.2 shows the movement of Enterprise Florida's branding through phases of the image. To determine how images and language shifted through phases, we used principles of QMA to analyse documents from the Enterprise Florida website in 2016, popular news sources (Florida newspaper and national newspapers that might have covered the fallout), and the Enterprise Florida website from the past. To do the latter, we used the Wayback Machine, an online tool that takes snapshots of what websites looked like before changes or alterations. We examined the images on old websites to see what led to the emergence of the orange tie and when it eventually disappeared. The earliest date on the Wayback Machine with images available is 2009. We selected random dates from 2009 through 2016 to see how the images associated with Enterprise Florida branding changed.

Regarding documents, we examined the language used and quotations from sources. For example, we noted that many females quoted in the stories we found adopted a negative tone towards the branding campaign. Through this triangulation, we were able to piece together how the orange tie campaign evolved from one that was to bolster the Florida business climate to one that excluded women from that success. As argued in prior work (Zavattaro, 2012), cities can go through phases of the image based on a combination of the language used in campaigns themselves, reaction to it, and the images. When the focus becomes too much on buzzwords and flashy images, a city moves further away from reality (see also Bellini *et al*., 2010). We applied the same logic during our analysis of the Florida case, and Figure 11.2 shows how the combination of language and imagery pushed the campaign into phase four and back after officials rebranded to move away from the controversial tie.

The controversy began as the state moved into phase three via the rebranding campaign. As a reminder, entities in phase two still have a connection to reality, yet they mask the truth. As the state began to slide into recession, business leaders in Enterprise Florida and top government officials tried to pull the state out through increasing tax breaks and other financial incentives. According to information found via our Wayback Machine search, the state focused on its innovation climate in 2009, even touting the state as a top location for business despite the harsh economic recession impacts. This is an example of an organization using language and images to cover up the reality of the state. As economic conditions began to improve, there was a movement towards more strategic brand identity. According to a press release from 2013, the 'Florida: The Perfect Climate' branding campaign featuring the orange tie was the state's first business brand attempt. With this, we can begin to see a move from phase two into phase three. It wasn't until the backlash began that there was a move into phase four.

To develop the brand, the state turned to North Star Destination Strategies, a business based in Tennessee specializing in creating brand campaigns for places. Many business leaders in the state criticized the North Star selection because it outsourced the task when there is plenty of marketing talent in Florida (Holan, 2013). According to Holan (2013), North Star officials interviewed more than

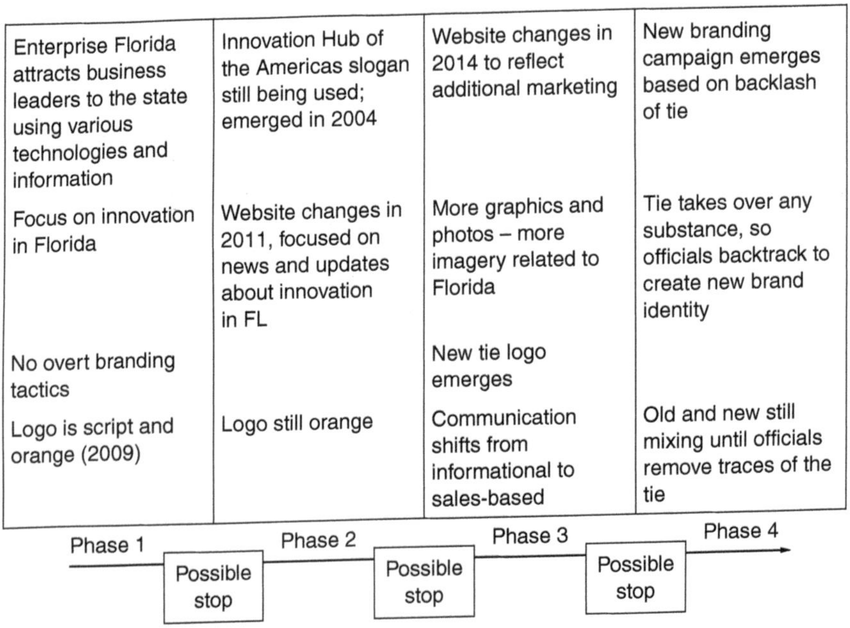

Phase 1	Phase 2	Phase 3	Phase 4
Enterprise Florida attracts business leaders to the state using various technologies and information	Innovation Hub of the Americas slogan still being used; emerged in 2004	Website changes in 2014 to reflect additional marketing	New branding campaign emerges based on backlash of tie
Focus on innovation in Florida	Website changes in 2011, focused on news and updates about innovation in FL	More graphics and photos – more imagery related to Florida	Tie takes over any substance, so officials backtrack to create new brand identity
No overt branding tactics		New tie logo emerges	
Logo is script and orange (2009)	Logo still orange	Communication shifts from informational to sales-based	Old and new still mixing until officials remove traces of the tie

Phase 1 → Possible stop → Phase 2 → Possible stop → Phase 3 → Possible stop → Phase 4

Figure 11.2 Florida's campaign through phases of the image.

116 people and conducted 26 focus groups, as well as did information-gathering exercises in and out of Florida. Findings from that research indicate that people outside of Florida think of the state primarily as a tourism entity (the Disney effect), and few people think of the state as high tech or innovative (Holan, 2013). Bellini *et al.* (2010) found similar problems with Tuscany's overall brand perceptions, so the finding in Florida parallels a global phenomenon when people only have a small association with a place that is much more. North Star worked with a Jacksonville-based agency On Ideas to implement the campaign, and it was that agency that designed the orange tie logo (Holan, 2013).

Based on Figure 11.1 on p. 147, the orange tie logo and campaign slipped into phase four. Officials did not intend for – and probably even think that – using such a masculine symbol would be problematic. Movement between phases is not usually intentional on the part of the brand creators. It is how people interpret that brand that shifts campaigns between phases. In this case, as the popular press reported, the image became the primary focus rather than the marketing or logic behind the branding strategy – to increase business ventures in the state. The image did not represent the business reality in the state so became meaningless given the harmful gendered connotations people had related to the image. Put simply: the orange tie image was removed from the demographic reality of the state's business climate where many women are CEOs and active within business communities. Based on our document analysis, we found an instance of an Enterprise Florida spokesman saying that 'the tie image was test surveyed in advance and found to be a widely accepted image for business' (Holan, 2013, para. 11). The article continued, noting the tie is a symbol of power, business acumen, and business smarts (Holan, 2013). As Rosica (2013) points out, the branding campaign sparked a social media battle with people falling on either side of the debate. He recounts Facebook posts in which one commenter noted that the logo seems to indicate the state is unwelcoming to women business leaders, while another wrote, '"Tie=long-standing symbol of professional business … women that have a problem with that need to just move on"' (Rosica, 2013, para. 4). This is a case where a seemingly benign image turns into a branding disaster.

In 2015, state officials began rethinking the branding campaign and phasing out the orange tie. In our view, officials began to realize just how harmful brands can be that exclude key demographics – women in this case. Female business leaders could not connect with the campaign because many did not see themselves reflected in the promotion. The idea was that the men run the business world in Florida and women were accessories at best, non-existent at worse. When officials pulled back the tie image, the branding campaign slid back into phase three. Again, this slide is not something officials thought consciously about. Rather, previous research shows that phase three often emerges when rebranding takes place (Zavattaro, 2012, 2014), and that is exactly what happened here. While the transition was taking place, some logos still used the orange tie, others replaced the tie with a black, upright 'I' instead. The impasse (Miller and Fox, 2007) was in full swing.

At the time of the rebranding start in 2015, the Enterprise Florida leader lobbied state lawmakers for additional funding to aggressively market the state to business interests (Turner, 2015). In 2014, Turner (2015) reports, state lawmakers failed to appropriate $20 million towards Enterprise Florida's marketing efforts centred upon The Perfect Climate for Business branding campaign. In 2015, Enterprise Florida officials wanted additional funding to roll out a new branding and marketing plan aimed specifically to bolster the aeronautical, space, and manufacturing sectors (Turner, 2015). In an interesting crossover, Enterprise Florida administrators indicated their willingness to borrow from Visit Florida's successful tourism branding strategies to improve economic conditions in the state (Turner, 2015). At this same time, Enterprise Florida officials noted that they did not plan to fully retire the tie-based logo, but it did eventually get phased out as the Perfect Climate brand struggled on (Rosica, 2013. This rebranding effort is characteristic of phase three, whereby agencies are still trying to find a solid identity upon which to build branding efforts.

In 2016, Enterprise Florida embarked on yet another rebranding campaign: *Florida – The Future is Here*. That this new branding strategy came about is not a surprise given the disaster related to the tie, along with a change in Enterprise Florida leadership. In March 2015, Enterprise Florida enlisted a new CEO, who also serves as the state's Secretary of Commerce, to further improve the state's business climate (Enterprise Florida, 2015). Part of his commitment was to launch a new brand within his first year, and the Florida – The Future is Here branding initiative achieves that goal (Trigaux, 2016). Accompanying the new branding effort is a marketing campaign titled Boundless:

> setting the overarching theme that Florida is home to the resources and attitudes that businesses need to flourish. Through imagery of Florida's key assets, the campaign brings just a few of the infinite opportunities to the forefront. Other campaign design elements reflect boundless optimism, potential, freedom and possibility.
>
> (Enterprise Florida, 2016b, para. 5)

Ads related to the campaign will cost $10 million. As an article in the *Palm Beach Post* notes, the new brand replaces the controversial tie campaign. One Florida official is quoted as saying, 'I found it (the new brand) to be much more reflective of the dynamic nature of our economy than orange ties and sand castles' (Palm Beach Post, 2016, para 6).

Business leaders hope the $10 million marketing and promotion budget will increase the state's visibility. Trigaux (2016, paras 8–9) puts it succinctly:

> To many, a new state business branding campaign cannot come quickly enough. Florida stopped marketing the business scene here more than a year ago, even though the state is enjoying big-name corporate relocations and job growth in the past year second only to larger California. A previous attempt in 2013 to create and market a business brand by Enterprise Florida

flubbed. The campaign's slogan was 'Florida. The Perfect Climate for Business.' But it featured people wearing orange ties, which felt dated and alienated some businesswomen who felt it was not inclusive. And too many of the visual scenes in the campaign featured Florida sand, which many business leaders criticized for sending the wrong message – that the state was still a place dominated by tourists and retirees.

Conclusion and discussion

The purpose of this chapter is to use a critical framework to understand a state-level branding campaign meant to attract economic development opportunities. For Florida, such branding and associated marketing endeavours are critical given the impact of the economic collapse, coupled with the state's image as a tourist heaven rather than a business one. As the case study showed, however, branding can sometimes go awry when the focus is on the images rather than the content. The image of an orange tie to connote business success alienated many female business leaders throughout the state, rendering the campaign itself relatively ineffective. It seems that officials did not learn lessons from the past, as the new branding campaign and tagline still was developed without including various stakeholder groups. Not including those who care about the place leads to problems with branding – some expert is paid a lot to tell you what you are (Kavaratzis and Hatch, 2013). A more participatory, inclusive approach from the beginning often leads to more successful place branding campaigns because everyone feels involved and part of something larger (Govers and Go, 2009). Simply changing an image will not help in terms of branding or marketing (Kavaratzis, 2004), as Florida is trying to do with the new campaign.

To better capture the importance of inclusive place branding, we offer possible ways forward derived from theory: collaborative public management and visual rhetoric.

Collaborative public management

Collaborative public management (CPM) 'describes the process of facilitating and operating in multi-organizational arrangements to solve problems that cannot be solved by single organizations' (O'Leary, Gerard and Bingham, 2006, p. 7). For branding and marketing, this collaboration is key (Eshuis and Edwards, 2012), lest people feel left out of the process. CPM ties to movements towards governance and away from traditional, top-down government. In governance settings, there is a focus on actors collaborating in formal and informal networks to achieve organizational and policy ends. In more traditional government settings, things happen in a top-down manner (as the orange tie campaign did).

When there is a focus on governance and collaboration, then branding efforts begin to make more sense for public administration. As Eshuis *et al.* (2013) argue, place branding is becoming a key governance strategy in light of market models of government that focus on importing business practices into the public sector. To correct for yet another top-down government intervention, the authors instead focus on how place marketing can bring together various stakeholder groups into collaborative settings. As they note, this is no easy task, as different people necessarily expect varying inputs and outcomes into place branding processes. That larger point, though, is that despite the difficulties, if place branding and marketing are done well it can bring people together in collaborative ways that might not have been available previously. When done this way, place branding can help stakeholders feel emotionally connected to a place and associated policies, which then can increase trust in government (Eshuis, Klijn and Braun, 2014). Such was not the case for Florida's exclusion of women in the place branding strategy.

More studies are needed to better understand how citizens meaningfully participate in city and state branding efforts – or if they still feel left out or contacted only for token opportunities to participate.

Visual rhetoric

It is not out of the ordinary for cities, states, nations, or organizations to change and alter a potentially harmful brand identity (Gertner and Kotler, 2004). For Florida, the battle state officials face is overcoming a tourism juggernaut that, in terms of real economic impact and worldwide perception, overshadows a business climate. If state officials are not careful, the state's image risks slipping into a stereotype, which, according to Gertner and Kotler (2004, p. 51), 'suggests a widely held image that is highly distorted, simplistic, and carries a favourable or unfavourable bias'. The 'Florida Man' stories cited above also do not help the state's image and movement into a stereotype of a state that has nothing to offer but crazy criminals, alligators, sweltering summer heat, and theme parks in the centre of the state.

In this instance, as the case study of the orange tie shows, images can become so powerful that they often dilute the intention behind the brand. We offer here the tools of visual rhetoric to include the importance of images into future place branding studies, realizing that brands are about more than images alone (Govers, 2013) but that images often can take on lives of their own for good or ill. Therefore, it becomes important for branding scholars and practitioners alike to realize the power of images in the place branding process. When image takes over for reality, the branding can potentially exclude everyone because they might not recognize what they love about their place. The image becomes the reality. That is the case that Orlando officials are fighting against. For many, Orlando *is* Disney World and nothing else. City and economic development officials on a local level are trying 'Orlando: You Don't Know the Half of It' as a way to speak to what else Orlando has to offer. Locals often are adamant that their city is more than theme parks and feel excluded from much of the tourism branding, yet the theme parks are what bring in the sixty-six million tourists who economically influence the city positively. This tension makes for an interesting catch-22 from a place branding standpoint.

Brand images usually come from (or ideally come from) extensive research and can become the most visible and often most loved (or most maligned) aspects of the process. Visual rhetoric, which developed in the 1970s from the discipline of rhetorical studies, 'is the actual image rhetors generate when they use visual symbols for the purpose of communicating' (Foss, 2005, p. 143). The process is an undeniable one that includes human intervention and interpretation. At its core, visual rhetoric as a scholarly endeavour is a critical approach to understanding how images can take on their own meanings within, and apart from, an overall rhetorical happening.

Future research can use both theories of CPM and visual rhetoric as ways to move towards more inclusive place branding strategies. CPM shows the importance of bringing together people from various standpoints to develop a brand identity together to ideally increase buy in and success. Visual rhetoric focuses the importance on creating meaningful images that also do not exclude people yet are unique to the place. Future research can focus on the role of these two theories within place branding, incorporating new avenues of theoretical thought into future empirical studies.

References

Altheide, D. L. and Schneider, C. J. (2013) *Qualitative Media Analysis*. 2nd edn. Thousand Oaks, CA: SAGE Publications.

Ashley, D. (1990) 'Marx and the excess of the signifier: Domination as production and simulation'. *Sociological Perspectives*, 33(1), pp. 129–146.

Baudrillard, J. (1994) *Simulacra and Simulation*. Ann Arbor: University of Michigan Press.

Bellini, N., Loffredo, A. and Pasquinelli, C. (2010) 'Managing otherness: The political economy of place images in the case of Tuscany', in Ashworth, G. and Kavaratzis, M. (eds), *Toward Effective Place Brand Management: Branding European Cities and Regions*, pp. 89–115.

Box, R. C. (1999) 'Running government like a business'. *American Review of Public Administration*, 29(1), pp. 19–43.

Braun, E., Eshuis, J. and Klijn, E. (2014) 'The effectiveness of place brand communication'. *Cities*, 41, pp. 64–70.

Broms, H. and Gahmberg, H. (1983) 'Communication to self in organizations and cultures'. *Administrative Science Quarterly*, 28(3), pp. 482–495.

Chan, C. and Marafa, L. M. (2013) 'A review of place branding methodologies in the new millennium'. *Place Branding and Public Diplomacy*, 9, pp. 236–253.

Christensen, L. T. (1995) 'Buffering organizational identity in the marketing culture'. *Organization Studies*, 16(A), pp. 651–672.

Constable, C. (2006) 'Baudrillard reloaded: Interrelating philosophy and film via *The Matrix Trilogy*'. *Screen*, 47, pp. 233–249.

Enterprise Florida. (2016a) 'Enterprise Florida launches "Florida – The Future is Here" branding campaign'. Available at: www.enterpriseflorida.com/news/enterprise-florida-launches-florida-the-future-is-here-branding-campaign/, 2016.

Enterprise Florida. (2016b) 'Bill Johnson'. Available at: www.enterpriseflorida.com/wp-content/uploads/EFI-Bio-Bill-Johnson.pdf

Enterprise Florida (2017) 'Peter Antonacci'. Available at: www.enterpriseflorida.com/wp-content/uploads/8.3.2017-Pete-Antonacci.pdf.

Eshuis, J., Klijn, E. and Braun, E. (2014) 'Place marketing and citizen participation: Branding as strategy to address the emotional dimension of policy making?'. *International Review of Administrative Sciences*, 80(1), pp. 151–171.

Eshuis, J., Braun, E. and Klijn, E. (2013) 'Place marketing as governance strategy: An assessment of obstacles in place marketing and their effects on attracting target groups'. *Public Administration Review*, 73(3), pp. 507–516.

Eshuis, J. and Edwards, A. (2012) 'Branding the city: The democratic legitimacy of a new mode of government'. *Urban Studies*, 50(5), pp. 1066–1082.

Fairclough, N. (1993) 'Critical discourse analysis and the marketization of public discourse: The universities'. *Discourse and Society*, 4(2), pp. 133–168.

Fay, D. L. (2016) 'Planning for a Payout Effectiveness of Special Purpose Entities as State Lottery Administrations'. *American Review of Public Administration*, 46(5), pp. 614–631.

Fay, D. L. and Zavattaro, S. M. (2016) 'Branding and isomorphism: The case of higher education'. *Public Administration Review*, 76(5), pp. 805–815.

Florida Chamber Foundation (2012) Florida business relocation information summary. Available at: www.flchamber.com/research/research-programs/florida-business-relocation-informational-summary/.

Foss, S. A. (2005) 'Theory of visual rhetoric', in Smith, K., Moriarty, S., Barbatsis, G. and Kenney, K. (eds), *Handbook of Visual Communication: Theory, Methods and Media*. Mahwah, New Jersey: Lawrence Erlbaum Associates, Inc., pp. 141–152.

Gertner, D. and Kotler, P. (2004) 'How can a place correct a negative image?'. *Place Branding*, 1(1), pp. 50–57.

Govers, R. (2013) 'Why place branding is not about logos and slogans'. *Place Branding and Public Diplomacy*, 9, pp. 71–75.

Govers, R. and Go, F. (2009) *Place Branding: Glocal, Virtual and Physical Identities, Constructed, Imagined and Experienced*. New York: Palgrave Macmillan.

Grunig, J. E. and Grunig, L. A. (1995) 'Models of public relations and communication', in Grunig, J. E. and Dozier, D. M. (eds), *Excellence in Public Relations and Communication Management*. New Jersey: Lawrence Erlbaum Associates.

Holan, M. (2013) Enterprise Florida rebuts critical report. Available at: www.bizjournals.com/tampabay/news/2013/02/05/enterprise-florida-rebuts-critical.html.

Huyssen, A. (1989) 'In the shadow of McLuhan: Jean Baudrillard's theory of simulation'. *Assemblage*, 10, pp. 6–17.

Kavaratzis, M. (2004) 'From city marketing to city branding: Towards a theoretical framework for developing city brands'. *Journal of Place Branding*, 7(1), pp. 58–73.

Kavaratzis, M. and Hatch, M. J. (2013) 'The dynamics of place brands: An identity-based approach to place branding theory'. *Marketing Theory*, 13(1), pp. 69–86.

Kelly, J. M. (2005) 'The dilemma of the unsatisfied customer in a market model of public administration'. *Public Administration Review*, 65(1), pp. 76–84.

Koller, V. (2008) 'The world in one city: Semiotic and cognitive aspects of city branding'. *Journal of Language and Politics*, 7(3), pp. 431–450.

Klijn, E., Eshuis, J. and Braun, E. (2014) 'The influence of stakeholder involvement on the effectiveness of place branding'. *Public Management Review*, 14(4), pp. 499–519.

Lucarelli, A. and Berg, P. O. (2011) 'City branding: A state-of-the-art review of the research domain'. *Journal of Place Management and Development*, 4(1), pp. 9–27.

Miller, H. T. and Fox, C. J. (2007) *Postmodern Public Administration, Revised edition*. New York: M. E. Sharpe.

O'Leary, R., Gerard, C. and Bingham, L. B. (2006) 'Introduction to the symposium on collaborative public management. *Public Administration Review*, 66(November 2006), pp. 6–9.

Office of Economic and Demographic Research (2016) 'Florida: An economic overview'. Available at: http://edr.state.fl.us/content/presentations/economic/FlEconomicOverview_5-3-16.pdf.

Office of Economic and Demographic Research (2009) 'Florida: An economic overview'. Available at: http://edr.state.fl.us/Content/presentations/economic/FlEconomicOverview_6-17-09.pdf.

Palm Beach Post (2016) 'Future is here for new Enterprise Florida branding campaign'. Available at: www.palmbeachpost.com/news/business/future-is-here-for-new-enterprise-florida-branding/nqFnz/.

Payne, E. (2016) 'Do you take reptiles? Customer throws alligator through drive-thru'. Available at: www.cnn.com/2016/02/09/us/florida-alligator-drive-through-window/index.html.

Pierre, J. (1995) 'The marketization of the state: Citizens, customers, and the emergence of the public market', in Peters, G. and Savoie, D. J. (eds), *Governance in a Changing Environment*. Canada: McGill-Queen's University Press.

Rosica, J. (2013) 'Enterprise Florida is dropping the tie from its logo'. Available at: http://saintpetersblog.com/has-enterprise-florida-dropped-the-tie-from-its-logo/.

Trigaux, R. (2016) 'Florida to launch fresher, better-funded business branding campaign'. Available at: www.tampabay.com/news/business/economicdevelopment/what-will-the-guy-behind-the-gator-nation-brand-do-for-floridas-business/2262976.

Turner, J. (2015) 'Florida may stow "tie" logo for marketing campaign'. Available at: www.tallahassee.com/story/news/politics/2015/05/31/florida-may-stow-tie-logo-marketing-campaign/28252535/?from=global&sessionKey=&autologin. (Accessed: 9 February 2016).

Ventriss, C. (2000) 'New Public Management: An examination of its influence on contemporary public affairs and its impact on shaping the intellectual agenda of the field'. *Administrative Theory and Praxis*, 22(3), pp. 500–518.

Visit Orlando. (2016) 'Orlando welcomed 66.1 million visitors in 2015'. Available at: http://media.visitorlando.com/pressrelease/index.cfm/2016/5/2/Orlando-Welcomed-66-Million-Visitors-in-2015/ (Accessed: 4 May 2016).

Waters, R. D. and Williams, J. M. (2011) 'Squaking, tweeting, cooing, and hooting: Analyzing the communication patterns of government agencies on Twitter'. *Journal of Public Affairs*, 11(4), pp. 353–363.

Zavattaro, S. M. (2014) *Place Branding Through Phases of the Image*. NYC: Palgrave Macmillan.

Zavattaro, S. M. (2012) 'Place marketing and phases of the image: A conceptual framework'. *Journal of Place Management and Development*, 5(3), pp. 212–222.

Zavattaro, S. M. (2010) 'Municipalities as public relations and marketing firms'. *Administrative Theory and Praxis*, 32(2), pp. 191–211.

12 Place branding as political research

From hidden agenda to a framework for analysis

Andrea Lucarelli

Introduction

Place branding is a diversified field of research. Whereas an increasing focus is placed on the way local residents and organizations are central in the re-production and usage of the branding efforts, the main focus is largely directed towards attempting to understand, analyse and explain the ways branding policies are produced and managed, as well as the different activities and efforts that emerge from the process of branding (see Lucarelli and Berg, 2011). This is problematic because regarding urban and branding policies as merely framed in city planning offices implies viewing other public bodies, private enterprise and local residents as simply passive users of branding policies. This view is further problematic because it neglects to analyse the appropriation patterns of public bodies, private enterprise and local residents, understood as political urban creators (Zukin, 2009); and in turn offer superficial views on branding policy formation, agency and change leading to a hasty view of the politics of branding, political actions and expressions.

This problem can be seen reflected into the literature in two ways; first it is related to an apparent lack of a *coherent political view* on place branding as a political phenomenon, its effects and implications; and second, it is linked to the presence of a *hegemonic discourse* on place branding as a form of economic-led neoliberal activity. More specifically, in relation to the former, the literature frames branding policies as either as progressive policies (e.g. Eshuis *et al.*, 2013; Wæraas *et al.*, 2014) or on the reverse, as the locus of structural conflicts between residents, planners and managers (e.g. Eisenschitz, 2010; Lewis, 2011). In relation to the latter, the hegemonic dominance of the usage of marketing 'approach' (with its specific vocabulary, ideas, and concepts) in analysing and conceptualizing place branding activities (e.g. Andersson, 2014) has produced a type of scholarship which 'uncritically' analyse branding polices as merely materializations of contemporary neoliberal philosophy affecting the realm of places.

Those two interlinked trajectories imply that place branding literature, somehow take for granted the 'marketing approach' of place branding – with its vocabulary, concept and ideas- as the common-best approach for conceptualizing and analysing place branding practices, or on reverse as the point of departure for critique, but without really going in-depth in regard to its political dimension. This view, it is here argued, not only lacks a truly political appreciation of place branding, but also results in false dichotomies within place branding research and practice. It leads, for instance, to conceptual 'exercises' attempting to spell out differences between consumption and production, public and private, economics and politics (Lucarelli and Brorström, 2013).

In order to unravel the *myopic stasis* in which place branding research is situated, and open the possibility for renewed critical place branding research, the present chapter makes two steps; first, it unpacks the constitutive dimension of the hegemonic discourse of place branding and its political dimension, and second, it offers a framework that can support researchers embracing a critical political research agenda for place branding.

Unpacking place branding as neoliberal marketing discourse affecting places

The mere existence of place branding as both a set of practices and theories could be seen as an example of the ways in which marketing practices and concepts have developed in contemporary society and are largely affecting different societal domains. In fact, the argument developed of the mainstream marketing literature on public sector, both in its societal or policy dimension (see e.g. Kotler and Levy, 1966; Kotler and Zaltman, 1971) sees the 'broadening of marketing orientation' from commercial realm to social realm (i.e. place) not only as possible and plausible but indeed necessary for flourishing of cities. This is mainly due to the increasing commercialization of the public sector, which is reflected in the adoption of the principle of increment in 'value' and 'benefit' for all the stakeholder involved (i.e. from company to consumer-citizens, from the government to the society). Marketing applied to place is thus not only necessary and plausible but should also be strategically and efficiently planned, implemented and reviewed.

Apart from the *narrative* about progress and communal benefit such 'orientation' suggests, one can see it as it more implicitly is grounded – and help to frame – a hegemonic *discourse* around place branding; place branding emerges as an example of economic-led imperatives and private interests fundamentally linked to a peculiar geopolitical and historical condition (i.e. post WWII) in which the narrative of the 'broadening' has flourished. The 'broadening', apart for being an important 'self-fulfilling' narrative, in that it creates and performs the conditions it is analysing, it also creates a narrative which maintains that place branding as an 'extension' – of the broadening – is a result of the increasing commercialization of the public sector formed by entrepreneurial principle informing a management style by 'number', 'quantification' and 'efficiency' for all the stakeholder involved.

The narrative framed by the 'broadening' argumentation has its inherent problem; it holds a deterministic view of neoliberalism and neoliberalization that sees it as a straightforward process embedded into every societal domain. Ironically, much of the critical literature dealing with place branding (see e.g. Broudehoux, 2007; Koller, 2008; Ward, 2000) have held fast the very same *narrative line* (see Harvey, 1989) present in the 'broadening' argumentation, even with a different much more negative type of deontological approach. In other words, those studies, by offering an understanding of the practices of place branding as an example of neoliberalization firmly embedded in the Marxist view of the labour being the main form colonizing the entire society, instead of offering an alternative explanation, have being facilitating the construction of the hegemonic discourse of place branding as a form of pure capitalist and economic-led activity. By offering an insightful debate constructing a more globalized view of neoliberalism (see Peck and Tickell, 2002), a more nuanced localized view (see Brenner and Theodore, 2002) or even a more spatially diversified view of neoliberalism (Jessop, 2002), critical place branding studies (see Lucarelli and Brorstöm, 2013) have been instrumental in recognizing the different shapes and forms that neo-liberalism can take (i.e. neo-statism, neo-corporatism, neo-communitarism). However, their approach have not helped to offer an analysis about the 'everyday' and mundane process of place branding as neoliberal apparatus; by being interested in the systemic, structural, capitalist nature of neoliberalism, critical studies have tended to put aside the type of analysis that would have instead helped to dig into the more micro practical, everyday criticalities of the practices of place branding as for example the framing of branding policies, or daily work of brand management officers.

However, as Agnew (1999), as do others, points out, places such as cities and urban agglomerates did not merely become more powerful due to neoliberalism and neoliberal policies, but have been historically and spatially framed and characterized beyond the labour-based (i.e. mercantilist, capitalist or neoliberal) structuring logic. In fact, the life of cities, regions and nations has historically emerged not merely as the total prevalence of the private sector over the public and non-commercial realm as a reflection of capitalist neo-liberalism (see Harvey, 1989), but rather as a hybridization process (Hodges, 2012; Sheller and Urry, 2003; Weintraub, 1997) in which public–private, economic-political, commercial- non-commercial logic is affecting each other emerging as complex organic practices.

Place branding as political research domain: towards a framework for analysis

The dominance of marketing oriented literature in place branding has helped to frame a hegemonic discourse based on economic deterministic rationale overshadowing the 'political' (i.e. here understood following Mouffe (2005) as the eruptive events that reveal 'politics' as the established, institutional means for organizing collective life). Its critical counterpart has been helpful in unmasking problems inherent with such deterministic view, but by holding fast a political-economic view privileging the labour and the capital, over politics and the political, has served to consolidate the hegemonic discourse of place branding as economic-led phenomenon. Such a view is problematic because, as pointed out by Castree (2006), it can create an impasse where a political analysis and critique is not possible, as the capital and labour are the main explanatory elements. It follows that only by 'credit' (i.e. *sdoganare*) the political dimension from the economic dimensions, still holding a view that conceptualized those as *ceteris paribus* (see Davies, 2014), a truly political analysis of the place branding as political apparatus could be performed.

This is done by adopting an archeo-geneological lens a la Foucault (1988); a lens which takes into consideration at the same time, on one hand the way the academic and popular literature has been instrumental in producing the ideas and argumentations constructing a certain view of place branding as product of neoliberalism, and on the other hand, recognizing place branding practices as fundamentally based on a 'scientific' assumption on the contemporary relations between economic and politics. It is a lens to use Davis (2014) words to build a framework which can consider politics at the centre, without failing to take into consideration the way neoliberalism has sought to disenchant politics by replacing it with economy.

Contextualizing and operationalizing the framework: policy, ideology and power

Previous conceptual studies on politics of place branding have built frameworks by departing either from empirical evidence (see e.g. Ooi, 2008; Therkelsen and Halkier, 2008) or from the adoption of a certain theoretical view or set of concepts (e.g. Marzano and Scott, 2009; Sevin, 2011) rather than departing from a critical assessment on the literature and unpacking its foundational underpinnings.

This is what is done here; namely by presenting a framework that is epistemologically sound and attached to the conditions, practices and activities in which place branding is unfolding. This is done because it allows one to ground a framework that is able to 'grasp' and analyse the 'crude' realities and everyday mundane politics practices happening in relation to branding of places.

In more practical term it is done by relaying on the broad discipline of marketing, not simply because place branding can be seen as the application of brand management to the realm of places but more crucially because marketing originates with a conceptual orientation profoundly embedded with a political rationale that can be linked to particular politico-theological implications (see Schwarzkopf, 2010, 2011).

The framework as presented below (see Figure 12.1) is based on four different pillars, one related to the needs to overcome the consumption–production dichotomy and the other three aimed at operationalizing such a non-dualist view in relation to three different political dimensions: policy process, ideology and power.

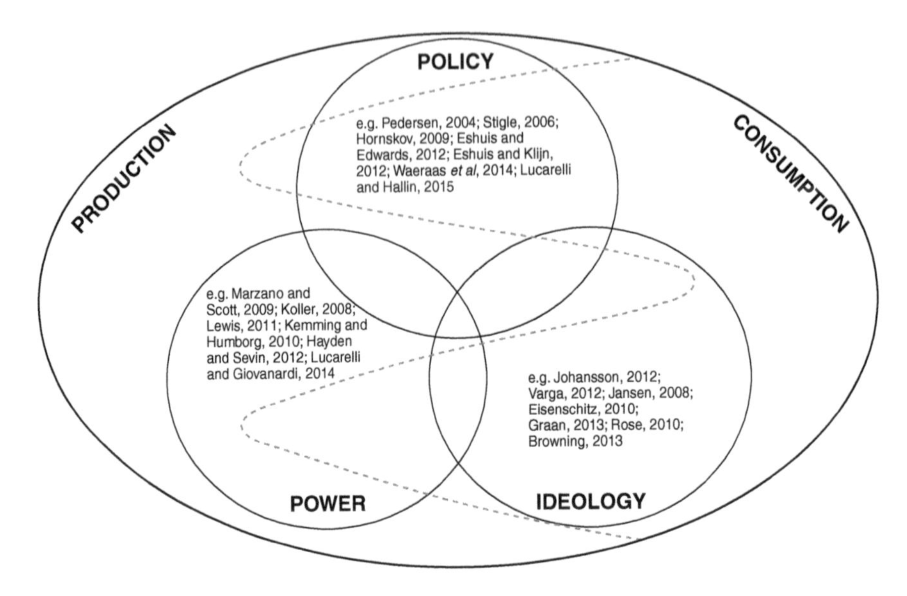

Figure 12.1 Breaking up the dichotomy consumption and production.

Breaking up the dichotomy consumption and production

Much of the extant literature focusing on place branding tends to rely on the consumption–production dichotomy. Such dichotomy, as suggested by Zukin (2009) in the case of cities, and by Kornberger (2010) in the case of place branding, is rather problematic since it fixes the view of public bodies and private enterprise as bare producers, and individuals and residents as bare consumers. The present framework suggests that place branding should be better seen as a political process where *the politics of consumption and production are conceptualized as two faces of the same coin.* This is not only corroborated by the shifting roles of consumers and producers contingent to a contemporary society (Ritzer and Jurgenson, 2010), but more crucially it can be seen as the conceptualization of the *blurring* of consumption and production (Firat and Venkatesh, 1995) not necessarily understood as a postmodern condition, but as an artificial hegemonic discourse constructed by the academic and popular literature on place branding; a discourse founded on the idea place branding essentially being a form economic-led practice (see Davis, 2014 for the same argument).

In more practical terms the present framework suggests one should analyse both a) how, where, when and why diverse types of stakeholder (e.g. institutions, organizations and individuals) repetitive, multimodal and multiple activities enfold and b) how, where, when and why such activities have a 'position' in the circuit of consumption–production in the moment in which place brands, images, efforts and policies are in the making. By doing so, it is then possible to shed light on different political practices, actions, reasons and modalities by diverse stakeholders.

Political dimension of place branding as policy process

Although place branding is firmly anchored on certain political premises few are those studies/stream, whether based on analytical or critical tradition, which performs a politically informed analysis. Among those, there are studies that approach the political dimension as *policy process*, or that conceptualize and analyse the policy process as foundational dimension of politics (Daigneault, 2014; Wilder and Howlett, 2014). At the crossroads between research on public administration, public policy and marketing, those studies adopt an *institutional and procedural* approach to politics based on an implicit Schumpeterian or neo-Schumpeterian view. *Policy process*, in other words, reflects the research, analysis and understanding of the political dimension as a form of public policy which involves decision (i.e. both action and no action) of government and other authorities, both public and hybrid, and includes laws, statutes, regulation, rule-in-use as examples of policies as products and processes (Daigneault, 2014). The aim of this approach is to identify the institutions and authorities that frame, design and build the content and forms of policies as well as to analyse the interaction between policies (i.e. place branding) and the actors involved (i.e. different stakeholders).

The studies employing a procedural view of politics, even those arguing for the centrality of the political dimension, have treated politics at an 'operational' level rather than at the ontological and epistemological level. It means that those studies perform an empirical and contextualized political analysis of the managerial, organizational and structural dimension of place branding. An example is Larson (2002) study of the Storsjosyran festival, analysed as form of relationship marketing in which the political process is understood as a public policy process based on gatekeeping and negotiation. Furthermore, this type of research is crucial for understanding the longevity and penetration of certain place brands compared to others. To do this requires investigation, not just of the communicative outcomes and the reception in targeted markets, but also of the processes through which the brands have been politically created as instrumental policy (e.g. Eshuis *et al.*, 2013; Eshuis and Edwards, 2012). As in the case of Therkelsen and Halkier (2008) in their study of branding of Aalborg by embracing a *policy process* 'approach' means to be attentive to the salient elements composing the policy process which are for the author's inclusion, preferred strategies and commitment.

Similarly, such understanding as *policy process*, allows, as suggested by Lucarelli and Hallin (2015) in the case of Stockholm, to offer an empirical analysis of branding as a form of regional development process. By embracing performative (vs. ostensive) analysis of the policy process and shifting the focus towards the political nature and value of the process of engagement, legitimization and co-production, those type of studies are based on a procedural conceptualization of politics proper to a peculiar political economic view (e.g. Anttiroiko, 2014). In fact, both the stream of literature that look at the effect of place branding as policy (e.g. Mayes, 2008) and the stream which attempt to dissect feature and consequences of place branding as policy for different stakeholders (see e.g. Barr, 2012; Berg and Björner, 2014; Hülsse, 2009) are adopting such a view.

Such understanding allows to bring to surface the argument that the success of a place branding process is totally dependent on the ability to handle and manage the political structure of interests around the brand (see e.g. Hornskov, 2007; Pedersen, 2004) where political stability should be seen as a prerequisite for a successful place branding campaign (Fan, 2006; Youde, 2009). Place branding could be thus analysed as a democratic legal policy process (Eshuis and Edwards, 2012; Eshuis and Klijn, 2011; Wæraas *et al.*, 2014), but also as a powerful broadband policy-instrument, with implications on many different policy areas internationally (Szondi, 2008; Van Ham, 2001) and locally, spanning from education and business to tourism and social inclusion (see Angell and Mordhorst, 2014; Coaffee and Rogers, 2008; Ryan *et al.*, 2002) in which participatory place branding (Kavaratzis, 2012) is seen a new strategy to bring inclusion in the political process.

To sum up, those studies adopting a view in terms of policy process help to highlight the procedural features and characteristics of branding practices and activities. Among those, there some that by endorsing a procedural and instrumental view, even if recognizing the centrality of politics, are treating it as one of many variables to take into consideration (Therkelsen and Halkier, 2008). But by endorsing a critical assessment of the policy process there are some who are helpful in offering insights for analysis related to the performative and institutional facet of the political dimension at different levels of institutionalization (Lucarelli and Hallin, 2015).

Political dimension of place branding as ideology

Schwarzkopf (2011) points out that branding, both as an academic discipline and as practice has been historically constructed around a particular ideology which can be tracked between medieval political theology and modern liberal political philosophy. In spite of such recognition and in spite of the different views about ideology (see Eagleton, 2006), ideology in the relation to politics, generally labelled as political ideology(ies), should be commonly understood as patterned, common forms of thinking about politics. Political ideologies should be seen as clusters of ideas, beliefs, opinions and values, usually held by groups, that provide directives, even plans, of action for public policy-making in an endeavour to uphold, justify, change or criticize the social and political arrangements of a state or other political communities. But ideologies, in relation to the political realm could also be seen as knowledge apparatus that serves the interests of those in power (Habermas, 1985). Despite those two different understandings, in the place branding research literature the former understanding is the most commonly used and practiced; with the latter instead embedded in the conceptualization of ideology as form of power (i.e. see the next subsection).

In the place branding research domain, there are a series of studies that approach the political dimension as *ideology*, or in other words, that conceptualize the *ideological* dimension as the foundational dimension of politics. The studies adopting such approach draw from both political science and political sociology for offering analysis of branding strategies based on political ideologies as for example neoliberalism. Those studies, by embracing an analytical approach that helps to explore the choices and beliefs any given combination of political norms and concepts, helps to open up and unpack such beliefs, to offer an account for them, and finally offers a way to map their complexity (e.g. Eisenschitz, 2010; Johansson, 2012; Kaneva, 2011; Varga, 2013).

Analysing the political dimension as ideology means drawing attention to the contextual relationship between ideology as identity action and identity as ideological action. For example, Eisenschitz (2010), by analysing the process of gentrification not as pragmatic activity, but rather the main neoliberal political activity being aimed at bringing prosperity to localities, allows the unpacking of place branding as an essentially political activity that demonstrates different class settlements by its impact on cities. Similarly, other studies endorsing this approach are interested in unpacking the embeddedness of place branding by certain ideological commitment (Aronczyk, 2013) and help to analyse how place branding activities, place brands and place branding efforts should be seen as politically-laden appropriation by subaltern interest groups and organizations (Dzenovska, 2005; Graan, 2013).

Such understanding of place branding allows one to bring to the surface an understanding of the politics of branding as a complex process constituting moral economics (Browning, 2013, 2014; Varga, 2013) and to unpack place branding as practices embedded in the economic capitalist rationale and calculus (see e.g. Broudehoux, 2007; Koller, 2008; Ward, 2000). Further, those studies have been helpful to analyse and conceptualize the politics of place branding as a form of ideological political propaganda (Jansen, 2008; O'Shaughnessy and O'Shaughnessy, 2000; Rose, 2010) or as pure ideology and ideological apparatus (Johansson, 2012). For this reason, they are very useful in unscrewing one of the main assumptions in the literature, namely that place-branding activities and place brands can be politically appropriated by interests and organizations not considered to be the prime-targets of the branding efforts (i.e. Graan, 2013). Those studies contextually locate their own research in a way that flesh out how the politics of place branding 'should be' or 'ought to be' analysed as ideological, normative and ethical activities co-constructive of its own political environment.

To sum up, those studies adopting a view of the political dimension in term of political ideologies, are very useful in offering both an analytical approach of political ideology without neglecting to critically contextualize the ideological dimension of place branding (Browning, 2014; Eisenschitz, 2010; Kaneva, 2011) by examining the ideological condition that make a particular set of place branding action possibly attractive or legitimate.

Political dimension of place branding as power politics

Despite the centrality of politics to all different stream of place branding research, 'politics' as both analytical unit of contextual frame is rarely explicitly addressed in the place branding literature. This is especially if one recognizes that political dimension of place branding could be seen as an apparatus that serves the interests of those in power (i.e. note here the difference as outlined before) or as the 'the general exposition on the meaning of politics at each level of analysis' (Earley, 2014, p. 83) materializing as oppressive or emancipatory. Such a view in regard to place branding implies one should recognize and analyse the political dimension as form of power-politics in which *power is* seen as the foundational nature of politics. The studies embracing such understanding recognize that not only knowledge and subjectivity are always politically constituted, but also more crucially that having an understanding of power is a prerequisite for analysing the political dimension of place branding at a different level (e.g. Hayden and Sevin, 2012; Van Ham, 2002). Despite the different in understanding of power, as 'power-politics' (see Clegg, 1989; Lukes, 1974) or as 'bio power' (Foucault, 2010), the centrality of power, both as an analytical and theoretical lens, in those studies is endorsed to unpack the relationship between social structures and political subjects. Power thus becomes the object of study in its own term, as for example research in place branding understanding of place branding as a political project and analysing its political outcomes (see e.g. Kemming and Humborg, 2010; Lewis, 2011). Lucarelli and Giovanardi (2014), in their analysis of the communicative process of brand governance clearly spell out the power relationship, framed by language, emerging as a negotiated and contested mechanism among different stakeholder. In similar fashion, but by looking at more macro-dimension, Hayden and Sevin (2012) in their analysis of Ankara public argumentation over the city brand meaning also highlight the power dimension included into the legitimacy and authority of the entire branding process.

In the broader place branding research domain, the studies strictly adopting a view of place branding as power politics are in relatively a minority compared to other view (i.e. *policy* and *ideology*). The reason can be several, but following my original argumentation much can depend on the embeddedness place branding research has with neoliberalism, which makes rather problematic both a purposeful and alternative analysis of the power dimension of politics. Despite this, by recognizing power as the general foundational nature of politics, and by recognizing power as being more than simply a 'unit of analysis', one can observe that this type of scholarship is wider. Among those studies analysing the political implication of power-politics, both empirically (e.g. Koller, 2008) or conceptually (e.g. Sevin, 2011) are a clear example. In similar vein, studies that analyse and conceptualize the politics of place branding as public diplomacy (see e.g. Van Ham, 2001; Wang, 2006; Browning, 2014) by assuming a view of the political dimension as a form of power, have been very instructive in unpacking a major assumption in the place branding literature, namely the dialectic between soft and hard power.

What is crucial here is that all those studies, have both empirically (e.g. Hayden and Sevin, 2012) and conceptually (e.g. Sevin, 2011) allow to highlight how the practise of place branding cannot be analysed properly without fleshing out how such practices are framed around a different ethical and normative worldview that are in play. Equally those studies could, in the future, as more marketing research is done by adopting a governmentality approach analyse the more specific process of the co-creation as a political form of power aimed at generating particular forms of consumer life and offer in-depth investigations of the nature and logic of consumption in relation to the political action of different consumers (see e.g. Bradshaw *et al.*, 2013).

To sum up, those few studies that recognize power as the foundational nature of politics, being inherently axiologically predicated on the issue of power and power relations, have been extremely insightful in paving the way for analyses aimed at revealing how place branding patterns are structured in ways that deviate markedly from articulations of citizen sovereignty. What in addition those studies have offered, even if partially, is an emancipatory view and research agenda that on one side has as its premise the concept of the 'political' embedded in the notion of power, seen either as 'power-over' or 'power in-between', that ultimately frame the political actions circumscribing therefore the possibility of free argentic action, on the other side those studies have elaborated a concept of the 'political' as reflection of the neoliberal and capitalist contemporary society.

Conclusion

The present chapter has attempted to make the case for a more conceptually rounded and empirically conscious research on the political dimension on place branding. By questioning the apparent paucity of research in place branding with an explicit focus on the politics of place branding it first critically assessed the reason behind it and second, by reviewing extant literature, it offered a framework that can support researchers who embrace a political research agenda for place branding. Such framework should not only be seen as way to summarize previous research, but rather as way to embark in future research. In this regard, the framework points out the primacy of concepts and theories of the political (Mouffe, 2005) and the context in which political activities emerge as branding practices. It further points out that a critical political place branding research agenda should be attentive to both the micro (e.g. resident acceptance of branding politics), meso (e.g. formation of branding strategies in city and consultancies offices) and macro dimension (e.g. intersection of branding policies with other policies as, for example, regionalization). All this is done by taking into consideration that different stakeholders are both producers and consumers of branding polices and actives at the same time. Finally, the framework points out that whereas the political dimension of place branding can be researched and analysed as ideology, power and policy at once, those three dimensions could appear all together in different modalities. Future studies might be seeking to analyse the political dimension of place branding in more than one modality (i.e. power, ideology, policy), in more than one case (e.g. comparing branding policies in different places) and at different levels of analysis (e.g. political interpretation of place branding polices in different stages of the branding process and by different stakeholders).

References

Agnew, J. (1999) 'Mapping political power beyond state boundaries: territory, identity, and movement in world politics'. *Millennium-Journal of International Studies*, 28(3), pp. 499–521.

Andersson, I. (2014) 'Placing place branding: an analysis of an emerging research field in human geography'. *Geografisk Tidsskrift-Danish Journal of Geography*, 114(2), pp. 143–155.

Angell, S. I. and Mordhorst, M. (2014) 'National Reputation Management and the Competition State: The cases of Denmark and Norway'. *Journal of Cultural Economy*, 8(2), pp. 184–201.

Anttiroiko, A. V. (2014) *The Political Economy of City Branding*. London: Routledge.

Aronczyk, M. (2013) *Branding the Nation: The Global Business of National Identity*. Oxford: Oxford University Press.

Barr, M. (2012) 'Nation branding as nation building: China's image campaign'. *East Asia*, 29(1), pp. 81–94.

Berg, P. O. and Björner, E. (2014) *Branding Chinese Mega-cities: Policies, Practices and Positioning*. London: Taylor and Francis.

Bradshaw, A., Campbell, N., and Dunne, S. (2013) 'The politics of consumption'. *ephemera*, 13(2), pp. 203–216.

Brenner, N. and Theodore, N. (2002) 'Cities and the Geographies of Actually Existing Neoliberalism'. *Antipode*, 34(3), pp. 349–379.

Broudehoux, A. M. (2007) 'Spectacular Beijing: The Conspicous Construction of an Olympic Metropolis'. *Journal of Urban Affairs*, 29(4), pp. 383–399.

Browning, C. S. (2013) 'Nation Branding, National Self-Esteem, and the Constitution of Subjectivity in Late Modernity'. *Foreign Policy Analysis*, 11(2), pp. 195–214.

Browning, C. S. (2014) 'Nation branding and development: poverty panacea or business as usual?' *Journal of International Relations and Development*, 19(1), pp. 50–75.

Castree, N. (2006) 'From neoliberalism to neoliberalisation: consolations, confusions, and necessary illusions'. *Environment and Planning A*, 38(1), pp. 1–6.

Clegg, S. (1989) *Frameworks of Power*. London: Sage.

Coaffee, J. and Rogers, P. (2008) 'Reputational risk and resiliency: The branding of security in place-making'. *Place Branding and Public Diplomacy*, 4(3), pp. 205–217.

Daigneault, P. (2014) 'Reassessing the concept of policy paradigm: Aligning ontology and methodology in policy studies'. *Journal of European Public Policy*, 21(3), pp. 453–469.

Davies, W. (2014) *The Limits of Neoliberalism: Authority, Sovereignty and the Logic of Competition*. London: Sage.

Dzenovska, D. (2005) 'Remaking the nation of Latvia: Anthropological perspectives on nation branding'. *Place Branding and Public Diplomacy*, 1(2), pp. 173–186.

Eagleton, T. (2006) *Criticism and Ideology: A Study in Marxist Literary Theory*. London: Verso.

Earley, A. (2014) 'Connecting contexts: A Badiouian epistemology for consumer culture theory'. *Marketing Theory*, 14(1), pp. 73–96.
Eisenschitz, A. (2010) 'Neo-liberalism and the future of place marketing'. *Place Branding and Public Diplomacy*, 6(2), pp. 79–86.
Eshuis, J. and Edwards, A. (2012) 'Branding the City: The Democratic Legitimacy of a New Mode of Governance'. *Urban Studies*, 50(5), pp. 1066–1082.
Eshuis, J., and Klijn, E. (2011) *Branding in Governance and Public Management.* London: Sage.
Eshuis, J., Braun, E. and Klijn, E. (2013) 'Place marketing as governance strategy: An assessment of obstacles in place marketing and their effects on attracting target groups'. *Public Administration Review*, 73(3), pp. 507–516.
Fan, Y. (2006) 'Branding the nation: What is being branded?' *Journal of Vacation Marketing*, 12(1), pp. 5–14.
Firat, A. F. and Venkatesh, A. (1995) 'Liberatory Postmodernism and the Reenchantment of Consumption'. *Journal of Consumer Research*, 22(3), pp. 239–267.
Foucault, M. (1988) *Technologies of the Self: A Seminar with Michel Foucault.* London: Sage.
Foucault, M. (2010) *The Birth of Biopolitics: Lectures At The College De France, 1978–1979 (Lectures At The College De France)*. London: Sage.
Graan, A. (2013) 'Counterfeiting the Nation? Skopje 2014 and the Politics of Nation Branding in Macedonia'. *Cultural Anthropology*, 28(1), pp. 161–179.
Habermas, J. (1985) *The Theory of Communicative Action: Lifeworld and System: A Critique of Functionalist Reason*. New York: Beacon Press.
Harvey, D. (1989) 'From managerialism to entrepreneurialism: The transformation in urban governance in late capitalism'. *Geografiska Annaler. Series B, Human Geography*, 71(1), pp. 3–17.
Hayden, C. and Sevin, E. (2012) 'The politics of meaning and the city brand: The controversy over the branding of Ankara'. *Place Branding and Public Diplomacy*, 8(2), pp. 133–146.
Hodges, M. (2012) 'The politics of emergence: Public–private partnerships and the conflictive timescapes of apomixis technology development'. *BioSocieties*, 7(1), pp. 23–49.
Hornskov, S. B. (2007) 'On the management of authenticity: Culture in the place branding of Oresund'. *Place Branding and Public Diplomacy*, 3(4), pp. 317–331.
Hülsse, R. (2009) 'The Catwalk Power: Germany's new foreign image policy'. *Journal of International Relations and Development*, 12(3), pp. 293–316.
Jansen, S. C. (2008) 'Designer nations: Neo-liberal nation branding – Brand Estonia'. *Social Identities*, 14(1), pp. 121–142.
Jessop, B. (2002) 'Liberalism, neoliberalism, and urban governance: A state-theoretical perspective'. *Antipode*, 34(3), pp. 452–472.
Johansson, M. (2012) 'Place branding and the imaginary: The politics of re-imagining a garden city', *Urban Studies*, 49(16), pp. 3611–3626.
Kaneva, N. (2011) 'Nation branding: Toward an agenda for critical research'. *International Journal of Communication*, 5, pp. 117–141.
Kavaratzis, M. (2012) 'From "necessary evil" to necessity: stakeholders' involvement in place branding'. *Journal of Place Management and Development*, 5(1), pp. 7–19.
Kemming, J. and Humborg, C. (2010) 'Democracy and nation brand (ing): Friends or foes?' *Place Branding and Public Diplomacy*, 6(3), pp. 183–197.
Koller, V. (2008) '"The world in one city": Semiotic and cognitive aspects of city branding'. *Journal of Language and Politics*, 7(3), pp. 431–450.

Kornberger, M. (2010) *Brand Society: How Brands Transform Management and Lifestyle*. London: Sage.

Kotler, P. and Levy, S. J. (1966) 'Broadening the Concept of Marketing'. *The Journal of Marketing*, 33(1), pp. 10–15.

Kotler, P. and Zaltman, G. (1971) 'Social marketing: An approach to planned social change'. *The Journal of Marketing*, 3(12).

Larson, M. (2002) 'A political approach to relationship marketing: Case study of the Storsjöyran Festival'. *International Journal of Tourism Research*, 4(2), pp. 119–143.

Lewis, N. (2011) 'Packaging political projects in geographical imaginaries: The rise of nation branding', in Pike, A. (ed.) *Brands and Branding Geographies*. London: Edward Elgar, pp. 264–271

Lucarelli, A. and Berg, P. O. (2011) 'City Branding – A state of the art review of the research domain'. *Journal of Place Management and Development*, 4(1), pp. 9–27.

Lucarelli, A. and Brorström, S. (2013) 'Problematizing place branding research: A metatheoretical analysis of the literature'. *The Marketing Review*, 13(1), pp. 65–81.

Lucarelli, A. and Giovanardi, M. (2014) 'The political nature of brand governance: a discourse analysis approach to a regional brand building process'. *Journal of Public Affairs*, 16(1), pp. 16–27.

Lucarelli, A. and Hallin, A. (2015) 'Brand transformation: a performative approach to brand regeneration'. *Journal of Marketing Management*, 31(1–2), pp. 84–106.

Lukes, S. (1974) *Power: A Radical View*. New York: Palgrave Macmillan.

Marzano, G. and Scott, N. (2009) 'Power in Destination Branding'. *Annals of Tourism Research*, 36(2), pp. 247–267.

Mayes, R. (2008) 'A place in the sun: The politics of place, identity and branding'. *Place Branding and Public Diplomacy*, 4(2), pp. 124–135.

Mouffe, C. (2005) *On the Political*. London: Verson.

O'Shaughnessy, J. and O'Shaughnessy, N. (2000) 'Treating the nation as a brand: Some neglected issues'. *Journal of Macromarketing*, 20(1), pp. 56–64.

Ooi, C. (2008) 'Reimagining Singapore as a creative nation: The politics of place branding'. *Place Branding and Public Diplomacy*, 4(4), pp. 287–302.

Peck, J. and Tickell, A. (2002) 'Neoliberalizing space'. *Antipode*, 34(3), pp. 380–404.

Pedersen, S. B. (2004) 'Place branding: Giving the region of Øresund a competitive edge'. *Journal of Urban Technology*, 11(1), pp. 77–95.

Ritzer, G. and Jurgenson, N. (2010) 'Production, consumption, prosumption: The nature of capitalism in the age of the digital "prosumer"'. *Journal of Consumer Culture*, 10(1), pp. 13–36.

Rose, J. (2010) 'The branding of states: The uneasy marriage of marketing to politics'. *Journal of Political Marketing*, 9(4), pp. 254–275.

Ryan, C., Morgan, N., Pritchard, A. and Pride, R. (2002) 'The politics of branding cities and regions: the case of New Zealand. ... *branding: Creating the ...*'. Available at: www.cabdirect.org/abstracts/20023033308.html (Accessed: 24 March 2015).

Schwarzkopf, S. (2010) 'The consumer as "voter," "judge," and "jury": Historical origins and political consequences of a marketing myth'. *Journal of Macromarketing*, 31(1), pp. 8–18.

Schwarzkopf, S. (2011) 'The political theology of consumer sovereignty: Towards an ontology of consumer society'. *Theory, Culture and Society*, 28(3), pp. 106–129.

Sevin, E. (2011) 'Thinking about place branding: Ethics of concept'. *Place Branding and Public Diplomacy*, 7(3), pp. 155–164.

Sheller, M. and Urry, J. (2003) Mobile transformations of public and private life'. *Theory, Culture and Society*, 20(3), pp. 107–125.

Szondi, G. (2008) 'Public diplomacy and nation branding: Conceptual similarities and differences'. Working Paper. Netherlands Institute of International Relations 'Clingendael'.

Therkelsen, A. and Halkier, H. (2008) 'Contemplating place branding umbrellas. The case of coordinated national tourism and business promotion in Denmark'. *Scandinavian Journal of Hospitality and Tourism*, 8(2), pp. 159–175.

Van Ham, P. (2001) 'The rise of the brand state'. *Foreign Affairs*, (5), pp. 2–6.

Van Ham, P. (2002) 'Branding territory: Inside the wonderful worlds of PR and IR theory'. *Millennium – Journal of International Studies*, 31(2), pp. 249–269.

Varga, S. (2013) 'The politics of nation branding: Collective identity and public sphere in the neoliberal state'. *Philosophy and Social Criticism*, 39(8) pp. 825–845.

Ward, K. G. (2000) 'State licence, local settlements, and the politics of branding the city'. *Environment and Planning C*, 18(3), pp. 285–300.

Weintraub, J. (1997) 'The theory and politics of the public/private distinction', in Weintraub, J. and Kumar, K. (eds) *Public and Private in Thought and Practice: Prospective on a Grand Dichotomy*. Chicago and London: Chicago University Press, pp. 1–17.

Wilder, M. and Howlett, M. (2014) 'The politics of policy anomalies: Bricolage and the hermeneutics of paradigms'. *Critical Policy Studies*, 8(2), pp. 183–202.

Wæraas, A., Bjørnå, H. and Moldenæs, T. (2014) 'Place, organization, democracy: Three strategies for municipal branding'. *Public Management Review*, pp. 1–23.

Youde, J. (2009) 'Selling the state': State branding as a political resource in South Africa'. *Place Branding and Public Diplomacy*, 5(2), pp. 126–140.

Zukin, S. (2009) *Naked City: The Death and Life of Authentic Urban Places*. London: Oxford University Press.

13 Conclusions

Inclusive place branding – towards an integrative research agenda

Massimo Giovanardi, Maria Lichrou and Mihalis Kavaratzis

Introduction

By now, the readers of this book have been exposed to a range of ways in which places are complex, and hence, should be considered as 'special' forms of products, to be handled with great care. The premise of the book was to explore and problematize inclusive forms of place branding in its current practices, as well as its future possibilities; to examine its aims and methods as well as its theoretical underpinnings and challenges. Throughout its chapters, this book has offered diverse insights into the potential of place branding's potential to go beyond economic interests and goals, to focus on residents, to engage diverse stakeholders, and to embrace contradictions and marginalized groups. We have not yet fully reached an exact definition of inclusive place branding; however, the book directs us towards a conception of inclusive place branding that is firmly situated in local contexts; cognizant of its political role; respectful of different communities' right to represent themselves; aware of representational ethics; appreciative of contradictions and alternative stories in the negotiation of place identity. Inclusive place branding is thus not a panacea that resolves the tensions involved in the branding of place. It is a branding process that seeks to actively include stakeholders and to resist naïve claims to identity, representation and participation.

Collectively, the thirteen contributions offered in the present book can be understood as a first step towards the systematization of a critical research agenda for place marketing and branding. Aware that such an effort would imply an enduring long-term plan rather than only a single, one-shot publication, we intend to propose a provisional research agenda that may guide marketers' future attempts to critically engage with the study and application of marketing and branding techniques to cities, regions and countries. This integrative research agenda emphasizes three main interrelated dimensions, each of which contributes the delineation of key aspects of the approach that this book appreciates as *inclusive place branding*. These three interrelated dimensions constitute the three crucial recurring themes that underpin the present book and can be distinguished into *strategic*, *cultural* and *socio-political*. Each dimension is discussed below, with the final goal to emphasize different perspectives of inclusivity within the current practices, policies and conceptualizations of place marketing and branding.

First, strategy, at least in the classical sense (Whittington, 2001), denotes a vision for a place and a plan of action that needs to be implemented tactically. Can place branding successfully unify diverse stakeholders' voices, agendas and desires to serve the interests of the many rather than the few while establishing, maintaining or enhancing the place's competitive advantages? Second, place branding draws heavily on the cultural milieu of a place and has a dialectical relationship with a place's identity (Kavaratzis and Hatch, 2013). Branding efforts capitalize on particular cultural meanings of place, but the branding process also impacts on the way particular interpretations of a place emerge. How is an inclusive effort different from more conventional top down approaches? Can the multitude of co-existing identities of a place be respected and incorporated as part of the process? Finally, as a public management activity, place branding is highly political in nature (Kalandides, 2011; Kavaratzis, 2012). This calls for democratic legitimacy of the process and outputs of the branding effort. Is place branding compatible with an inclusive democratic governance of places? These are complex issues that are not resolvable within a single book. Yet, we hope that this book has been inspiring in exploring some inclusive alternatives in theory and practice. It is also important to note that the book is edited during a pivotal moment for place branding; a period in which a participatory turn is gradually moving from the margins towards the core of the discipline. We are therefore in the midst of an ongoing process, the outcomes of which we have not yet witnessed, but which promises much for more responsible and democratic place branding processes. The collection of chapters presented in this book contributes rich conceptual and empirical insights to this dialogue, weaving together interdisciplinary perspectives and empirical contexts. Remarkably, these contributions show that inclusivity can be proactively achieved when the process of place brand stakeholder engagement is facilitated, in an attempt to embrace the diverse communities it may affect. The chapters exposed the nuances of inclusivity; the tensions and contradictions involved, revealed instances of inclusive initiatives and identified opportunities for inclusive place branding theory and practice. Their implications are discussed in the following sections.

The *strategic* dimension of inclusivity

Pursuing an inclusive approach to place branding entails recognition of the dynamics through which spatial products 'function' and evolve, which reverberates in the way these are operated and managed by place managers. This strategic dimension seems to capture the challenges evoked by what Warnaby, Meadway and Bennison (2010) call place product's 'strategic fissures'. These strategic fissures originate from the 'differences in the backgrounds/agendas/perspectives of stakeholders, which create the potential for competing visions/alternative views on how a place product is managed and operate' (p. 1377).

The chapters by Jan Brown and Garry Warnaby, Richard Koeck and Dominic Medway clearly showed that the variety and differences among place brand stakeholders contribute to create a *sui-generis* governance, which cannot be explained and governed through a simplistic application of marketing principles and protocols. The idea of place brand *co-creation* is consistently identified as a pillar of a more nuanced understanding of place brand governance, whereby a bottom-up approach to the identification and selection of stakeholders is expected to pave the way for a more transparent and effective marketing-oriented place development. Drawing on the work of Michel de Certeau, Warnaby *et al.* (Chapter 8) proposed a conceptual shift from the 'map' to the 'tour'; the tour being an appropriate metaphor for putting the needs and views of a wider array of place users and consumers centre stage. This conceptual shift is consistent with a wider paradigm shift in marketing that views place as a service ecosystem from an S-D logic perspective (Brown, Chapter 5). Combined, these two chapters offered some valuable conceptual aid that could help place managers, consider and give credit to a wider number of visions for a place, rooted in an 'expanded' and more refined understanding of the stakeholder concept. As the chapters by Staci Zavattaro and Daniel Fay and Kevin Fox Gotham and Cate Irvin show, this recognition has inescapable implications for the elaboration of strategic goals and implementation of place marketing and branding campaigns. The contested case of Florida's 'Orange Tie' illustrated by Zavattaro and Fay clearly points to the failures brought about by a top-down approach to the elaboration and delivery of place brand essence. Superficial and hurried interventions may neglect what is meaningful for the stakeholders who are mostly affected by place branding campaigns, resulting in awkward situations of internal opposition against the main place aspects being communicated. The recalibration of the Florida place branding strategy reported provides some optimistic signs that it would be possible to prevent, or at least to try to rebalance, internal opposition and conflicts by deploying a more respectful attitude towards what is meaningful for the stakeholders mostly affected by place branding.

Consistently, an augmented care for the different, often diverging strategic orientations characterizing various local stakeholders is a main point stemming from Gotham and Irvin's chapter on post-disaster rebranding in New Orleans. Besides touching upon the controversial issue of social inequalities and gentrification that the branding discourse brings with it, their discussion of the reimaging strategies also identifies some seminal opportunities for place planners to include marginalized cultures in the place marketing repertoire of a city, and to nurture new place-based identities. This recognition is deeply connected to a second dimension of inclusivity, which more explicitly pertains to the realm of cultural processes contributing to defining places.

The *cultural* dimension of inclusivity

If the concept of co-creation appears to be a strong conceptual proposal that recognizes the strategic importance to consider and involve a wider number of place co-owners and co-producers, the underlying cultural dynamics of this process also warrants some careful consideration. Kavaratzis and Ashworth (2015) described the relationship between 'place culture' and 'place brands' as inherently uneven and controversial, by proposing to view it through the metaphor of the 'hijacking'. However, they proceeded to identify a 'refined appreciation of the role of place brands in the production of culture as well as of the cultural nature of place brands' (Kavaratzis and Ashworth, 2015, p. 155). Resonating with that effort, this book has sought to critically discuss the extent to which inclusivity can be achieved in place branding and at which cost. This has been done by offering some novel empirical perspectives to the issues of representativeness and negotiations, which arise as soon as a place becomes an object of branding. In line with Harvey (1993), in fact, places can be seen as arenas of multi-layered and multipurpose meanings (Harvey, 1993).

Annette Therkelsen demonstrated that inclusive place branding needs to be culturally situated and 'in tune with place practices' (p. 115). Investigating the food narratives employed by Danish coastal destinations, she warns against the conformity trap evident in the adoption of ambiguous geographical markers and similar expressions. This results in generic branding that does little if anything to differentiate these destinations. Therkelsen identified the lack of inclusivity as a contributing factor to the development of these generic brands, because the lack of stakeholder participation can result in a brand not being firmly situated in the local context. Inclusion of stakeholders in the place branding process offers opportunities for meaningfully differentiated place brand narratives.

Given the reliance of place branding on representations of people, cultures and identities, we draw attention to the notion of representational ethics discussed by Borgerson and Schroeder (2002). Marketers must avoid 'bad faith' in representational practices, which refers to the process of essentializing others, by reducing people, cultures and identities to stereotypical representations of the exotic other (Borgerson and Schroeder, 2002). Such eroticizing discourses may be compelling in, say, attracting tourists to a place (e.g. Echtner and Prasad, 2003). However, they may also constrain the possibilities of local populations to accomplish the full potential of their human existence. Representational practices can shape how not only external audiences, but also inhabitants of particular places come to view themselves. Inclusive place branding practices should prioritize the interests of those who live in a place. If we accept that the purpose of the whole place branding effort is to improve the lives of places' inhabitants, then this is a critical task.

Indigenous peoples and cultures are very often the object of the *tourist gaze*. Presenting an Indigenist paradigm, Skye Akbar and Freya Higgins-Desbiolles discussed Aboriginal and Torres Strait Islander tourism operators' resistance to inappropriate top-down approaches to tourism development, and advancement of their own, bottom-up approaches, codes of conduct, and tourism bodies. In doing so, the authors offered a compelling case for the inclusion of Indigenous Peoples' concerns in place branding processes. This is not simply about including Indigenous voices in the branding process; it is about recognizing the right of Indigenous People to represent themselves; it is about recognizing and advancing Indigenous Rights and respecting 'the right ways to engage with Indigenous issues and Indigenous Peoples' (p. 32). The chapter offers lessons from Indigenous practices and knowledge for inclusive place marketing.

Cecillia Cassinger and Åsa Thelander explored in depth the challenges involved in participatory branding programmes. Focusing on a small post-industrial Swedish city plagued by economic decline, they offered insights into how and why even well intending participatory programmes can fail to engage a multitude of perspectives, and may even become exclusionary. In countering the negative media surrounding their city, the residents selected to participate in the programme reproduced what they deemed positive imagery, and excluded representations that triggered negative connotations. It is however, these excluded representations or 'absent spaces', the authors claim, that 'include many different strands of discourses, which could lead to novel meanings of the city' (p. 32). We should therefore truly embrace the contradictions and articulate alternative histories and stories in order to achieve inclusivity.

Place branding theory has also been accused of overlooking 'absent spaces'. The political nature of marketing is often excluded from accounts of place branding strategies and efforts. In order to achieve a truly inclusive place branding, this aspect needs to be brought to the foreground.

The *political* dimension of inclusivity

Since the first emergence of the 'classic' critical human geographers (e.g. Kearns and Philo, 1993), the political dimension of place branding has been as a sort of 'sword of Damocles' for marketing scholars interested in places. Seen from the angle of inclusivity, the realm of the political can be considered as the institutional and operational 'gateway' whereby the place branding process is managed and moderated, which thus contributes to establishing the varying degrees of participation or exclusion that characterizes both the design and 'dissemination' of place brands. To be frank, marketing scholarship about place marketing largely co-habits with an underlying stream of alternative research, which highlights power-related issues affecting the marketing of locations, not only in the area of destination branding (e.g. Marzano and Scott, 2009), but also regional branding (e.g. Lucarelli and Giovanardi, 2016) and place branding in general (Mayes, 2008).

Johan Gromark's case study of the branding of Stockholm as the 'Capital of Scandinavia' (SCS) offered a 'tasty' empirical illustration of place branding politics at an international level. Detailing the development of and reactions to the slogan 'Stockholm – the Capital of Scandinavia', he illustrated how place branding can be accused of narcissistic tendencies. While the slogan has proved successful in attracting attention and has endured protests and reactions, the author questions the ethical standing of the claim.

At a more abstract level of intervention, Aram Eisenschitz made his doubts about the exercise of an inclusive place branding approach explicit. He claimed that the willingness to create an agenda for inclusive place marketing programmes depends on the implementation of 'explicitly political approaches' (p. 147). Andrea Lucarelli's chapter further developed this political conceptual inquiry by offering a thorough systematization of scientific appreciations of the political in place branding. This chapter offers a useful reference point for political studies scholars and marketing researchers interested in taking forward the rigorous examination of the politics of branding as applied to places. It should be noted that a political perspective to inclusiveness is not always simple to operationalize, not only in terms of research approach and design, but also –and especially – in terms of those specific institutional contexts (and related expectations) in which researchers may operate. The growing body of literature on place branding practices in China (e.g. Berg and Björner, 2014), for example, has a lot of politics-related facets to be further scrutinized through a rigorous politically sensitive lens.

Disillusionment towards the concept of participatory place branding was expressed in Eva Maria Jernsand and Helena Kraff's chapter. While appreciating the potential of the concept, they observed that 'participatory' and 'participation' are often being uncritically incorporated in the language of place marketers. The authors challenge the idea that participatory approaches can be straightforwardly proposed and implemented. Rather than a pessimistic celebration of the flaws in participatory place branding mechanisms, this challenge should serve as a further call for refining the research and application of the participatory agenda.

Inevitably, the political dimension begs the question: are branding and participatory democracy compatible? On one hand, it would be naïve to assume that participatory branding programmes are a form of inclusive democratic governance, in spite of good intentions and, in many cases, excellent efforts to include diverse perspectives. On the other hand, inclusivity and diversity of perspectives have often been treated as an Achilles heel in branding, which seeks to express a single unified vision for a place. Yet, the legitimacy of the place branding effort requires at least consent among the various stakeholders. We have seen that various communities resist or even fight against branding efforts and assert their rights to place. The Australian Aboriginals discussed by Akbar and Higgins-Desbiolles (Chapter 3) are an illustration of this, but many other cases of resistance have emerged. Media reports on movements by residents who are taking action as a result of feeling excluded from the place branding developments abound, from East Los Angeles and East London, to Dublin, to Berlin to Barcelona and elsewhere. Grassroots initiatives such as participatory budgeting in Porto Alegre and Boston's Dudley Street Neighbourhood Initiative discussed by Eisenschitz (Chapter 4) are worthy of our attention as alternatives to established models. Similarly, to the 'absent spaces' discussed by Cassinger and Thelander, embracing the contradictions may increase our awareness about power asymmetries and, ultimately, may create disciplinary spaces in which place branding discourses and practices can be continuously reworked and updated.

Moving forward

Overall, the integrative research agenda proposed here can be understood as a provisional constructive response to the needs posed to place scholars and managers by place complexity in its various manifestations. The focus on inclusivity hints at the value of including the diverse stakeholders of place in the process of place branding. This is essential if place branding is to gain any democratic legitimacy and is to be seriously considered by institutional actors as a means to improve the life conditions of local communities. Furthermore, inclusivity opens up opportunities for a more systematic consideration of meaningfully different place brand narratives, both internally and externally. This, as we saw, requires firmly connecting the brand with the actual needs of communities; relinquishing control to the stakeholders affected by the branding process; establishing ethical representational practices that respect the rights of different communities and identities involved; and advancing inclusive democratic governance.

The suggested conceptual foundation of place branding based on the strategic, cultural and political role of inclusivity intends to rebalance the prevalent normative and prescriptive marketing models applied to places and destinations. Those models are primarily interested in addressing 'how-to' types of questions, such as 'how to build strong brands?' (e.g. Govers and Go, 2009, p. 254), in an effort to control the dynamicity and unpredictability of places by focusing on the techniques and procedures to achieve that goal. However, reflecting on the value of inclusivity is not just a sociological or geographical intellectual exercise per se, because it can also be seen as a constructive step towards a more complete understanding of the mechanisms underpinning this very dynamicity and unpredictability of places, as compared to commercial products or services. For decades, we have seen the two streams of literature proceeding in parallel, often disjointed ways. Now, we see an emerging, more mature awareness of the need to combine managerially-oriented thinking, which focuses on techniques and procedures, with a more nuanced account of how places function and their inherently multi-layered, contested and negotiated nature. This more mature awareness can (and *should*) inform practice and facilitate the process of place branding planning and implementation nowadays. As recommended by recent self-reflective accounts of practitioners (Goulart *et al.*, 2017), branding places entails that researchers and consultants are prepared to deal with the contradictions of place brands' fuzzy governance and ambiguities, by acknowledging those as part of their everyday 'hazards of the job' in coping with place complexity.

The contributions in this book have shown that a drastic attempt to reduce or limit this complexity through the use of branding is not always possible or even legitimate for marketers and place managers. Instruments to make this attempt more legitimate and effective, and ultimately possible, have been illustrated. Often, these instruments are not simply pure marketing techniques or protocols that can be applied straightforwardly to locales, cities, regions and nations, but require the existence or implementation of processes of civic and social inclusion. The fascination that participatory approaches have exerted on place branding researchers and practitioners is remarkable, but has also warranted some criticism that this book has contributed to investigations with respect to contemporary discussions on marketing, co-creation and inclusion.

Rather than dismissing civic participation as useless or unsuccessful, we should be augmenting the ways in which marketers explore citizens' views and attitudes about places and their future in their branding programmes. In other words, more work is necessary to reconsider the specific application of participatory planning tools to the realm of place branding (see also Kavaratzis, 2012). In this respect, one of the most promising directions that contemporary geography is exploring is 'the right to the city' concept, which was first proposed by Henri Lefevbre and then extended by geographers interested in the strategic development of places (see Masuda and Bookman, 2016). In this view, marketers should then be prepared to witness different simultaneous manifestations of counter-branding happening within a place, as those manifestations probably indicate that an official place branding exercise might have not done enough to include all the stakeholders in a public confrontation about the future of the place before the campaign went 'on air'. More specifically, Vanolo (2017) highlights the need to study how inhabitants and other city users can be actively empowered, suggesting that place brands can be seen as a particular form of *urban commons*. This book demonstrates that the desirability of bottom-up approaches to the place branding/marketing process is not a taboo any more. Indeed, the quest for inclusivity is one of the most demanding conceptual and practical challenges that are currently being debated in the literature. If anything, a remarkable number of obstacles to civic participation in place branding are still under scrutiny (see Insch and Stuart, 2015).

In spite of the wide empirical coverage offered to the readers and the variety of critical approaches and perspectives discussed, there is room for expansion of the research agenda (as Nadia Kaneva also suggests in her closing commentary). First, some of the conceptual propositions offered should still find their home in terms of empirical or practical application. Hence, we encourage the development of a more applied and in-context exploration of the theoretical proposals advanced by the present book. Second, we recognize that the inclusive place branding practices reported from around the world happened in specific cultural and institutional contexts and, as often occurs, little can be said to guarantee that their application into different contexts would produce similar outcomes or results. Thus, a more systematic research effort is necessary to compare practices of inclusive place branding throughout the globe. In particular, we emphasise the need for a more diversified empirical coverage that is able to better render what places are doing in developing countries and how they are approaching the branding game at a similarly accelerated speed as in the Western democracies. Third, we would like to clarify that the spirit animating the idea of an inclusive place branding should not be seen as the prerogative of interpretivist scholars and qualitative researchers. Rather, it should be the duty of all those involved in place branding. Even though the contributions offered in the present book are grounded in an interpretivist research paradigm, we would like to encourage researchers to incorporate and operationalize the sensibility for place branding inclusiveness into research approaches that also involve measurement. We appreciate that these final thoughts do not just hint to minor concerns. The initial effort propelled by this book now lies in the hands of our colleagues, researchers and practitioners, and the readers. We hope that the book will motivate many to accept the challenge of moving place branding towards a more inclusive future.

References

Berg, P. O. and Björner, E. (eds). (2014) *Branding Chinese Mega-Cities: Policies, Practices and Positioning*. Cheltenham: Edward Elgar Publishing.

Borgerson, J. L. and Schroeder, J. E. (2002) 'Ethical issues of global marketing: avoiding bad faith in visual representation'. *European Journal of Marketing*, 36(5–6), pp. 570–594.

Echtner, C. M. and Prasad, P. (2003) 'The context of third world tourism marketing'. *Annals of Tourism Research*, 30(3), pp. 660–682.

Goulart Sztejnberg, R. and Giovanardi, M. (2017) 'The ambiguity of place branding consultancy: working with stakeholders in Rio de Janeiro'. *Journal of Marketing Management*, pp. 1–25. DOI: http://dx.doi.org/10.1080/0267257x.2017.1319404.

Govers, Robert and Go, Frank. (2009) *Place Branding: Glocal, Virtual and Physical Identities, Constructed, Imagined and Experienced*. Basingstoke, UK: Palgrave Macmillan.

Harvey, D. (1993) 'From space to place and back again: Reflections on the condition of postmodernity', in Bird, J., Curtis, B., Putnam, T., Robertson, J. and Tickner, L. (eds), *Mapping the Futures: Local Cultures, Global Change*. London: Routledge, pp. 3–29.

Insch, A. and Stuart, M. (2015) 'Understanding resident city brand disengagement'. *Journal of Place Management and Development*, 8(3), pp. 172–186.

Kalandides, A. (2011) 'City marketing for Bogotá: a case study in integrated place branding'. *Journal of Place Management and Development*, 4(3), pp. 282–291.

Kavaratzis, M. (2012) 'From "necessary evil" to necessity: stakeholders' involvement in place branding'. *Journal of Place Management and Development*, 5(1), pp. 7–19.

Kavaratzis, M. and Ashworth, G. (2015) 'Hijacking culture: the disconnection between place culture and place brands'. *Town Planning Review*, 86(2), pp. 155–176.

Kavaratzis, M. and Hatch, M. J. (2013) 'The dynamics of place brands: An identity-based approach to place branding theory'. *Marketing Theory*, 13(1), pp. 69–86.

Kearns, G. and Philo, C. (1993) 'Culture, history, capital: A critical introduction to the selling of places', in *Selling Places: The City as Cultural Capital, Past and Present*. Oxford: Bergamon Press, pp. 1–32.

Lucarelli, A. and Giovanardi, M. (2016) 'The political nature of brand governance: A discourse analysis approach to a regional brand building process'. *Journal of Public Affairs*, 16(1), pp. 16–27.

Marzano, G. and Scott, N. (2009) 'Power in destination branding'. *Annals of Tourism Research*, 36(2), pp. 247–267.

Masuda, J. R. and Bookman, S. (2016) 'Neighbourhood branding and the right to the city'. *Progress in Human Geography*, https://doi.org/10.1177/0309132516671822.

Mayes, R. (2008) 'A place in the sun: The politics of place, identity and branding'. *Place Branding and Public Diplomacy*, 4(2), pp. 124–135.

Vanolo, A. (2017) *City Branding: The Ghostly Politics of Representation in Globalising Cities*. Taylor & Francis.

Warnaby, G., Medway, D. and Bennison, D. (2010) 'Notions of materiality and linearity: The challenges of marketing the Hadrian's Wall place "product"'. *Environment and Planning A*, 42(6), pp. 1365–1382.
Whittington, R. (2001) *What is strategy-and does it matter?* London: Cengage Learning EMEA.

14 Closing commentary

Between brand utopias and lived experience

Nadia Kaneva

Who doesn't love a parade?

On 29 October 2016, tens of thousands of people flooded the Paseo de la Reforma and the Zócalo, Mexico City's main plaza, to take part in the first ever Day of the Dead Parade. The Parade featured hundreds of actors and dancers with elaborately painted faces, skeleton costumes, a sea of scull masks, giant marionettes, colourful floats, and pulsating music. Over 1,000 volunteers had worked for weeks to put on the show, funded by Mexico's Tourism Ministry, and the spectacular event delivered positive coverage in many international media.

Although the Day of the Dead is a centuries-old Mexican tradition, recognized by UNESCO as part of the Intangible Cultural Heritage of Humanity, it had never been celebrated as a massive street carnival before. In fact, the Parade might have never come to life at all, had it not been for Hollywood and its James Bond movie franchise, which had invented a fictional Day of the Dead Parade for the opening scenes of its latest instalment, *Spectre*. The film, which reportedly received $20 million in incentives from the Mexican government, was released globally on 6 November 2015, only days after traditional Mexican celebrations that honour the dead. It featured the first Mexican 'Bond Girl' as well as plenty of spectacular footage from Mexico City – elements that had been added to the script, allegedly, in exchange for Mexico's financial support (Estevez, 2015; Janowitz, 2016).

One CNN reporter described the Parade as a case of 'life imitating art' (Scott, 2016). But Mexican officials and producers of the Parade saw it as a strategic marketing intervention, intended to bank on the popularity of *Spectre* with global audiences and to draw in international tourists. Mexico's Tourism Minister Enrique de la Madrid Cordero told a gathering of travel agents, 'We have to invent the Day of the Dead carnival because, after the James Bond movie, tourists are going to come looking for the carnival and they're not going to find it' (quoted in Janowitz, 2016). In an interview for CNN, Alejandra González Anaya, one of the Parade's creative directors, described the event as part of a deliberate rebranding effort for Mexico and its capital city:

> We're really trying to find a new brand, a new identity, rescuing the old and creating another option for the world to be able to come to our country rather than take a trip to the carnival of Rio or the carnival of Venice. Now there's also the Day of the Dead in Mexico.
>
> (Quoted in Scott, 2016)

The Mexican government's financial backing of *Spectre* and the Parade generated plenty of controversy on social media (Agren, 2016), but that didn't stop the crowds of local residents from flocking to the streets on the day of the Parade and enjoying the festivities, along with the tourists. In interviews with foreign media, some residents shared their delight, noting that the carnival had given them a new way to express and celebrate Mexican culture and identity (e.g. BBC, 2016; Al Jazeera English, 2016).

What does this fascinating example reveal about the nature of place marketing at the present juncture? And what new questions does it suggest for scholars interested in advancing a critical research agenda on the branding of places? To begin with, this example vividly illustrates that, when it comes to the marketing of places, the task of separating 'product' from 'promotion' is particularly difficult. This is especially so in the context of globalized media networks and industries, whose business model depends on the production, circulation, and consumption of made-for-the-screen commodity-signs that are designed to appeal to audiences across borders. In this case, what exactly was the product and what was the promotion? Considering that many news reports described the Parade as inspired by *Spectre*, was the elaborate carnival simply a media pseudo-event that extended the global publicity strategy for the film? Or was Mexico's investment in the film a sophisticated form of 'product placement' whereby Mexico City and the Day of the Dead tradition became the 'products' on display for global viewers?

To complicate things further, do the synergies of commercial cultural production and promotion represent the diverse identities and interests of the residents of a place? In other words, how did the government's decision to replicate the atmosphere of the film for the benefit of foreign tourists affect the lives of local people? And, regardless of the intentions behind it, how did the Parade – as a mediated spectacle and an actual event – transform the authentic meaning of the traditional family holiday it was supposed to represent? Did the skeleton tuxedo and scull mask, which Bond wears in the film's opening scene, reduce the Day of the Dead to a macabre costume party that anyone could enjoy, provided they donned the right garb?

Finally, can we truly separate 'promotion' from 'culture' in this example? Was the creative appropriation of a Mexican cultural tradition in the film part of a marketing strategy to extend the appeal of *Spectre* to Latin American audiences? Was it a genuine artistic decision by the film's writers? Or was it a clever use of nation branding intended to generate widespread visibility for Mexico through the film's global distribution? Were the Parade's film-inspired costumes and floats true expressions of Mexican culture? Or were they mere simulacra of cultural identity, which emanated from Hollywood's myth-making machine?

Promotion, profit, participation

What these diverse questions have in common is that they abandon a dominant positivist perspective of place branding that has dominated the field of marketing research. As editors of this volume document in their introduction, the positivist approach to place marketing is instrumentalist and functionalist in nature. It assumes that cities, countries, and regions are not very different from consumer products and services and, therefore, that they can be promoted in similar ways. This approach views promotion as a means to an end, where the end is, ultimately, the generation of economic value. This value can be measured in terms of revenues from tourism, direct investment, or business development, whereas any social, cultural, and environmental consequences are largely ignored or treated as impediments to be contained and managed.

By contrast, a critical perspective on place marketing – as the one suggested in this volume – recognizes that any 'profits' that may result from the promotion of a place are difficult to define and measure, not least because it is hard to pin down who 'owns' a city or a country, who is responsible for its 'management', and whose interests should be prioritized in its development and promotion. As the chapters in this volume illustrate, not all constituents in a place benefit equally, or at all, from place branding efforts. Based on this recognition, the editors propose an alternative approach, which they have termed 'inclusive place branding'. Introducing the idea of inclusivity allows them to shift the analysis of place promotion from a focus on 'competition' to a focus on 'participation'. In turn, a wide variety of stakeholders can be recognized as important actors in the production, promotion, and consumption of places and, at least in theory, their various interests and claims may be better incorporated in the dynamic processes of place branding.

Highlighting participation as an integral part of place branding extends a broader conversation within the marketing and branding literature on the productive powers of consumers as active agents who are involved in the co-creation, co-development, and co-ownership of brands (e.g. Prahalad and Ramaswamy, 2004; Kozinets *et al.*, 2008; Lawrence *et al.*, 2013). The idea of participation has been making inroads in the social sciences with scholars from various disciplines adopting the methods of Participatory Action Research (PAR) to address complex social problems (e.g. Kindon *et al.*, 2007; Ozanne and Saatcioglu, 2008; Lawson *et al.*, 2015).

Broadly speaking, the notion of participation is attractive for many reasons. It invokes democratic values, openness, and collaboration. Yet, participation is not an unproblematic idea in and of itself. A critique of branding and promotional cultures, which originates outside of the marketing field, problematizes the ways in which consumer participation is converted into added value for brands and, ultimately, into profit for private companies (Arvidsson, 2005; Lury, 2004; Marshall, 2002). This line of critique examines the ways in which brands extract profit from basic human sociality. Using iconic consumer brands, such as Apple and Starbucks, as the basis of his analysis, sociologist Adam Arvidsson argues that:

> an important part of brand management consists of building intertextual, physical and virtual spaces that pre-structure and anticipate the agency of consumers. Within these spaces consumers are given contours of and raw material for the exercise of their productive agency.
>
> (2005, p. 247)

For Arvidsson, this exercise of consumer agency, i.e. the active participation of consumers in branded spaces and experiences, is the source of the '*ethical surplus* – a social relation, a shared meaning, an emotional involvement that was not there before' (2005, p. 237, emphasis in original), which forms the basis of brands' economic value. In other words, following Arvidsson, participation is a form of immaterial, uncompensated labour that is essential for the production of brand value. In my view, Arvidsson's argument could be extended productively to the analysis of place branding. Consider, again, Mexico City's creation of the Day of the Dead Parade. The Bond-inspired, tradition-laced, publicity event of the Parade exemplifies the 'intertextual, physical, and virtual space' that Arvidsson describes. The Parade was manufactured for the purposes of generating brand value for Mexico City by materializing the fictional carnival from *Spectre*. But it was the social interactions of performers, local citizens, tourists, and global media audiences that became the true source of that brand value. In fact, without the participation of all of these groups, the production of brand value would have been impossible. In that sense, the participation of various constituents in the Parade was a form of immaterial labour that produced the shared meanings, experiences, memories, and emotions that transformed Mexico City from a place to a *place brand*. At the same time, these unrecognized 'producers' of the brand did not share equally, or at all, in the economic value, or profit, that they had helped to generate. Nevertheless, participation does have its rewards, although they may not come in the form of economic capital. Kavaratzis (2004) points out that what distinguishes city marketing from city branding is the latter's intersection with identity and community building. Rather than being a purely economic tool, place branding claims to be a means for 'achieving community development, reinforcing local identity and identification of the citizens with their city and activating all social forces to avoid social exclusion and unrest' (Kavaratzis, 2004, p. 70). Understood in this way, place branding is a process of cultural production, which cannot be separated from basic human practices of meaning making. These dynamics are clearly reflected in the statements of organizers and participants in the Day of the Dead Parade, which were referenced above.

In this context, the Day of the Dead Parade is a vivid reminder that the social construction of places, identities, and cultures is, at the present time, intimately intertwined with the workings of markets. In this particular case, we can see the intersections of a market for global entertainment and a market for international tourism, both of which encroach on the efforts of a city and a nation to articulate and express its cultural identities. Perhaps most provocatively, this example also illustrates that, as the boundaries between commerce and culture have become ever more porous, so have the boundaries between fantasy and reality, the world of branded utopias and the embodied world of living in a particular place and time.

Between brand utopias and lived experience

From this vantage point, located at the intersection of brand utopias and embodied, everyday life, I offer some thoughts on what might be productive directions for future critical research on place branding. The preliminary list of questions below is far from exhaustive; nevertheless, it aims to expand upon, as well as push beyond, the themes emerging from the contributions in this volume. What situates these questions within a critical research tradition is a refusal to accept that markets are neutral or natural systems. Rather, these questions are informed by the foundational belief that markets are, and have always been, social, and therefore political, constructions (Bourdieu, 2005; Storr, 2009). In light of this, the suggestions below are not directly concerned with generating practical recommendations for branding and marketing practitioners in the field. Rather, the questions I propose aim to highlight the social, political, and cultural contexts within which place branding is inevitably embedded.

With this in mind, an agenda for critical research on place marketing and branding must begin by questioning some of the foundational assumptions about the nature of markets and their role in the social lives of places. How do specific markets come into being and how do they interact with other forms of social organization at a given place and time? How do different markets intersect and overlap and how does that change the production and distribution of value? In the example of Mexico City, sketched out above, place branding clearly activated multiple market dynamics at the same time. Some of these are easy to see, while others remain hidden and, as a result, may be harder to theorize and research. Beyond the obvious market for tourists, there are various markets for labour – both material and immaterial – that made the Day of the Dead Parade possible. For instance, how did this publicity event influence the market for creative services in Mexico and the relationships between the public sector and the private, promotional industries? Why did the producers of the Parade use volunteers to put on the show and how were they able to recruit and motivate so many local residents to donate their time and energies? Furthermore, if it were to become an annual event, how would the Parade affect the economic fortunes of local street vendors, taxi drivers, tour guides, and other small businesses? Would it enhance or diminish their ability to earn a living? These types of questions are relevant beyond the example of Mexico City and they get to the heart of developing more inclusive approaches to place branding and development.

Second, a critical research agenda on place branding needs to examine the various 'alternative markets' that operate within and among places. It is no secret, for instance, that places attract various 'undesirable' visitors, including sex tourists, drug tourists, migrants, and refugees. This spawns a variety of legal or extra-legal markets that service these populations. However, such developments are rarely, if ever, acknowledged in official place branding strategies. An even more troubling dimension of alternative markets concerns the illicit markets that enable human trafficking, organ trafficking, drug trafficking, and arms trafficking. These 'dark markets' also shape the development of places but are not accounted for in marketing research. At the same time, some place branding programs aim to divert attention from the reality of illicit markets and their negative social impact. In the case of Mexico, place-branding campaigns have been part of a long-term effort to counteract the country's troubled reputation for drug-related violence. In short, critical approaches to place branding need to investigate how alternative and illicit markets intersect with the development and promotion of places and consider the consequences of these intersections for a wide range of social groups.

Third, it is clear that place branding intersects with a global market for the production, circulation, and consumption of mediated commodity-signs. I have argued elsewhere that global media outlets constantly churn out commodity-signs of and about places with the primary purpose of generating profit for the media corporations that own them (Kaneva, 2015 and 2017). Commodity-signs are produced not only by promotional campaigns, but are generated through various technological and industrial protocols, which reflect journalistic, artistic, commercial, political, or personal agendas. They use different genre conventions and are often contradictory in nature. How and why certain commodity-signs gain greater visibility is determined, in part, by the logics of the media markets within which they circulate. Yet, the affordances of media markets and industries are largely absent from current discussions of place branding. This direction for research would require place-branding scholars to move beyond a conceptualization of media as mere vehicles for message delivery and to recognize the multifaceted processes of mediation that underlie the symbolic and cultural production of places.

Finally, an important line of critical research on place branding needs to continue to examine the intersections of markets and identities. Once again, the Day of the Dead Parade provides an apt illustration of the complexities of these intersections. Was the Parade an authentic expression of Mexican culture and identity or a tourist-friendly, media-savvy simulation of it? To be sure, commercialized performances of local culture are not unique to Mexico. From ayahuasca ceremonies in Peru, to yoga retreats in India, to guided tours of urban slums in South Africa, many places offer opportunities for tourists, who are willing to pay, to partake in more or less stylized and sanitized expressions of local ways of life.

Recently, the rise of the so-called 'sharing economy' has opened up new, highly mediated, opportunities for locals to commodify, package, and profit from their personal lives and experiences. For example, the popular site Airbnb, which describes itself as an 'online marketplace and hospitality service', now lists more than just homes for rent. The site includes a section labelled, 'Experiences', where locals offer various 'authentic' and immersive activities which travellers can pay to enjoy. For instance, one can hire a salsa dancer in Havana and go out dancing with her and her friends; meet a 'real samurai' in Tokyo for a sparring match with swords; or have a drink and dig through vinyl records with a professional DJ in London. Airbnb's most recent advertising campaign slogan is, 'Don't go there. Live there'. (Richards, 2016). In short, what the company purports to sell is nothing less than *living* in a particular place.

These examples link back to my earlier observations on the difficulty of defining who owns and manages a place and its brand. They also illustrate, once again, the complexity of separating the commercial and the promotional from what was once simply known as 'living' in a place. At the same time, critical analyses of place branding have documented that, in many cases, there are dramatic differences between the fanciful brand narratives that cities and nations project and the actual living conditions of local populations (e.g. Browning, 2016; Greenberg, 2010; Iordanova, 2007; Kaneva, 2017 and forthcoming). This is especially prevalent in post-colonial and post-conflict settings, where place branding is often presented as a solution to developmental challenges. The long-term political and psychological consequences of living with such disparities remain to be fully explored and understood.

In this context, to what extent is the commercialization of lived experience empowering or exploitative for the residents of a place? How are cultural symbols, identities, and traditions transformed once they are subject to market exchange? And what are the social costs for communities when particular aspects of local life become reified and essentialized for the benefit of the 'paying customer'? One way to begin to formulate answers to some of these questions may require further engagement with theories of performance and performativity, which have attracted the attention of marketing researchers fairly recently (e.g. Maclaran *et al.*, 2009; Tadajewski, 2010; Mason *et al.*, 2015). A focus on performativity opens up new avenues for understanding the ways in which place branding extracts value from, and simultaneously transforms, the very nature of belonging to and living in a place.

Ultimately, critical approaches to place branding must interrogate the consequences of the multi-dimensional interactions between brand utopias and lived experience. What is really at stake here is the nature and quality of contemporary life itself. It remains to be seen whether the idea of inclusive place branding might help to reconcile some of the tensions and contradictions I have outlined above. As we look ahead, perhaps the most important promise for inclusive place branding is that it might encourage marketing scholars and practitioners to engage with the world they seek to influence in ways that are more reflexive, culturally sensitive, and socially responsible.

References

Agren, D. (2016) 'Mexico City's James Bond-inspired Day of the Dead parade gets mixed reviews', *Guardian*. 30 October. Available at: www.theguardian.com/world/2016/oct/29/day-of-the-dead-parade-james-bond-mexico-city (Accessed: 10 June 2017).

Al Jazeera English (2016) 'Mexicans celebrate first Day of the Dead procession', video. *Al Jazeera English*. 30 October. Available at: www.youtube.com/watch?v=gmFYuyvyivI (Accessed: 10 June 2017).

Arvidsson, A. (2005) 'Brands: A critical perspective'. *Journal of Consumer Culture*, 5(2), pp. 235–258.

BBC (2016) 'Mexico City stages first Day of the Dead parade', *BBC*. 29 October. Available at: www.bbc.com/news/world-latin-america-37813562 (Accessed: 10 June 2017).

Bourdieu, P. (2005) *The Social Structures of the Economy*. Cambridge: Polity.

Browning, C. (2016) 'Nation branding and development: Poverty panacea or business as usual?'. *Journal of International Relations and Development*, 19(1), pp. 50–75.

Estevez, D. (23 March 2015) 'Controversy over 007's new film as Mexico denies script changes but admits economic assistance'. *Forbes*. Available at: www.forbes.com/sites/doliaestevez/2015/03/23/controversy-over-007s-new-film-as-mexico-denies-script-changes-but-admits-economic-assistance/#75c8e2e921b0 (Accessed: 10 May 2017).

Greenberg, M. (2010) 'Branding, crisis, and utopia: Representing New York in the age of Bloomberg', in Aronczyk, M. and Powers, D. (eds), *Blowing Up the Brand: Critical Perspectives on Promotional Culture*. New York: Peter Lang.

Iordanova, D. (2007) 'Cashing in on Dracula: Eastern Europe's hard sells'. *Framework* 48(1), pp. 46–63.

Janowitz, N. (2016) 'James Bond's fake Day of the Dead parade was so cool Mexico wants to do it for real'. *Vice News*. 8 July. Available at: https://news.vice.com/article/james-bonds-fake-day-of-the-dead-parade-was-so-cool-mexico-wants-to-do-it-for-real (Accessed: 15 May 2017).

Kaneva, N. (2015) 'Nation branding and commercial nationalism: A critical perspective', in Volcic, Z. and Andrejevic, M. (eds), *Commercial Nationalism: Selling the Nation and Naitonalizing the Sell*. New York and London: Palgrave Macmillan, pp. 175–189.

Kaneva, N. (2017) 'The branded national imagination and its limits: Insights from the post-socialist experience'. *Strategic Review for Southern Africa*, 39(1), pp. 116–138.

Kaneva, N. (forthcoming) 'Simulation nations: Nation brands and Baudrillard's theory of media'. *European Journal of Cultural Studies*.

Kavaratzis, M. (2004) 'From city marketing to city branding: Towards a theoretical framework for developing city brands'. *Place Branding*, 1(1), pp. 58–73.

Kindon, S. L., Pain, R. and Kesby, M. (eds) (2007) *Participatory Action Research Approaches and Methods: Connecting People, Participation and Place*. London: Routledge.

Kozinets, R. V., Hemetsberger, A. and Schau, H. J. (2008) 'The wisdom of consumer crowds: Collective innovation in the age of networked marketing'. *Journal of Macromarketing*, 28(4), pp. 339–354.

Lawrence, B., Fournier, S. and Brunel, F. (2013) 'When companies don't make the ad: A multimethod inquiry into the differential effectiveness of consumer-generated advertising'. *Journal of Advertising*, 42(4), pp. 292–307.

Lawson, H. A., Caringi, J. C., Pyles, L., Jurkowski, J. M. and Bozlak, C. T. (eds) (2015) *Participatory Action Research*. New York: Oxford University Press.

Lury, C. (2004) *Brands: The Logos of the Global Economy*. London: Routledge.

Maclaran, P., Miller, C., Parsons, E. and Surman, E. (2009) 'Praxis or performance: Does critical marketing have a gender blind-spot?' *Journal of Marketing Management*, 25(7–8), pp. 713–728.

Marshall, P. D. (2002) 'The new intertextual commodity', in Harries, D. (ed.), *The New Media Book*. London: BFI Publishing, pp. 69–92.

Mason, K., Kjellberg, H. and Hagberg, J. (2015) 'Exploring the performativity of marketing: Theories, practices and devices'. *Journal of Marketing Management*, 31(1–2), pp. 1–15.

Ozanne, J. L. and Saatcioglu, B. (2008) 'Participatory action research'. *Journal of Consumer Research*, 35(3), pp. 423–439.

Prahalad, C. K. and Ramaswamy, V. (2004) *The Future of Competition: Co-Creating Unique Value with Customers*. Boston, MA: Harvard Business School Press.

Richards, K. (2016) 'Put away the selfie stick and live like a local, urges Airbnb's new campaign', *Adweek*. 19 April. Available at: www.adweek.com/brand-marketing/put-away-selfie-stick-and-live-local-urges-airbnbs-new-campaign-170920 (Accessed: 10 June 2017).

Scott, C. (28 October 2016) 'Mexico City didn't have a Day of the Dead parade. Then they saw "Spectre,"' *CNN*. Available at: www.cnn.com/travel/article/mexico-city-day-of-the-day-parade/index.html (Accessed: 15 May 2017).

Storr, V. H. (2009) 'Social construction of the market'. Working Paper, Mercatus Center at George Mason University, No. 09–44, November 2009. Available at: http://mercatus.org/publication/social-construction-market (Accessed: 10 June 2017).

Tadajewski, M. (2010) 'Critical marketing studies: logical empiricism, "critical performativity" and marketing practice'. *Marketing Theory*, 10(2), pp. 210–222.

Index

Note: page locators in **bold** and *italics* represents figures and tables, respectively.

For Product Safety Concerns and Information please contact our EU
representative GPSR@taylorandfrancis.com
Taylor & Francis Verlag GmbH, Kaufingerstraße 24, 80331 München, Germany